WHO WANTS TO BE A

# MILLIONAIRE

WHO WANTS TO BE A

# ENTERTAINMENT

# ENTERTAINMENT

B■XTREE

First published 2002 by Boxtree
an imprint of Pan Macmillan Ltd
Pan Macmillan, 20 New Wharf Road, London N1 9RR
Basingstoke and Oxford
Associated companies throughout the world
www.panmacmillan.com

ISBN 07522 15027

Produced under license from Celador International Limited

1 3 5 7 9 8 6 4 2

A CIP catalogue record for this book is
available from the British Library.

Designed and typeset by seagulls
Printed and bound by Mackays of Chatham plc, Kent

# CONTENTS

# How to play

The brand new *Who Wants To Be A Millionaire? Quiz Book* designed exclusively for all Entertainment buffs is finally here. Brace yourself for 1,000 new questions especially themed around Entertainment topics. Whether you play on your own or compete with your friends, start with Fastest Finger First and remember to use your lifelines wisely. The *Who Wants To Be A Millionaire? Entertainment* challenge awaits you.

## FOR 1 PLAYER

As on *Who Wants To Be A Millionaire?*, the aim of the game is to reach £1 Million. But before you can even go on to play the game, you must first correctly answer a question from the Fastest Finger First section. You have just 30 seconds to put the letters in the correct order. When the time's up, follow the page reference at the bottom of the page to find out if you can take your place in the hotseat and begin your climb for the cash!

### Once in the hotseat

Start with a question worth £100 and once you have decided on your final answer (and you're absolutely sure...) follow the page reference at the bottom of the page to find out if you're right. If your answer is correct, you can play to win £200 and start making your way up that famous Money Tree. The page where each money level begins is listed in the answer section.

As on the programme you have three Lifelines to help you on your way to £1 Million. You don't *have* to use them, but remember, each Lifeline can only be used once, so don't use them if you don't need to.

### Fifty-Fifty

This option takes away two incorrect answers leaving the correct answer and the one remaining incorrect answer. The page reference at the bottom of each page will tell you where to look for the remaining answers.

### Phone-A-Friend

If you have a telephone to hand (and a willing friend!) ring him/her up to help you out. You have 30 seconds (and no cheating please...) to read the question to your friend and for them to tell you what they think the answer is. If there's someone else around, ask them to time your call for you.

### Ask The Audience

This works in exactly the same way as on *Who Wants To Be A Millionaire?* except we've already asked the audience so you don't have to! Simply follow the page reference at the bottom of each page to find out what our audience thought. But in the end, the decision is yours.

If you answer incorrectly at any time, you are out of the game. £1,000 and £32,000 are 'safe havens', but if you answer a question incorrectly and you have not reached £1,000 then not only are you out of the game but you will leave without a penny! If you have reached one (or both) of these havens and you answer a question incorrectly, then, depending on the stage you have reached in the game, you will leave with either £1,000 or

£32,000. If at any point during the game you are unsure of an answer and don't want to risk being out of the game, you can 'stick' at the amount you have won so far and that will be your final score. As you play, use the score sheets at the back of the book to keep a running record of the amount you have won and the Lifelines you have used.

## FOR 2–5 PLAYERS

Players should take it in turns at being 'Chris Tarrant' and posing questions to the other contestants. The rules are the same as for a single player (see pages 6–7). If someone reaches £1 Million that person is the winner and the game is over. Otherwise, once everyone else is out, the person who has won the most money is the winner.

Are you ready to play? Good. With all that money at stake, we're sure we don't need to tell you to think very carefully before you give your final answer. Good luck and be sure to remember at all times the motto for *Who Wants To Be A Millionaire?* – it's only easy if you know the answer!

# FASTEST FINGER FIRST

# FASTEST FINGER FIRST

## 1

Starting with the earliest, put these TV series starring John Thaw in the order in which they were first broadcast.

- A: Inspector Morse
- B: Redcap
- C: The Sweeney
- D: Kavanagh QC

## 2

Place these 'Star Wars' films in order of increasing episode number.

- A: The Empire Strikes Back
- B: The Phantom Menace
- C: Attack of the Clones
- D: Return of the Jedi

## 3

Starting with the earliest, put these Queen singles in the order in which they first became top ten hits in the UK charts.

- A: Another One Bites the Dust
- B: Radio Gaga
- C: Bohemian Rhapsody
- D: A Kind of Magic

## 4

Starting with the oldest, put these Hollywood actors in order of their dates of birth.

- A: Danny DeVito
- B: Matt Damon
- C: Brad Pitt
- D: Harrison Ford

## 5

Starting with the quietest, put these musical instructions in order of loudness.

- A: Fortissimo
- B: Mezzopiano
- C: Forte
- D: Pianissimo

Answers on page 265

# FASTEST FINGER FIRST

## 6

Staring with the earliest, put these playwrights
in the order they lived and worked.

◆A: William Shakespeare ◆B: Oscar Wilde

◆C: Harold Pinter ◆D: Aristophanes

## 7

Starting with the most recent, put these celebrity
couples in the order in which they married each other.

◆A: Chris Evans & Billie Piper ◆B: Madonna & Guy Ritchie

◆C: Paul McCartney & Heather Mills ◆D: David Beckham & Victoria Adams

## 8

Starting with the earliest, place these 'Star Trek'
captains in the order they first appeared on British TV.

◆A: Kathryn Janeway ◆B: Jonathan Archer

◆C: James T Kirk ◆D: Jean-Luc Picard

## 9

Starting with the oldest, put the
Beatles in order of their dates of birth.

◆A: George Harrison ◆B: John Lennon

◆C: Ringo Starr ◆D: Paul McCartney

## 10

Starting with the earliest, put these musicals
in the order in which they were first performed.

◆A: Cats ◆B: West Side Story

◆C: Oklahoma! ◆D: Hair

**?** Answers on page 265

# FASTEST FINGER FIRST

## 11

Starting with the most recent, put these celebrity couples in the order they separated.

- A: Liz Hurley & Hugh Grant
- B: Nicole Kidman & Tom Cruise
- C: Madonna & Sean Penn
- D: Cindy Crawford & Richard Gere

## 12

Starting with the earliest, put these events from the history of the BBC in order.

- A: First colour TV service begins
- B: BBC2 goes on air
- C: Launches television service
- D: Becomes British Broadcasting Corporation

## 13

Starting with the least, put these musical instruments in order according to the number of strings each normally has.

- A: Guitar
- B: Harp
- C: Balalaika
- D: Violin

## 14

Starting with the earliest, place these quiz programmes in the order they first appeared on British TV.

- A: Mastermind
- B: A Question of Sport
- C: University Challenge
- D: Who Wants To Be A Millionaire?

## 15

Starting with the fewest, put these films in order of the number of episodes in the series.

- A: Godzilla
- B: The Carry Ons
- C: Star Trek
- D: Nightmare on Elm Street

Answers on page 265

# FASTEST FINGER FIRST

## 16

Starting with the earliest, place these TV dramas in the chronological order of the period in which they are set.

- A: When The Boat Comes In
- B: Poldark
- C: I, Claudius
- D: Colditz

## 17

Starting with the lowest, put these films in order according to the numbers in their titles.

- A: 101 Dalmatians
- B: 24 Hour Party People
- C: Terminator 2: Judgment Day
- D: One Flew Over the Cuckoo's Nest

## 18

Starting with the earliest, put these Kylie Minogue singles in the order they reached No 1 in the UK charts.

- A: Tears On My Pillow
- B: Spinning Around
- C: I Should Be So Lucky
- D: Can't Get You Out of My Head

## 19

Starting with the youngest, put these members of the Jacksons in the order they were born.

- A: Marlon
- B: Janet
- C: Michael
- D: Jackie

## 20

Starting with the earliest, put these BBC Radio 4 programmes in the order they normally appear on a weekday.

- A: Book at Bedtime
- B: PM
- C: Today
- D: The World at One

Answers on page 265

# FASTEST FINGER FIRST

## 21

Starting with the earliest, place these programmes in the order they first appeared on British TV.

◆A: Newsnight
◆B: The Sky at Night
◆C: The Generation Game
◆D: Top of the Pops

## 22

Starting with the furthest south, put these ITV companies in order of the areas to which they broadcast.

◆A: Grampian
◆B: Granada
◆C: Meridian
◆D: London Weekend

## 23

Starting with the earliest, put these pop stars in order of their dates of birth.

◆A: Elvis Presley
◆B: Chuck Berry
◆C: David Bowie
◆D: Mick Jagger

## 24

Starting with the closest, put these opera houses in order according to their proximity to London.

◆A: La Scala, Milan
◆B: Sydney Opera House
◆C: The Metropolitan, New York
◆D: Glyndebourne, West Sussex

## 25

Starting with the earliest, place these police dramas in the order they first appeared on British TV.

◆A: The Bill
◆B: Z Cars
◆C: The Sweeney
◆D: Dixon of Dock Green

Answers on page 265

# FASTEST FINGER FIRST

## 26

Starting with the lowest, put these notes of the tonic sol-fa scale in ascending order.

- A: Fah
- B: Ray
- C: Soh
- D: Me

## 27

Starting with the earliest, put these BBC1 weekday programmes in the order of their regular time-slots.

- A: Kilroy
- B: Breakfast
- C: BBC News at Ten O'Clock
- D: Neighbours

## 28

Starting with the first, put these elements of a theatrical performance in order.

page 15

- A: Opening night
- B: Dress rehearsal
- C: Press preview
- D: Read through

## 29

Starting with the earliest, put these Richard Attenborough films in the order in which he directed them.

- A: Cry Freedom
- B: A Bridge Too Far
- C: Shadowlands
- D: Gandhi

## 30

Starting with the highest, put these singing voices in order.

- A: Contralto
- B: Baritone
- C: Tenor
- D: Soprano

**?** Answers on page 265

# FASTEST FINGER FIRST

## 31

Starting with the earliest, put these programmes starring Ronnie Barker in the order in which they were first broadcast on British TV.

- A: Open All Hours
- B: Clarence
- C: Porridge
- D: Going Straight

## 32

Place these Australian series in the reverse chronological order in which they were first screened in the UK.

- A: Neighbours
- B: Home and Away
- C: Prisoner: Cell Block H
- D: Sons and Daughters

## 33

Starting with the earliest, put these ballet dancers in order of their date of birth.

- A: Wayne Sleep
- B: Vaslav Nijinsky
- C: Darcey Bussell
- D: Margot Fonteyn

## 34

Starting with the lowest, put these quiz shows in order of the number of players that usually make up each team.

- A: Have I Got News For You
- B: Countdown
- C: University Challenge
- D: A Question of Sport

## 35

Starting with the earliest, put these actors in the order in which they first won the Best Actor Oscar.

- A: Ben Kingsley
- B: Gene Hackman
- C: Gary Cooper
- D: Nicolas Cage

Answers on page 265

# FASTEST FINGER FIRST

## 36

Starting with the earliest, put these David Lean films in the order in which he directed them.

- A: The Bridge on the River Kwai
- B: A Passage to India
- C: Great Expectations
- D: Lawrence of Arabia

## 37

Starting with the earliest, put these comic book characters in the order they first appeared in print.

- A: Andy Capp
- B: Dick Tracy
- C: Superman
- D: Popeye

## 38

Put these George Michael singles in the order in which they were Top 10 hits in the UK.

- A: Fastlove
- B: Faith
- C: Careless Whisper
- D: Praying for Time

## 39

Starting with the earliest, arrange these films in the order of the time in which they are set.

- A: Grease
- B: Gone with the Wind
- C: Gladiator
- D: The Guns of Navarone

## 40

Put these words in order to complete a famous Shakespeare line, 'O Romeo, Romeo...'.

- A: Romeo
- B: Art
- C: Thou
- D: Wherefore

Answers on page 265

# FASTEST FINGER FIRST

## 41

Starting with the earliest, place these TV medical programmes in chronological order of when they were first screened in the UK.

- A: Dangerfield
- B: Emergency Ward 10
- C: Doctor Finlay's Casebook
- D: Casualty

## 42

Starting with the earliest, put these songs in the order they won the Academy Award for Best Song.

- A: My Heart Will Go On
- B: White Christmas
- C: Born Free
- D: Fame

## 43

Starting with the earliest, place these former soap stars in the order of when they had their first UK No 1 single.

- A: Kylie Minogue
- B: Nick Berry
- C: Jason Donovan
- D: Martine McCutcheon

## 44

Starting with the first, put these stages of a play in chronological order.

- A: Final curtain
- B: Act I
- C: Prologue
- D: Act III

## 45

Starting with the earliest, put these actresses in the order of their date of birth.

- A: Greta Garbo
- B: Melanie Griffith
- C: Judy Garland
- D: Whoopi Goldberg

Answers on page 265

# FASTEST FINGER FIRST

## 46

**Starting with the earliest, place these four operas in the order in which they were first performed.**

- A: Pirates of Penzance
- B: Don Giovanni
- C: Tosca
- D: Billy Budd

## 47

**Place these words in sequence to make the title of a TV comedy series.**

- A: Dead
- B: The
- C: Donkey
- D: Drop

## 48

**Starting with the earliest, put these events in the life of Steven Spielberg in chronological order.**

page 19

- A: Wins Oscar for 'Schindler's List'
- B: Makes TV movie 'Duel'
- C: Attends California State College
- D: 'Jaws' released

## 49

**Starting with the earliest, put these opera singers in order according to their year of birth.**

- A: Bryn Terfel
- B: Maria Callas
- C: Enrico Caruso
- D: Luciano Pavarotti

## 50

**Starting with the least, put these films in order according to the number of Oscars they won.**

- A: Attack of the Killer Tomatoes
- B: The Godfather
- C: One Flew Over the Cuckoo's Nest
- D: Gone With the Wind

Answers on page 265

# FASTEST FINGER FIRST

## 51

Starting with the earliest, place these TV programmes in the order they would normally appear during a day's transmission by the BBC.

- A: Newsnight
- B: Kilroy
- C: The National Lottery Draw
- D: Breakfast

## 52

Working from least to most, place these film stars in order according to the number of times they have been married.

- A: Cher
- B: Gwyneth Paltrow
- C: Elizabeth Taylor
- D: Liza Minnelli

## 53

Starting with the earliest, put these Madonna singles in the order in which they were first released in the UK.

- A: Don't Tell Me
- B: Material Girl
- C: Holiday
- D: Ray of Light

## 54

Put these composers in alphabetical order according to their surnames.

- A: Karlheinz Stockhausen
- B: Franz Schubert
- C: Arnold Schoenberg
- D: Erik Satie

## 55

Starting with the earliest, put these films in the order in which they were released.

- A: Alien3
- B: Alien
- C: Aliens
- D: Alien Resurrection

Answers on page 265

# FASTEST FINGER FIRST

## 56

Put these comic book super-heroes in alphabetical order.

◆A: Silver Surfer    ◆B: Superman

◆C: Swamp Thing    ◆D: Spider-Man

## 57

Starting with the earliest, put these events
in the history of cinema in order.

◆A: Mickey Mouse makes first film appearance    ◆B: Eisenstein directs 'Battleship Potemkin'

◆C: George Lucas directs 'Star Wars'    ◆D: Cinemascope launched

## 58

Starting with the earliest, put these actors in
the order they played Hamlet on the big screen.

◆A: Mel Gibson    ◆B: Kenneth Branagh

◆C: Laurence Olivier    ◆D: Nicol Williamson

## 59

Put these words in the correct order to make a series
of films starring Michael J Fox and Christopher Lloyd.

◆A: To    ◆B: Future

◆C: The    ◆D: Back

## 60

Starting with the earliest, put these groups in the
order in which Eric Clapton recorded with them.

◆A: Blind Faith    ◆B: Cream

◆C: The Yardbirds    ◆D: Derek and the Dominos

❓ Answers on page 265

# FASTEST FINGER FIRST

## 61

Starting with the youngest,
put these Michaels in order of age.

A: Michael Parkinson

B: Michael Jackson

C: Michael Douglas

D: Michael J Fox

## 62

Starting with the earliest, put these films
in the order they won the Best Picture Oscar.

A: Oliver!

B: Rain Man

C: Ben-Hur

D: Rocky

## 63

page 22

Starting with the least, place these TV comedy programmes
in the order of how many main comedians they involved.

A: Monty Python's Flying Circus

B: Alas Smith and Jones

C: The Man from Auntie

D: Not the Nine O'Clock News

## 64

Starting with the earliest, put these Russell Crowe
films in the order in which they were made.

A: LA Confidential

B: A Beautiful Mind

C: Romper Stomper

D: The Insider

## 65

Starting with the most northerly, put these
TV shows in the order of where they are set.

A: Only Fools And Horses

B: Rab C Nesbitt

C: 'Allo 'Allo

D: Bread

Answers on page 265

# FASTEST FINGER FIRST

## 66

Starting with the earliest, put these composers in the order of their dates of birth.

- A: Edward Elgar
- B: George Frederick Handel
- C: Aaron Copland
- D: Frédéric Chopin

## 67

Put these words in order to form the name of a US rock band.

- A: Hot
- B: Peppers
- C: Chili
- D: Red

## 68

Starting with the earliest, put these Spice Girls singles in the order in which they were released in the UK.

- A: Who Do You Think You Are?
- B: Goodbye
- C: Viva Forever
- D: Wannabe

## 69

Arrange these sci-fi film titles in alphabetical order.

- A: Star Wars
- B: Stargate
- C: Starman
- D: Starship Troopers

## 70

Starting with the earliest in the day, put these BBC Radio 5 Live programmes in chronological order.

- A: Up All Night
- B: Morning Reports
- C: Drive
- D: The Midday News

**?** Answers on page 265

# FASTEST FINGER FIRST

## 71

Put these words in the order they appear in a famous line from the 1972 film 'The Godfather'.

- A: Refuse
- B: Offer
- C: Can't
- D: Make

## 72

Starting with the earliest, put these tenors in the order of their dates of birth.

- A: Placido Domingo
- B: José Carreras
- C: Beniamino Gigli
- D: Luciano Pavarotti

## 73

Starting with the shortest, put these TV shows in order of the length of each episode.

- A: Rainbow
- B: The Incredible Hulk
- C: The Clangers
- D: Batman

## 74

Starting with the earliest, put these events in Elizabeth Taylor's life in chronological order.

- A: Is the voice of Maggie on 'The Simpsons'
- B: Wins Oscar for 'Butterfield 8'
- C: Appears in 'Lassie Come Home'
- D: Marries Richard Burton

## 75

Going from east to west, put these pop acts in order of the country from which the they originated.

- A: Beach Boys
- B: Beatles
- C: Björk
- D: INXS

Answers on page 265

# FASTEST FINGER FIRST

## 76

Starting with the earliest, put these
Will Smith films in the order of their release.

- A: Enemy of the State
- B: Ali
- C: Men in Black
- D: Wild Wild West

## 77

Put these words in order to form the
title of a long-running TV programme.

- A: Is
- B: Life
- C: This
- D: Your

## 78

Starting with the earliest, put these jazz
personalities in the order of their dates of birth.

- A: Dizzy Gillespie
- B: Jools Holland
- C: Louis Armstrong
- D: John Dankworth

## 79

Put these TV quiz shows in alphabetical order.

- A: Crosswits
- B: Celebrity Squares
- C: Countdown
- D: Catchphrase

## 80

Starting with the earliest, put these actors
in the order in which they were knighted.

- A: Anthony Hopkins
- B: Laurence Olivier
- C: Henry Irving
- D: Sean Connery

Answers on page 265

# FASTEST FINGER FIRST

## 81

Starting with the most recent, put these composers in the order in which they were born.

A: Giuseppe Verdi
B: Arthur Sullivan
C: Philip Glass
D: Wolfgang Amadeus Mozart

## 82

Starting with the earliest, put these childrens' TV characters in the order they first released a single.

A: Roland Rat
B: Mr Blobby
C: Teletubbies
D: Bob the Builder

## 83

Starting with the least, put these artists in order according to the number of UK No 1s they have had.

A: Donna Summer
B: Elvis Presley
C: Roy Orbison
D: Michael Jackson

## 84

Starting with the earliest, put these crime series in the order in which they were first screened on UK television.

A: The Bill
B: Prime Suspect
C: Dixon of Dock Green
D: Kojak

## 85

Arrange these words according to the order in which they appear in the title of a classic film starring Jack Lemmon and Tony Curtis.

A: It
B: Like
C: Hot
D: Some

Answers on page 265

# FASTEST FINGER FIRST

## 86

Starting with the earliest, put these directors in the order in which they first won the Best Director Oscar.

- A: Richard Attenborough
- B: Sam Mendes
- C: David Lean
- D: Francis Ford Coppola

## 87

Place these words in sequence to give the name of a French play, film and musical.

- A: Folles
- B: Aux
- C: La
- D: Cage

## 88

Starting with the earliest, put these singles featuring Paul McCartney in the order in which they were No 1 in the UK.

page 27

- A: Ebony and Ivory
- B: Ferry 'Cross the Mersey
- C: Pipes of Peace
- D: Mull of Kintyre

## 89

Put these comedy shows in alphabetical order.

- A: Sorry!
- B: Smack The Pony
- C: Soap
- D: Seinfeld

## 90

Starting with the earliest, put these events in the life of Ronald Reagan in order.

- A: Marries Jane Wyman
- B: Has screen test for Warner Bros
- C: Becomes president of the United States
- D: Marries Nancy Davis

**?** Answers on page 265

# FASTEST FINGER FIRST

## 91

Put these ITV companies in reverse alphabetical order.

- A: Anglia Television
- B: HTV
- C: Yorkshire Television
- D: Ulster Television

## 92

Starting with the earliest, place these Gerry Anderson productions in the order they first appeared on British television.

- A: Stingray
- B: Joe 90
- C: Thunderbirds
- D: Fireball XL5

## 93

Put these TV Batman villains in alphabetical order.

- A: The Joker
- B: The Riddler
- C: The Penguin
- D: Cat Woman

## 94

Starting with the earliest, put these Oasis singles in the order they were No 1 in the UK charts.

- A: D'you Know What I Mean
- B: All Around the World
- C: Some Might Say
- D: Don't Look Back in Anger

## 95

Starting with the smallest, put these musical instruments in order according to their size.

- A: Harmonica
- B: Ukulele
- C: Piano
- D: Cello

Answers on page 265

# FASTEST FINGER FIRST

## 96

**Starting with the earliest, put these David Jason shows in the order in which they first appeared on British television.**

◆A: The Darling Buds of May   ◆B: Open All Hours

◆C: Only Fools and Horses   ◆D: Danger Mouse

## 97

**Place these words in the order they appear in the title of a famous Rolf Harris song.**

◆A: Sport   ◆B: Kangaroo

◆C: Down   ◆D: Tie

## 98

**Starting with the earliest, place these actors in the order they played Batman on the big screen.**

◆A: George Clooney   ◆B: Michael Keaton

◆C: Adam West   ◆D: Val Kilmer

## 99

**Put these words in the order they appear in the title of a much loved sitcom.**

◆A: Mothers   ◆B: Some

◆C: 'Em   ◆D: 'Ave

## 100

**Starting with the earliest, put these films starring Hugh Grant in the order in which they were released.**

◆A: Notting Hill   ◆B: About a Boy

◆C: Impromptu   ◆D: Four Weddings and a Funeral

**?** Answers on page 265

| 15 | £1 MILLION |
|----|-----------|
| 14 | £500,000 |
| 13 | £250,000 |
| 12 | £125,000 |
| 11 | £64,000 |
| 10 | £32,000 |
| 9 | £16,000 |
| 8 | £8,000 |
| 7 | £4,000 |
| 6 | £2,000 |
| 5 | £1,000 |
| 4 | £500 |
| 3 | £300 |
| 2 | £200 |
| 1 ◆ | £100 |

# 1 ◆ £100

## 1

Which of these frightening creatures were the subject of the film 'Jurassic Park'?

A: Sharks

B: Dinosaurs

C: Aliens

D: Hollywood agents

## 2

In which country was the actor and comedian Billy Connolly born?

A: England

B: Scotland

C: Ireland

D: Wales

## 3

Which of these would you normally use to play a violin?

A: Knot

B: Bow

C: Twine

D: Shackle

## 4

Complete the name of the 1980s pop group, Duran...?

A: One Hundred

B: Boys

C: Club

D: Duran

## 5

Which of the following is a well-known cereal advertising slogan?

A: Crash, bang, wallop!

B: Snap! Crackle! Pop!

C: Plink plink fizz!

D: Crunch, munch, ouch!

50:50 Go to page 241   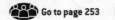 Go to page 253    Answers on page 265

# 1 ◆ £100

## 6

The person who supervises the actors, camera crew and other staff on a film set is known as what?

- A: Detector
- B: Defector
- C: Director
- D: Dissector

## 7

Which of the Spice Girls is Victoria Beckham?

- A: Scary
- B: Posh
- C: Sporty
- D: Baby

## 8

Complete the name of this TV comedy double-act, Little and...?

page **33**

- A: Littler
- B: Often
- C: Tall
- D: Large

## 9

Which of the following are actors traditionally said to tread?

- A: Boards
- B: Planks
- C: Shelves
- D: Dole queues

## 10

How is the tent in which a circus is held commonly known?

- A: Big end
- B: Big dipper
- C: Big cheese
- D: Big top

50:50 Go to page 241    Go to page 253    ? Answers on page 265

# 1 ♦ £100

## 11

**Which of these is a cowboy character played in over sixty films by William Boyd?**

A: Scootalong Cassidy
B: Shrugalong Cassidy
C: Runalong Cassidy
D: Hopalong Cassidy

## 12

**With which of the following are Anna Pavlova and Dame Margot Fonteyn associated?**

A: Opera
B: Ballet
C: Film directing
D: Stand-up comedy

## 13

**Which of these does the conductor of an orchestra traditionally do during a performance?**

A: Play the violin
B: Wave a baton
C: Clap wildly
D: Sweep the floor

## 14

**What name is given to the storyline of a film?**

A: Plan
B: Policy
C: Scheme
D: Plot

## 15

**Which Greg became Director-General of the BBC in 2000?**

A: Ditch
B: Trench
C: Hole
D: Dyke

 **50:50** Go to page 241    Go to page 253    **?** Answers on page 265

## 16

**A short comic play is known as what?**

A: Paint

B: Sketch

C: Colour

D: Draw

## 17

**Which brother of Paul Ross is also a TV presenter?**

A: Joseph

B: Jonathan

C: Adrian

D: Rupert

## 18

**In music, how would you normally play a triangle?**

A: Strum it

B: Blow into it

C: Press its keys

D: Strike it

## 19

**What 'Killed the Radio Star' according to Buggles' 1979 No 1 single?**

A: Audio

B: Billy-o

C: Rodeo

D: Video

## 20

**In which country is the soap 'Neighbours' set?**

A: USA

B: Canada

C: England

D: Australia

50:50 Go to page 241    Go to page 253    ? Answers on page 265

# 1 ◆ £100

## 21

What was it 'good to' do according to the 1990s
British Telecom advertising campaign?

A: Natter
B: Chat
C: Rabbit
D: Talk

## 22

Which Dawn has teamed up with Jennifer
Saunders in many TV comedy shows?

A: German
B: French
C: Spanish
D: Swiss

## 23

What common setting links the TV programmes
'Porridge', 'Prisoner: Cell Block H' and 'The Governor'?

A: Holiday camp
B: Health farm
C: Prison
D: School

## 24

Which married lady was made
famous by Caroline Aherne?

A: Mrs Merton
B: Mrs Beeton
C: Mrs Thatcher
D: Mrs Mopp

## 25

To which of the following does
the term 'silver screen' refer?

A: Cinema
B: Circus
C: Theatre
D: Television

 50:50 Go to page 241      Go to page 253      ? Answers on page 265

# 1 ◆ £100

## 26

Which popular cartoon character
used his ears to fly in a 1941 film?

◆A: Pluto      ◆B: Dumbo

◆C: Rocko      ◆D: Jimbo

## 27

Who 'Investigates' in the title of a BBC
drama series starring Patricia Routledge?

◆A: Milly Philpott      ◆B: Hatty Spendthrift

◆C: Polly Prendergast      ◆D: Hetty Wainthropp

## 28

Which of these is a musical group
comprising four players?

◆A: Duo      ◆B: Trio

◆C: Quartet      ◆D: Sextet

## 29

Kate Winslet and Leonardo DiCaprio find love
aboard which of these in a 1997 blockbuster?

◆A: Orient Express      ◆B: Titanic

◆C: Concorde      ◆D: Clapham Omnibus

## 30

Which catchphrase does Fred Flintstone use?

◆A: Yabba dabba diddy!      ◆B: Yabba dabba doo!

◆C: Yabba dabba don't!      ◆D: Yabba dabba d'oh!

 50:50 Go to page 241    Go to page 253     Answers on page 265

# 1 ◆ £100

## 31

**What is the title of Andrew Lloyd-Webber and Tim Rice's musical about Eva Peron?**

◆A: Conchita ◆B: Evita

◆C: Ryvita ◆D: Danny DeVito

## 32

**Which Friday is the title of the first of a series of horror films, featuring the ice hockey mask-wearing Jason?**

◆A: Friday the 1st ◆B: Friday the 8th

◆C: Friday the 13th ◆D: Friday the 29th

## 33

**Whose 'Flying Circus' featured John Cleese, Graham Chapman, Michael Palin, Terry Jones, Eric Idle and Terry Gilliam?**

◆A: Para Handy's ◆B: Monty Python's

◆C: Bill Cotton's ◆D: Rowan and Martin's

## 34

**Which of these is the name of the group fronted by Beyoncé Knowles?**

◆A: Destiny's Child ◆B: Fortune's Baby

◆C: Fate's Nipper ◆D: Kismet's Toddler

## 35

**Complete the title of the 1977 John Travolta film, 'Saturday Night...'?**

◆A: Headache ◆B: Earache

◆C: Tummy ache ◆D: Fever

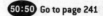 50:50 Go to page 241  Go to page 253  ? Answers on page 265

# 1 ◆ £100

## 36

**Which annual film festival takes place in the south of France?**

A: Tinnes
B: Jarres
C: Cannes
D: Pottes

## 37

**In which of these TV soaps is the Queen Vic the local pub?**

A: Coronation Street
B: Emmerdale
C: Brookside
D: EastEnders

## 38

**Which of the following did Ludwig van Beethoven become towards the end of his life ?**

page
39

A: Polish
B: Deaf
C: A doctor
D: A professional footballer

## 39

**Who was the comedy partner of Ernie Wise?**

A: Frankie Howerd
B: Eric Sykes
C: Des O'Connor
D: Eric Morecambe

## 40

**Which of these is a rapid succession of notes played on a drum?**

A: Drumroll
B: Drumbun
C: Drumsandwich
D: Drumpasty

# 1 ◆ £100

## 41

**Who is the helmeted baddie in 'Star Wars', 'The Empire Strikes Back' and 'Return of the Jedi'?**

- A: Dave Voider
- B: Dirk Vaster
- C: Dolph Vinger
- D: Darth Vader

## 42

**Which playwright was 'In Love' in the title of a 1998 multi Oscar-winning comedy starring Gwyneth Paltrow and Joseph Fiennes?**

- A: Shakespeare
- B: Pinter
- C: Coward
- D: Molière

## 43

**For which band does Charlie Watts play drums, Keith Richard play guitar and Mick Jagger sing?**

- A: The Rolling Stones
- B: Simply Red
- C: The Who
- D: Depeche Mode

## 44

**Which American film actress's name is synonymous with an inflatable life jacket?**

- A: Mae North
- B: Mae South
- C: Mae East
- D: Mae West

## 45

**What did Ian Dury want to be hit with in the title of his 1978 No 1 single?**

- A: Walking stick
- B: Big stick
- C: Rhythm stick
- D: Hockey stick

**50:50** Go to page 241  Go to page 253  Answers on page 265

# 1 ◆ £100

## 46

**Which of these is a musical term used to describe a series of repeated chords?**

- A: Miff
- B: Riff
- C: Tiff
- D: Skiff

## 47

**In 'Star Wars', what does Han Solo tell Luke Skywalker he hopes will be with him?**

- A: Furs
- B: Farce
- C: Fish
- D: Force

## 48

**Which term means both the place where tickets are sold at a cinema and the amount of money a film brings in?**

- A: Sack office
- B: Bag office
- C: Box office
- D: Tin office

## 49

**Complete the title of the musical, 'Fiddler on the...'?**

- A: Landing
- B: Conservatory
- C: Stairs
- D: Roof

## 50

**Which of these TV series starred a dog?**

- A: Skippy
- B: Black Beauty
- C: Daktari
- D: Lassie

50:50 Go to page 241   Go to page 253   ? Answers on page 265

# 1 ◆ £100

## 51

What is the traditional name for the side or back entrance to a theatre used by the actors?

A: Stage window
B: Stage curtain
C: Stage left
D: Stage door

## 52

Which of these is a famous 19th century Parisian dance?

A: Willwill
B: Cancan
C: Wontwont
D: Shouldshould

## 53

In panto, which of these is traditionally Aladdin's mother?

A: Widow Hankey
B: Widow Manky
C: Widow Thanky
D: Widow Twankey

## 54

Which of the following words is used to describe musical instruments such as the violin, cello and double bass?

A: Roped
B: Stringed
C: Cabled
D: Barbed

## 55

According to the Beatles' 1964 song, 'It's Been a Hard Day's...'?

A: Work
B: Living
C: Night
D: Journey

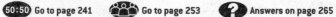

50:50 Go to page 241   Go to page 253   ? Answers on page 265

# 1 ◆ £100

## 56

Which British weekly magazine contains television and radio listings?

A: Radio Telegraph
B: Radio Independent
C: Radio Times
D: Radio News

## 57

What did Bernard Matthews describe as 'bootiful!' in a series of television advertisements?

A: Cars
B: Lager
C: Turkeys
D: His wife

## 58

Which of the following is a famous London concert hall?

A: V & A
B: Royal Albert Hall
C: Hayward Gallery
D: The Tate Modern

## 59

What was Rick Astley 'Never Gonna' do according to the title of his 1987 UK No 1 single?

A: Give You a Headache
B: Give You a Present
C: Give You Up
D: Give You a Break

## 60

Which comedy show of the 1980s and 1990s lampooned politicians with latex puppets?

A: Coughing Picture
B: Dribbling Venue
C: Spitting Image
D: Spluttering Vista

 50:50 Go to page 241    Go to page 253     Answers on pages 265 & 266

# 1 ◆ £100

## 61

In which musical are King Arthur, Queen Guinevere and Sir Lancelot principal characters?

A: Virgin
B: Railtrack
C: Camelot
D: Kingfisher

## 62

Which musical is based on the Gospel according to St Matthew?

A: Evita
B: 42nd Street
C: Godspell
D: Gentlemen Prefer Blondes

## 63

What is the catchphrase of the cartoon rabbit Bugs Bunny?

A: Cowabunga!
B: I tawt I taw a puddy tat
C: What's up, Doc?
D: Sufferin' succotash!

## 64

Which of these is a type of African-American music that originated in the early 1900s?

A: Blues
B: Greens
C: Yellows
D: Pinks

## 65

With which instrument is Sir Elton John chiefly associated?

A: Violin
B: Saxophone
C: Trombone
D: Piano

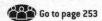 50:50 Go to page 241    Go to page 253     ? Answers on page 266

## 66

Which of these does a guitar normally have?

A: Mouthpiece

B: Reed

C: Strings

D: Keys

## 67

How did Frank Sinatra say he'd done it in the title of his famous 1969 hit?

A: One Way

B: The Wife's Way

C: My Way

D: Any Which Way

## 68

Which part does Kathy Staff play in TV's 'Last of the Summer Wine'?

A: Nora Daffy

B: Nora Dotty

C: Nora Potty

D: Nora Batty

## 69

What type of creature is Flipper in the 1960s TV series of the same name?

A: Dolphin

B: Octopus

C: Shark

D: Turtle

## 70

Which cartoon character eats spinach for strength?

A: Incredible Hulk

B: Superman

C: He-Man

D: Popeye

50:50 Go to page 241    Go to page 253    ? Answers on page 266

# 1 ♦ £100

## 71

Who had a hit with 'Born in the USA'?

A: Bruce Summersteen

B: Bruce Autumnsteen

C: Bruce Wintersteen

D: Bruce Springsteen

## 72

Which of these is a Channel 4 teen drama series?

A: Hollyelms

B: Hollyoaks

C: Hollymaples

D: Hollyashes

## 73

Who was Paul Simon's long-running musical partner?

A: Art Blakey

B: Art Tatum

C: Art Malik

D: Art Garfunkel

## 74

Which of these characters is played by William Shatner in a long-running TV show?

A: Captain Chaos

B: Captain Kirk

C: Captain Kremmen

D: Captain Fantastic

## 75

A fiddle is a colloquial term for which musical instrument?

A: Piano

B: Harp

C: Violin

D: Clarinet

50:50 Go to pages 241 & 242    Go to page 253    ? Answers on page 266

# 1 ◆ £100

## 76

**Which army sergeant was played by Phil Silvers in the long running TV series, 'The Phil Silvers Show'?**

A: Milko | B: Wilko
C: Silko | D: Bilko

## 77

**By what name are the puppet characters Bill and Ben also known?**

A: The Hosepipe Men | B: The Rake Men
C: The Wheelbarrow Men | D: The Flowerpot Men

## 78

**Which of these is a famous British dancer?**

A: Wayne Sleep | B: Wayne Doze
C: Wayne Nap | D: Wayne Forty-Winks

## 79

**Billy Ray Cyrus had a worldwide line-dancing hit in 1992 with 'Achy Breaky...'?**

A: Heart | B: Head
C: Elbow | D: Pelvis

## 80

**Which of these is an orchestral instrument?**

A: French horn | B: French guitar
C: French drum | D: French triangle

**50:50** Go to page 242　 Go to page 254　**?** Answers on page 266

# 1 ◆ £100

## 81

From which country does the fictional
TV character Dame Edna Everage hail?

- A: USA
- B: Australia
- C: England
- D: Scotland

## 82

Which BBC drama series is set in a hospital?

- A: Accident
- B: Disaster
- C: Mishap
- D: Casualty

## 83

A room or building equipped for
filming is known as a what?

- A: Studio
- B: Workhouse
- C: Laboratory
- D: Office

## 84

Which TV series is set in New York's
High School for the Performing Arts?

- A: Acclaim
- B: Notice
- C: Fame
- D: Success

## 85

Complete the title of the TS Eliot work on which a famous Andrew
Lloyd-Webber musical is based, 'Old Possum's Book of Practical...'?

- A: Dogs
- B: Elephants
- C: Giraffes
- D: Cats

 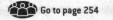

# 1 ◆ £100

## 86

Which 'Lady' was a No 1 hit for Chris de Burgh?

◆A: Lady in Bed  ◆B: Lady with Bread

◆C: Lady in Red  ◆D: Lady in Shed

## 87

Complete the title of the BBC
comedy sci-fi series, 'Red...'?

◆A: Goblin  ◆B: Elf

◆C: Hobbit  ◆D: Dwarf

## 88

Which Freddie was the lead singer with Queen?

◆A: Neptune  ◆B: Pluto

◆C: Mercury  ◆D: Saturn

50:50 Go to page 242　　Go to page 254　　❓ Answers on page 266

| 15 | £1 MILLION |
|----|------------|
| 14 | £500,000 |
| 13 | £250,000 |
| 12 | £125,000 |
| 11 | £64,000 |
| 10 | £32,000 |
| 9 | £16,000 |
| 8 | £8,000 |
| 7 | £4,000 |
| 6 | £2,000 |
| 5 | £1,000 |
| 4 | £500 |
| 3 | £300 |
| 2 ◆ | £200 |
| 1 ◆ | £100 |

# 2 ◆ £200

### 1

**Which George is the star of 'The Perfect Storm' and 'Three Kings'?**

A: George Best
B: George Clooney
C: George Michael
D: George Formby

### 2

**Who duetted with Cher on their 1960s hit single 'I Got You Babe'?**

A: Sonny
B: Rainy
C: Cloudy
D: Snowy

### 3

**Which popular series made a return to the small screen in 2002?**

A: Au Revoir, Duck
B: Auf Wiedersehen, Pet
C: Ciao, chum
D: Adios, chuck

### 4

**Whose catch-phrase was 'Just like that!'?**

A: Tommy Cooper
B: Tommy Trinder
C: Tommy Cannon
D: Terry-Thomas

### 5

**Which of these is a short film which advertises another?**

A: Trailer
B: Caravan
C: Camper
D: Truck

50:50 Go to page 242     Go to page 254     ? Answers on page 266

### 6

**Who owned an 'Amazing Technicolor Dreamcoat' in the title of the hit musical?**

◆A: Moses  ◆B: Joseph

◆C: Aaron  ◆D: Elvis

### 7

**Which of these had a No 1 hit single in 1999 with 'Flying Without Wings'?**

◆A: Northlife  ◆B: Southlife

◆C: Eastlife  ◆D: Westlife

### 8

**What does the title of a 2002 British film encourage you to do 'Like Beckham'?**

◆A: Backheel It  ◆B: Bend It

◆C: Bleach It  ◆D: Break It

page
**53**

### 9

**Complete the name of the drag queen played by Paul O'Grady, 'Lily...'?**

◆A: Rage  ◆B: Wild

◆C: Savage  ◆D: Fury

### 10

**Which classic rock group featured Robert Plant on vocals and Jimmy Page on guitar?**

◆A: Led Balloon  ◆B: Led Dirigible

◆C: Led Airship  ◆D: Led Zeppelin

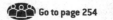 **50:50** Go to page 242    Go to page 254     **?** Answers on page 266

# 2 ◆ £200

## 11

**What is the surname of Rodney and Del in the TV series 'Only Fools and Horses'?**

A: Foot

B: Hoof

C: Trotter

D: Paw

## 12

**Who had a 1956 UK No 1 hit with 'Singing The Blues'?**

A: Tommy Iron

B: Tommy Copper

C: Tommy Bronze

D: Tommy Steele

## 13

page
54

**According to the 1980s television advertisement, the TSB was the 'bank that likes to say...'?**

A: Hello

B: Yes

C: Sorry

D: You're overdrawn again

## 14

**Which of these was a popular British dance of the 1930s?**

A: Chelsea Stroll

B: Lambeth Walk

C: Greenwich Step

D: Westminster Wander

## 15

**Who achieved fame as a film tramp with a smudge moustache, twirling cane and bowler hat?**

A: Charlie Parker

B: Charlie Sheen

C: Charlie Higson

D: Charlie Chaplin

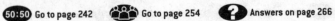

50:50 Go to page 242    Go to page 254    ? Answers on page 266

# 2 ◆ £200

## 16

Which of these is a Shakespeare play?

- A: Weight for Weight
- B: Size for Size
- C: Measure for Measure
- D: Volume for Volume

## 17

Complete the title of the song from 'South Pacific', 'There Is Nothing Like A...'?

- A: Dame
- B: Game
- C: Grain
- D: Drain

## 18

Which fictional detective made the actor David Suchet a household name?

- A: Wolfe
- B: Wimsey
- C: Holmes
- D: Poirot

## 19

George Formby sang 'When I'm Cleaning...'?

- A: Doors
- B: Windows
- C: Bathrooms
- D: The Dog

## 20

Which of the following is the actress daughter of Hollywood legend Tony Curtis?

- A: Carrie Ann
- B: Jamie Lee
- C: Peggy Sue
- D: Billie Jo

 50:50 Go to page 242     Go to page 254    ? Answers on page 266

## 21

**Complete the title of Puccini's famous opera, 'Madame...'?**

A: Grasshopper
B: Dragonfly
C: Moth
D: Butterfly

## 22

**Which of the following is the name used for a non-speaking film actor, normally used in a crowd scene?**

A: Extra
B: Bonus
C: Tip
D: Perk

## 23

**In which 1979 film did Mel Gibson play policeman Max Rockatansky?**

A: Mild Max
B: Mellow Max
C: Mad Max
D: Mental Max

## 24

**Which of these goes before 'drum' to give the name of a type of percussion instrument?**

A: Saucepan
B: Frying pan
C: Kettle
D: Colander

## 25

**Kermit the Frog, Miss Piggy and Fozzie Bear regularly appeared on which TV show?**

A: The Muppet Show
B: Spitting Image
C: The Sooty Show
D: Play School

50:50 Go to page 242    Go to page 254    ? Answers on page 266

# 2 ◆ £200

## 26

Which 1941 film starred Humphrey Bogart as private eye Sam Spade on the hunt for a valuable statuette?

A: The Turkish Pigeon
B: The Russian Seagull
C: The Maltese Falcon
D: The Welsh Parrot

## 27

Complete the title of Andrew Lloyd-Webber's musical, 'The Phantom of the...'?

A: Ballet
B: Musical
C: Drama
D: Opera

## 28

Which of these would describe a play with a grim humour?

A: White comedy
B: Blue comedy
C: Red comedy
D: Black comedy

## 29

Elton John and Kiki Dee's 1976 No 1 single was 'Don't Go Breaking My...'?

A: Knee
B: Brain
C: Heart
D: Neck

## 30

Which of these was a film starring Daniel Day-Lewis?

A: My Right Knee
B: My Big Toe
C: My Left Foot
D: My Trembling Lip

50:50 Go to page 242  Go to page 254 ? Answers on page 266

### 31

What name is given to the highest balcony in a theatre which contains the cheapest seats?

- A: Stalls
- B: Pit
- C: Gallery
- D: Circle

### 32

Which of these is a deadpan stand-up comedian?

- A: Heavy D
- B: Sandra Dee
- C: Jack Dee
- D: Kiki Dee

### 33

What is 'All You Need' according to the title of the 1967 Beatles single?

- A: Money
- B: Good Looks
- C: Fame
- D: Love

### 34

Complete this line from Shakespeare's 'Hamlet', 'To be or not to be, that is the...'?

- A: Thing
- B: Problem
- C: Snag
- D: Question

### 35

Which of these was not a destination in the Crosby-Hope-Lamour 'Road' films?

- A: Singapore
- B: Hong Kong
- C: Zanzibar
- D: Cleethorpes

50:50 Go to page 242　Go to page 254　? Answers on page 266

# 2 ◆ £200

## 36

**Complete the title of Jimmy Saville's popular TV series, 'Jim'll...'?**

- A: Make It
- B: Break It
- C: Mix It
- D: Fix It

## 37

**Which of these is not one of the 'Three Tenors'?**

- A: Luciano Pavarotti
- B: José Carreras
- C: Bob Dylan
- D: Placido Domingo

## 38

**The text and graphic information broadcast on television is known as what?**

- A: Teletype
- B: Teleprint
- C: Telepress
- D: Teletext

## 39

**Which of these was a No 1 hit for Chuck Berry in 1972?**

- A: My Clang-a-lang
- B: My Boom-a-room
- C: My Splash-a-lash
- D: My Ding-a-ling

## 40

**Who is the sidekick of the animated cartoon hero Dangermouse?**

- A: Penfold
- B: Fourfold
- C: Blindfold
- D: Centrefold

**50:50** Go to page 242　　**👥** Go to page 254　　**❓** Answers on page 266

# 2 ◆ £200

## 41

Which of these is a 1963 stage musical which initially starred Tommy Steele in the leading role?

- A: Half a Penny
- B: Half a Twopence
- C: Half a Threepence
- D: Half a Sixpence

## 42

Complete the title of the disaster film starring Steve McQueen and Paul Newman, 'The Towering...'?

- A: Inferno
- B: Mountain
- C: Iceberg
- D: Budget

## 43

Which of these shares its name with the lowest register of male singing voice?

- A: Badger
- B: Boddingtons
- C: Bass
- D: Beamish

## 44

Ken Barlow is the longest-running character in which soap opera?

- A: EastEnders
- B: Casualty
- C: Coronation Street
- D: Neighbours

## 45

What is the surname of the singing duet, Ike and Tina, who had a 1960s hit with 'River Deep Mountain High'?

- A: Turkey
- B: Tumour
- C: Turtle
- D: Turner

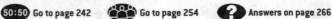 50:50 Go to page 242     Go to page 254    ? Answers on page 266

# 2 ◆ £200

page
61

## 46

Which British TV cop show took its title from the rhyming slang which included the name of an infamous barber?

- A: The Sweeney
- B: The Sorbie
- C: The Clarke
- D: The Sassoon

## 47

In which soap opera did Mike Reid play Frank Butcher?

- A: EastEnders
- B: Home and Away
- C: Brookside
- D: Neighbours

## 48

Complete the title of the 1965 film starring Michael Caine, 'The Ipcress...'?

- A: Hammer
- B: Saw
- C: Chisel
- D: File

## 49

Which Disney cartoon character is the uncle of Huey, Dewey and Louie?

- A: Mickey Mouse
- B: Pluto
- C: Goofy
- D: Donald Duck

## 50

What name is given to the inanimate objects that appear on the stage of a theatre?

- A: Supports
- B: Props
- C: Bolsters
- D: Extras

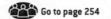 50:50 Go to page 242    Go to page 254     Answers on page 266

# 2 ◆ £200

## 51

Which of the following was the Lone Ranger's sidekick?

- A: Tripitaka
- B: Tonto
- C: Tarzan
- D: Tantor

## 52

In which 1950s classic western does
Alan Ladd famously ride off into the sunset?

- A: Wayne
- B: Gawain
- C: Dwayne
- D: Shane

## 53

Which Victoria wrote and starred in the
award-winning TV series 'dinnerladies'?

- A: Forest
- B: Wood
- C: Copse
- D: Grove

## 54

In which series did David Hasselhoff
star alongside Pamela Anderson?

- A: Baywatch
- B: Seawatch
- C: Beachwatch
- D: Peninsulawatch

## 55

Which popular 1980s group was formed
by George Michael and Andrew Ridgeley?

- A: Wham!
- B: Slam!
- C: Clam!
- D: Spam!

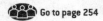 **50:50** Go to page 242     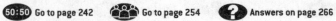 Go to page 254     **?** Answers on page 266

# 2 ◆ £200

## 56

Complete the title of this 1988 film, 'When Harry Met...'?

A: Larry          B: Jerry

C: Molly          D: Sally

## 57

Which of the following is a popular
time-travelling fictional character?

A: Doctor Who          B: Doctor What

C: Doctor Why          D: Doctor Wherefore

## 58

According to Gloria Gaynor's 1979 chart-topper, 'I Will...'?

A: Survive          B: Triumph

C: Excel          D: Succeed

## 59

Which two initials go before the name Barnum to
give the title character of the musical 'Barnum'?

A: A N          B: P T

C: C S          D: W H

## 60

What name is given to a film sound track
commentary by an unseen narrator?

A: Voice-under          B: Voice-over

C: Voice-aside          D: Voice-nearby

 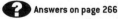

# 2 ◆ £200

## 61

Which word means to adjust a radio
signal to the desired frequency?

A: Jingle
B: Tune
C: Lilt
D: Melody

## 62

In the Laurel and Hardy films, Oliver Hardy's catchphrase
was 'Here's another fine... you've gotten me into'?

A: Pickle
B: State
C: Mess
D: Situation

## 63

Which musical is set in a village in the highlands of
Scotland and only appears for 24 hours each century?

A: Brigadier
B: Brigand
C: Brigadoon
D: Brigantine

## 64

Complete the title of the TV sitcom, 'Some Mothers Do...'?

A: Breed 'Em
B: Rear 'Em
C: 'Ave 'Em
D: Shoot 'Em

## 65

Which Stevens had a 1981 hit with 'This Ole House'?

A: Shakin'
B: Quakin'
C: Wakin'
D: Flakin'

50:50 Go to pages 242 & 243    Go to page 254    Answers on page 266

# 2 ◆ £200

page
65

## 66

By what name is the actor and comedian Robert Davis better known?

A: Jasper Cabbage

B: Jasper Potato

C: Jasper Onion

D: Jasper Carrott

## 67

Complete this musical duo, Flanders and...?

A: Drake

B: Moorhen

C: Swann

D: Goose

## 68

When written down, a piece of music is usually divided up into a number of what?

A: Bars

B: Cafés

C: Restaurants

D: Pubs

## 69

According to the 1981 film, who 'Always Rings Twice'?

A: The Postman

B: The Gasman

C: The Milkman

D: The Paperboy

## 70

J R and Bobby Ewing, residents of Southfork Ranch, were characters in which soap?

A: Dallas

B: Falcon Crest

C: Dynasty

D: Thirtysomething

50:50 Go to page 243    Go to page 255    ? Answers on page 266

# 2 ◆ £200

## 71

Complete the title of Sandy Shaw's 1967 Eurovision Song Contest winner, 'Puppet on a...'?

- A: Cable
- B: Rope
- C: Chain
- D: String

## 72

What is the profession of TV's Ally McBeal?

- A: Dentist
- B: Lawyer
- C: Policewoman
- D: Soldier

## 73

Who played the female lead in the film 'Pretty Woman'?

- A: Sandra Bullock
- B: Julia Roberts
- C: Liz Hurley
- D: Kathy Burke

## 74

Complete the title of the long-running West End musical, 'Blood...'?

- A: Cells
- B: Ties
- C: Brothers
- D: Feuds

## 75

Which of these is a film starring Vinnie Jones and Brad Pitt, and directed by Guy Ritchie?

- A: Snatch
- B: Grab
- C: Lunge
- D: Throw

# 2 ◆ £200

## 76

How are anarchic students Rik, Neil, Mike and Vyvyan collectively known in their BBC sitcom?

A: The Proud Ones
B: The Live Ones
C: The Young Ones
D: The Big Ones

## 77

Which of the following eventually triumphed in the 2002 hit TV show 'Pop Idol'?

A: Will Young
B: Darius Danesh
C: Zoe Birkett
D: Gareth Gates

## 78

In the world of radio, what name is given to the range of wavelengths between two given limits?

page 67

A: Tape
B: String
C: Band
D: Chain

## 79

Complete the title of the classic western, 'The Magnificent...'?

A: One
B: Twenty
C: Seven
D: Hundred

## 80

In 'Emmerdale', what is The Woolpack?

A: Hospital
B: Pub
C: Library
D: Prop sheep

 50:50 Go to page 243   Go to page 255    Answers on page 266

# 2 ◆ £200

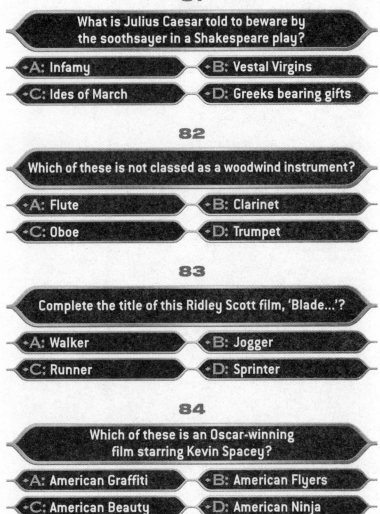

## 81

**What is Julius Caesar told to beware by the soothsayer in a Shakespeare play?**

A: Infamy

B: Vestal Virgins

C: Ides of March

D: Greeks bearing gifts

## 82

**Which of these is not classed as a woodwind instrument?**

A: Flute

B: Clarinet

C: Oboe

D: Trumpet

## 83

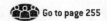

**Complete the title of this Ridley Scott film, 'Blade...'?**

A: Walker

B: Jogger

C: Runner

D: Sprinter

## 84

**Which of these is an Oscar-winning film starring Kevin Spacey?**

A: American Graffiti

B: American Flyers

C: American Beauty

D: American Ninja

**50:50** Go to page 243   Go to page 255   **?** Answers on page 266

| 50:50 | | |
|---|---|---|
| **15** | **£1 MILLION** | |
| 14 | £500,000 | |
| 13 | £250,000 | |
| 12 | £125,000 | |
| 11 | £64,000 | |
| **10** | **£32,000** | |
| 9 | £16,000 | |
| 8 | £8,000 | |
| 7 | £4,000 | |
| 6 | £2,000 | |
| **5** | **£1,000** | |
| 4 | £500 | |
| **3** | ◆ | **£300** |
| 2 | ◆ | £200 |
| 1 | ◆ | £100 |

# 3 ◆ £300

**1**

Which of these is a romantic film comedy starring Cher and Nicolas Cage?

- A: Frostbitten
- B: Sunburnt
- C: Windswept
- D: Moonstruck

**2**

What name is given to a film actor's stand-in?

- A: Doppelgänger
- B: Duplicate
- C: Second
- D: Double

**3**

Which of these TV comedy series stars Clive Dunn as Corporal Jones?

- A: 'Allo, 'Allo!
- B: Hi-De-Hi!
- C: Are You Being Served?
- D: Dad's Army

**4**

Who had a UK No 1 hit in 2000 with 'Stan'?

- A: Emenin
- B: Enimen
- C: Enemin
- D: Eminem

**5**

Which of these singing stars has won a Best Actress Oscar?

- A: Billie Piper
- B: Kylie Minogue
- C: Britney Spears
- D: Cher

50:50 Go to page 243  Go to page 255  **?** Answers on page 266

# 3 ◆ £300

**6**

What kind of 'pie' provided the title of a hit 1999 movie?

A: Blackberry Pie

B: Humble Pie

C: Pork Pie

D: American Pie

**7**

Which member of 'The Simpsons' has a blue beehive hairstyle?

A: Bart

B: Homer

C: Lisa

D: Marge

**8**

What is the first name of the actor Kiefer Sutherland's famous actor father?

A: Donald

B: David

C: Damian

D: Denzil

**9**

Which of these is a stage musical based on the Thornton Wilder play, 'The Matchmaker'?

A: Hello, Holly

B: Hello, Dolly

C: Hello, Molly

D: Hello, Polly

**10**

Lionel Richie was the lead singer with which group?

A: The Captains

B: The Admirals

C: The Rear Admirals

D: The Commodores

50:50 Go to page 243    Go to page 255    ? Answers on page 266

# 3 ◆ £300

## 11

**Which of these is the title of a classic American sci-fi series from the 1950s and 1960s?**

- A: The Afternoon Zone
- B: The Twilight Zone
- C: The Morning Zone
- D: The Midday Zone

## 12

**What did Madonna call her first-born daughter?**

- A: Lourdes
- B: Mecca
- C: Ganges
- D: Vaticana

## 13

**Which of these is the title of a stylish cop show of the 1980s?**

- A: Cleveland Homicide
- B: Miami Vice
- C: San Francisco Narcotics
- D: Milwaukee Fraud

## 14

**Complete the title of the film musical, 'Seven Brides for Seven...'?**

- A: Brothers
- B: Fathers
- C: Uncles
- D: Grandads

## 15

**Which of these is a list of those responsible for the production of a film or television programme?**

- A: Debits
- B: Receipts
- C: Credits
- D: Withdrawals

 50:50 Go to page 243    Go to page 255     Answers on page 266

# 3 ◆ £300

## 16

Which of the following are actors said
to have done when they forget their lines?

A: Dusted
B: Downed
C: Feathered
D: Fluffed

## 17

The name of which material is used
as a slang term for the cinema?

A: Celluloid
B: Nylon
C: Vinyl
D: Perspex

## 18

Which of these characters features
in the film 'The Wizard of Oz'?

A: Iron Duke
B: Lead Soldier
C: Tin Man
D: Brass Monkey

## 19

What word refers to a group of actors or entertainers?

A: Pod
B: Herd
C: Gaggle
D: Troupe

## 20

Which band caused controversy in
1984 with their single 'Relax'?

A: Davy Goes to Holyrood
B: Charlie Goes to Cricklewood
C: Jerry Goes to Holyhead
D: Frankie Goes to Hollywood

50:50 Go to page 243    Go to page 255    ? Answers on page 266

# 3 ◆ £300

## 21

**Complete the name of the drag comedy duo, 'Hinge and...'?**

- A: Buttress
- B: Bulwark
- C: Bracket
- D: Brace

## 22

**Which of the following is a popular pantomime character?**

- A: Buttons
- B: Pockets
- C: Zipper
- D: Poppers

## 23

**As which of the following are professional dancers sometimes referred?**

- A: Trotters
- B: Hoofers
- C: Clawers
- D: Pawers

## 24

**Which of these is the title of a long-running Broadway musical first performed in 1975?**

- A: A Washing Line
- B: A Pencil Line
- C: A Fine Line
- D: A Chorus Line

## 25

**Meg Ryan and Tom Hanks starred in the 1998 romantic comedy, 'You've Got...'?**

- A: Love
- B: Mail
- C: Cold Hands
- D: Dandruff

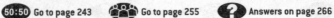 50:50 Go to page 243   Go to page 255   ? Answers on page 266

**26**

Which of the following is a character in the
Tennessee Williams play 'Cat on a Hot Tin Roof'?

- A: Big Daddy
- B: Mick McManus
- C: Giant Haystacks
- D: Kendo Nagasaki

**27**

Who is the regular partner of Dave Stewart
in the pop group 'Eurythmics'?

- A: Madonna
- B: Celine Dion
- C: Kylie Minogue
- D: Annie Lennox

**28**

Which of the following is associated with
the phrase 'Not a lot of people know that'?

- A: Sean Connery
- B: Richard Attenborough
- C: Magnus Magnusson
- D: Michael Caine

**29**

What does an actor do when departing from the script?

- A: Ad hoc
- B: Ad sum
- C: Ad lib
- D: Ad infinitum

**30**

Complete the title of the Mike Myers film,
'Austin Powers: International Man of...'?

- A: Mystery
- B: Ministry
- C: Mastery
- D: Misery

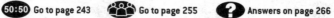

**50:50** Go to page 243　　Go to page 255　　? Answers on page 266

# 3 ◆ £300

## 31

Which of the following is a romantic comedy starring Gregory Peck and Audrey Hepburn?

A: Vegas Vacation
B: Brighton Break
C: Greenland Getaway
D: Roman Holiday

## 32

What are 'alive with the sound of music' in the song from the popular musical of the same name?

A: The valleys
B: The trees
C: The hills
D: The rivers

## 33

Which of the following 'Stole Christmas' in the title of the Dr Seuss film and cartoon?

A: Grump
B: Grouch
C: Grinch
D: Grool

## 34

What is the subject matter of the BBC's long-running Saturday afternoon show 'Grandstand'?

A: Opera
B: Pop music
C: Sport
D: Stand-up comedy

## 35

Who are Tom and Barbara's neighbours in the 1970s TV comedy 'The Good Life'?

A: Terry and June
B: George and Mildred
C: Jerry and Margot
D: Homer and Marge

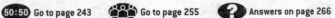

50:50 Go to page 243    Go to page 255    ? Answers on page 266

# 3 ◆ £300

## 36

Of which pop group are Liam and
Noel Gallagher both members?

A: Oasis

B: Desert

C: Palmtree

D: Sandstorm

## 37

Which pop songstress had a
2001 hit with 'I'm a Slave 4 U'?

A: Britney Swords

B: Britney Spears

C: Britney Slings

D: Britney Arrows

## 38

What name is given to a short extract from a film?

A: Cut

B: Crop

C: Clip

D: Snip

## 39

Which of these words is used to mean
an unrehearsed musical performance?

A: Buttering

B: Marmalading

C: Jamming

D: Honeying

## 40

Break dancing and body popping are both dance forms
of which urban culture which originated in the 1970s?

A: Hip-skip

B: Hip-hop

C: Hip-jump

D: Hip-hip-hooray

50:50 Go to page 243    Go to page 255    ? Answers on page 266

# 3 ◆ £300

## 41

Which British actress starred as the spiteful
Alexis Carrington Colby in 'Dynasty'?

- A: Joan Collins
- B: Vanessa Redgrave
- C: Judi Dench
- D: Maggie Smith

## 42

Davy Jones and Mike Nesmith were
members of which 1960s pop group?

- A: The Chimps
- B: The Apes
- C: The Gorillas
- D: The Monkees

## 43

What substance, invented in 1865, is
synonymous with theatrical make-up?

- A: Greasepaint
- B: Turpentine
- C: Cod liver oil
- D: Talcum powder

## 44

With which of the following would
you most associate the ukelele?

- A: Ronnie Scott
- B: George Formby
- C: Yehudi Menuhin
- D: Roy Castle

## 45

Which of these is Dr David Banner's TV alter ego?

- A: The Incredible Bulk
- B: The Incredible Skulk
- C: The Incredible Sulk
- D: The Incredible Hulk

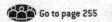 50:50 Go to page 243     Go to page 255    ? Answers on page 266

# 3 ◆ £300

## 46

The comedy singing duo Flanagan and Allen sang about being 'Underneath the...'?

- A: Arches
- B: Heels
- C: Toes
- D: Ankles

## 47

What name is given to someone who plays the flute?

- A: Fluter
- B: Flutter
- C: Flautist
- D: Fluteer

## 48

Which of the following is an arts complex by the river Thames in London, incorporating the Royal Festival Hall?

- A: North Bank
- B: West Bank
- C: South Bank
- D: East Bank

## 49

The creator of 'Star Trek' was Gene...?

- A: Blackberry
- B: Raspberry
- C: Loganberry
- D: Roddenberry

## 50

Which of the following would you hear sung in the hit musical 'Oliver!'?

- A: Mud, glorious mud
- B: Food, glorious food
- C: Slums, glorious slums
- D: Cash, glorious cash

# 3 ◆ £300

## 51

What does the 'V' stand for in the abbreviation VHS?

- A: Video
- B: Virtual
- C: Vortex
- D: Vital

## 52

Which comedian regularly used the catchphrase, 'Nice to see you, to see you nice'?

- A: Jimmy Tarbuck
- B: Bob Monkhouse
- C: Bruce Forsyth
- D: Russ Abbott

## 53

According to the title of an opera by Mozart, which musical instrument was 'Magic'?

- A: Flute
- B: Synthesizer
- C: Electric guitar
- D: Drum machine

## 54

Which spoof radio DJ duo was created by Harry Enfield?

- A: Bangers and Smash
- B: Smashie and Nicey
- C: Smashing and Lovely
- D: Smash and Grab

## 55

Complete the name of the 1980s pop group, Adam and the...?

- A: Bees
- B: Spiders
- C: Bugs
- D: Ants

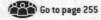 50:50 Go to page 243    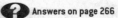 Go to page 255    ? Answers on page 266

# 3 ◆ £300

## 56

Which soft drink was often advertised as 'the real thing'?

A: Tizer
B: Irn Bru
C: Coca-Cola
D: Pepsi

## 57

What is the other profession of the actor 'The Rock', star of the film 'The Scorpion King'?

A: Stonemason
B: Wrestler
C: Prison Guard
D: Geologist

## 58

Which island is particularly renowned as a popular destination for nightclubbers?

A: Sardinia
B: Ibiza
C: Malta
D: Guernsey

## 59

What did the Beastie Boys 'Fight For Your Right' to do in the title of their 1987 UK hit?

A: Vote
B: Free Expression
C: Party
D: Education

## 60

Who is Sharon's sister in the TV sitcom 'Birds of a Feather'?

A: Tracey
B: Linda
C: Susan
D: Sarah

50:50 Go to pages 243 & 244     Go to page 255     Answers on page 266

# 3 ◆ £300

## 61

What is the name of the darts-based
quiz show presented by Jim Bowen?

A: Double Top

B: Trebles All Round

C: Bullseye

D: Oche!

## 62

Which of these is a successful musical
based on a story by Victor Hugo?

A: Les Misérables

B: Les Incroyables

C: Les Desirables

D: Les Impossibles

## 63

To which of the following do the lines,
'We can rebuild him; we have the technology' refer?

A: Robocop

B: Six Million Dollar Man

C: Terminator

D: David Beckham

## 64

Which of these is a Gilbert and Sullivan
operetta set in Japan?

A: The Subaru

B: The Mikado

C: The Mitsubishi

D: The Shogun

## 65

Complete the title of the 1996
Oscar winning film, 'The English...'?

A: Doctor

B: Nurse

C: Surgeon

D: Patient

50:50 Go to page 244      Go to page 256      ? Answers on page 266

# 3 ◆ £300

## 66

Which singer had hits with 'Bat Out of Hell',
'Dead Ringer for Love' and 'Not a Dry Eye in the House'?

A: Nut Roast

B: Lamb Chop

C: Veggie Burger

D: Meat Loaf

## 67

In television, what name is given to a sample episode of a
projected series which is produced to test audience reaction?

A: Guide

B: Conductor

C: Pilot

D: Navigator

## 68

Who was 'Indahouse' in a 2002 film?

page
83

A: Warren G

B: Mel B

C: Ali G

D: George W Bush

## 69

In the US cartoon, which moose is the sidekick
of the character Rocky, the flying squirrel?

A: Bulloyster

B: Bullmussel

C: Bullwhelk

D: Bullwinkle

## 70

Which shabby item of clothing was the
trademark of the TV detective 'Columbo'?

A: Anorak

B: Bowler hat

C: Bow tie

D: Raincoat

 50:50 Go to page 244    Go to page 256    ? Answers on page 266

# 3 ◆ £300

## 71

What was the composer Beethoven's first name?

- A: Wolfgang
- B: Herman
- C: Ludwig
- D: Siegfried

## 72

Which super-hero was born on the planet Krypton?

- A: Superman
- B: Batman
- C: Spider-Man
- D: Super Mario

## 73

Who is Shakespeare's 'Prince of Denmark'?

- A: Hamlet
- B: Hansel
- C: Harquil
- D: Hurley

## 74

Which of these classic comedy characters was played by Leonard Rossiter?

- A: Norman Stanley Fletcher
- B: Reginald Perrin
- C: Mr Humphries
- D: Victor Meldrew

## 75

What form of transport does Steve McQueen use in his final attempt to escape in the 1963 film 'The Great Escape'?

- A: Horse and cart
- B: Hot air balloon
- C: Submarine
- D: Motorcycle

 50:50 Go to page 244   Go to page 256   ? Answers on page 266

# 3 ◆ £300

## 76

Which TV personality regularly hosts BBC's 'Children in Need' charity programme?

- A: Terry Wogan
- B: Cilla Black
- C: Des O'Connor
- D: Jonathan Ross

## 77

Complete the name of the Welsh pop group, Manic Street...?

- A: Preachers
- B: Evangelists
- C: Gospellers
- D: Bible Thumpers

## 78

Which occupation does Jim Carrey have in the title of a 1994 film?

page 85

- A: Pet Defender
- B: Pet Detective
- C: Pet Defector
- D: Pet Detector

## 79

The Battersby family – Les, Janice, Toyah and Leanne – appear in which soap opera?

- A: Coronation Street
- B: Crossroads
- C: Emmerdale
- D: Brookside

## 80

With which group is singer Errol Brown chiefly associated?

- A: Hot Coffee
- B: Hot Tea
- C: Hot Toddy
- D: Hot Chocolate

50:50 Go to page 244    Go to page 256    ? Answers on page 266

| 50:50 | | |
|---|---|---|
| **15** | **£1 MILLION** | |
| 14 | £500,000 | |
| 13 | £250,000 | |
| 12 | £125,000 | |
| 11 | £64,000 | |
| **10** | **£32,000** | |
| 9 | £16,000 | |
| 8 | £8,000 | |
| 7 | £4,000 | |
| 6 | £2,000 | |
| **5** | **£1,000** | |
| **4 ◆** | **£500** | |
| 3 ◆ | £300 | |
| 2 ◆ | £200 | |
| 1 ◆ | £100 | |

# 4 ◆ £500

## 1
Which word can go before pipe, stop and grinder?

A: Saxophone
B: Drum
C: Trombone
D: Organ

## 2
What name is used to describe India's film-making industry?

A: Bollywood
B: Dollywood
C: Gandhiwood
D: Delhiwood

## 3
Produced by ex-Monkee Michael Dolenz, what was the name of the robot in an ITV children's series in the early 1980s?

A: Copper Colin
B: Iron Ian
C: Metal Mickey
D: Silver Sid

## 4
Which of these is a play by William Shakespeare?

A: One Night
B: Last Night
C: Twelfth Night
D: Fright Night

## 5
By what stage name is the US singer Stanley Burrell better known?

A: M C Nail
B: M C Screw
C: M C Hammer
D: M C Mallet

50:50 Go to page 244  Go to page 256  Answers on page 267

# 4 ◆ £500

## 6

Which of the following is an acting technique in which performers aspire to identify with the motivation of their character?

- A: Motion
- B: Method
- C: Mode
- D: Manner

## 7

Who presents Channel 4's long-running numbers and letters quiz 'Countdown'?

- A: Bob Holness
- B: Richard Whiteley
- C: Michael Parkinson
- D: Chris Tarrant

## 8

Which of these is a comedy western directed by Mel Brooks?

- A: Smoking Stirrups
- B: Flaming Stetsons
- C: Blazing Saddles
- D: Sizzling Spurs

## 9

Complete the name of the pop group, 'Simple...'?

- A: Ideas
- B: Thoughts
- C: Brains
- D: Minds

## 10

Which of these characters was made famous by the comedian Sacha Baron Cohen?

- A: Ali Baba
- B: Muhammad Ali
- C: Ali McGraw
- D: Ali G

50:50 Go to page 244    Go to page 256    ? Answers on page 267

# 4 ◆ £500

## 11

Complete the title of the successful
1990s musical, 'Five Guys Named...'?

- A: Joe
- B: Poe
- C: Moe
- D: Bo

## 12

On a feature film set, what is a boom?

- A: Microphone
- B: Camera
- C: Stunt explosion
- D: Unhappy director

## 13

Which phrase was used to describe a 1980s fashion and music movement
which included groups such as Duran Duran and Spandau Ballet?

- A: New Sentimental
- B: New Sceptic
- C: New Romantic
- D: New Cynic

## 14

In music, which word means the degree
of highness or lowness of a tone?

- A: Throw
- B: Cast
- C: Pitch
- D: Lob

## 15

Which character is played by Jennifer Saunders
in the TV series, 'Absolutely Fabulous'?

- A: Edina Storm
- B: Edina Typhoon
- C: Edina Hurricane
- D: Edina Monsoon

 50:50 Go to page 244    Go to page 256    ? Answers on page 267

# 4 ◆ £500

## 16

Robbie WIlliams, Gary Barlow and Mark Owen
were all members of which boy band?

- A: East 17
- B: Take That
- C: Westlife
- D: Boyzone

## 17

With which cinema genre are
Hammer Films chiefly associated?

- A: Musical
- B: Documentary
- C: Comedy
- D: Horror

## 18

Which hobby does former TV comedian
Bill Oddie now pursue as a 'professional'?

page
**91**

- A: Stamp collecting
- B: Pottery
- C: Fishing
- D: Bird-watching

## 19

What are Randall and Hopkirk in the
TV series 'Randall and Hopkirk (Deceased)'?

- A: Soldiers
- B: Doctors
- C: Firefighters
- D: Private detectives

## 20

Which of these is a 1990 gangster
film directed by Martin Scorsese?

- A: Nicechaps
- B: Goodfellas
- C: Fineblokes
- D: Excellentmen

 **50:50** Go to page 244      Go to page 256      **?** Answers on page 267

# 4 ◆ £500

## 21

What are actors proverbially encouraged
to break before going on stage?

A: Leg

B: Neck

C: Arm

D: Wrist

## 22

Which of the following performers was referred
to as 'The Pelvis' for his on-stage posturing?

A: Frank Sinatra

B: Elvis Presley

C: Dean Martin

D: Luciano Pavarotti

## 23

Complete the title of this comedy duo, Baddiel and...?

A: Livingstone

B: Mowlam

C: Skinner

D: Banks

## 24

Which of these dancers became
famous for appearing in 'Riverdance'?

A: Margot Fonteyn

B: Wayne Sleep

C: Michael Flatley

D: Darcey Bussell

## 25

Who is the star of the 'Alien' movies?

A: Kate Winslet

B: Goldie Hawn

C: Sigourney Weaver

D: Helena Bonham Carter

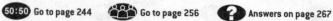
**50:50** Go to page 244    Go to page 256    **?** Answers on page 267

# 4 ◆ £500

## 26

Which sport formed the background to the 1990s TV comedy series 'Outside Edge'?

A: Tennis
B: Golf
C: Rugby Union
D: Cricket

## 27

Def Leppard and Iron Maiden are best known for what kind of music?

A: Jazz
B: Disco
C: Heavy metal
D: Latin American

## 28

Which EastEnders actress had a No 1 hit with 'Perfect Moment'?

A: Wendy Richard
B: Barbara Windsor
C: Martine McCutcheon
D: Letitia Dean

## 29

A musical, based on a story by Ian Fleming, opened in London's West End in 2002 starring which famous fictional car?

A: Herbie
B: KITT
C: Chitty Chitty Bang Bang
D: Batmobile

## 30

Which of these countries became the adopted home of film stars Mel Gibson, Nicole Kidman and Russell Crowe?

A: Australia
B: Canada
C: South Africa
D: New Zealand

50:50 Go to page 244     Go to page 256      Answers on page 267

# 4 ◆ £500

## 31

In which of the following is the TV drama 'Bad Girls' set?

A: School
B: Beautician's
C: Supermarket
D: Prison

## 32

Whom did Eric Clapton shoot, according to his 1974 hit single?

A: The Judge
B: The Marshal
C: The Lawyer
D: The Sheriff

## 33

In the title of the musical, on which 'Street' would you meet the characters Peggy Sawyer and Billy Lawyer?

A: 19th
B: 42nd
C: 50th
D: 67th

## 34

Which Californian suburb has the zipcode 90210, in the title of a 1990s US TV series?

A: Bel Air
B: Hollywood
C: Beverly Hills
D: Malibu

## 35

In which film does Bruce Willis play a child psychologist treating a boy who can see dead people?

A: The Seventh Seal
B: The Sixth Sense
C: The Fifth Wheel
D: The Third Degree

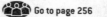 50:50 Go to page 244    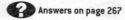 Go to page 256    ? Answers on page 267

# 4 ◆ £500

## 36

Which group had a 1960s hit with 'Monday Monday'?

- A: Aunties and the Uncles
- B: Brothers and the Sisters
- C: Grandpas and the Grandmas
- D: Mamas and the Papas

## 37

By which more common name is the
Royal Victoria Hall in London known?

- A: Teenaged Vic
- B: Middle-aged Vic
- C: Old Vic
- D: Baby Vic

## 38

In which South American country
is the musical 'Evita' set?

- A: Argentina
- B: Brazil
- C: Chile
- D: Peru

## 39

What is the nickname of the surgeon Captain Pierce,
played by Alan Alda, in the TV series 'M*A*S*H'?

- A: Hawkeye
- B: Bullseye
- C: Eagle-eye
- D: Popeye

## 40

Complete the title of the Stephen Sondheim musical,
'A Funny Thing Happened on the Way to...'?

- A: The Colosseum
- B: The Forum
- C: The Circus Maximus
- D: The Via Appia

 50:50 Go to page 244    Go to page 256    ? Answers on page 267

# 4 ◆ £500

## 41

Which of the following does Mickey Mouse put under his spell to help him with his chores in the children's favourite 'Fantasia'?

- A: Brooms
- B: Aerosols
- C: Washing machines
- D: Hoovers

## 42

Who was the lead singer of the Supremes?

- A: Diana Dors
- B: Dyan Cannon
- C: Diana Ross
- D: Diane Keaton

## 43

Wolf, Jet, Scorpio and Hunter were muscle-bound participants in which game show?

- A: The Krypton Factor
- B: It's a Knockout
- C: Gladiators
- D: Shooting Stars

## 44

With which pop star did Tim Rice co-write the lyrics and music for the film 'The Lion King'?

- A: Phil Collins
- B: Eric Clapton
- C: George Michael
- D: Elton John

## 45

What were Sister Sledge, according to the title of their 1979 hit single?

- A: Lost in Music
- B: Lost in Fog
- C: Lost in Love
- D: Lost in Peckham

50:50 Go to page 244     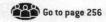 Go to page 256      Answers on page 267

# 4 ◆ £500

## 46

**In which 1998 film does part of a comet hit the Earth?**

- A: Light Brush
- B: Deep Impact
- C: Glancing Blow
- D: Heavy Contact

## 47

**Who played Basil Fawlty's wife in the TV sitcom, 'Fawlty Towers'?**

- A: Connie Booth
- B: Felicity Kendal
- C: Prunella Scales
- D: Penelope Keith

## 48

**In which country are the Kirov Ballet Company based?**

- A: Russia
- B: China
- C: North Korea
- D: Vietnam

## 49

**With which instrument was the entertainer Liberace usually associated?**

- A: Guitar
- B: Trumpet
- C: Piano
- D: Vibraphone

## 50

**What is the name of Kylie Minogue's 2002 album that includes the hit 'Can't Get You Out of My Head'?**

- A: Sneezing
- B: Aches and Pains
- C: Fever
- D: Sore Throat

50:50 Go to page 244     Go to page 256     Answers on page 267

# 4 ◆ £500

## 51

Which sitcom sees Rene Artois running a café in occupied France during WWII?

- A: Secret Army
- B: 'Allo 'Allo!
- C: Robin's Nest
- D: Are You Being Served?

## 52

Gene Kelly was the star which of these films?

- A: Rain Man
- B: Singin' in the Rain
- C: Black Rain
- D: Purple Rain

## 53

Which of the following is an airy spirit in Shakespeare's 'The Tempest'?

- A: Ariel
- B: Bold
- C: Persil
- D: Radion

## 54

For what does the second 'B' in BBC stand?

- A: British
- B: Broadcasting
- C: Broadband
- D: Beeb

## 55

Complete the name of the popular 1980s group, Fine Young...?

- A: Savages
- B: Headhunters
- C: Maneaters
- D: Cannibals

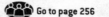 50:50 Go to page 244     Go to page 256    ? Answers on page 267

# 4 ◆ £500

## 56

What was Clint Eastwood in the title of his 1992 western?

- A: Unannounced
- B: Unforgiven
- C: Unamused
- D: Unpaid

## 57

By what name was Ben Elton known in his 1990s TV comedy sketch series?

- A: The Man from Auntie
- B: The Man from Mummy
- C: The Man from Granny
- D: The Man from Uncle

## 58

What sort of animal is Felix, the cartoon creation of Otto Messmer?

- A: Mouse
- B: Dog
- C: Cat
- D: Pig

## 59

Complete the title of Prokofiev's symphonic fairy tale, 'Peter and the...'?

- A: Lion
- B: Tiger
- C: Elephant
- D: Wolf

## 60

Which of these was a No 1 single in 1977 for Kenny Rogers?

- A: Lucille
- B: Loretta
- C: Lorna
- D: Lucinda

50:50 Go to page 244     Go to page 257     Answers on page 267

# 4 ◆ £500

## 61

What is the name of the FBI agent played by David Duchovny in the TV series 'The X Files'?

- **A: Fox Mulder**
- **B: Wolf Mulder**
- **C: Bear Mulder**
- **D: Badger Mulder**

## 62

Where do the TV characters Kyle, Kenny, Cartman and Stan live?

- **A: North Park**
- **B: South Park**
- **C: East Park**
- **D: West Park**

## 63

Complete this famous trio of record producers, Stock, Aitken and...?

- **A: Waterman**
- **B: Boatman**
- **C: Bargeman**
- **D: Seaman**

## 64

In which British city would you find the Barbican arts and entertainment complex?

- **A: London**
- **B: Leeds**
- **C: Glasgow**
- **D: Manchester**

## 65

Which 'Only Fools and Horses' actor subsequently starred in the TV series, 'Goodnight Sweetheart'?

- **A: David Jason**
- **B: Buster Merryfield**
- **C: Roger Lloyd Pack**
- **D: Nicholas Lyndhurst**

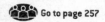 **50:50** Go to page 245  Go to page 257 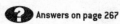 **?** Answers on page 267

# 4 ◆ £500

## 66

What did Mikhail Baryshnikov famously do in 1974?

- ◆A: Break the long jump record
- ◆B: Defect to the west
- ◆C: Reach the North Pole
- ◆D: Walk on the moon

## 67

In 2002, who made a tearful acceptance speech after becoming the first black American to win a Best Actress Oscar?

- ◆A: Angela Bassett
- ◆B: Jada Pinkett-Smith
- ◆C: Halle Berry
- ◆D: Whitney Houston

## 68

What was Jeff Goldblum turned into in the 1986 remake of that title?

- ◆A: The Wasp
- ◆B: The Bee
- ◆C: The Ant
- ◆D: The Fly

## 69

Which of the following was a hit for the 1980s pop diva Sade?

- ◆A: Smooth Operator
- ◆B: Suave Mover
- ◆C: Dodgy Geezer
- ◆D: Slimy Character

## 70

Complete the title of the famous musical, 'Guys and...'?

- ◆A: Gals
- ◆B: Dolls
- ◆C: Maids
- ◆D: Molls

50:50 Go to page 245    Go to page 257    ? Answers on page 267

# 4 ◆ £500

## 71

In Rossini's Seville-based opera,
what is the occupation of Figaro?

- A: Baker
- B: Barber
- C: Policeman
- D: Hot dog seller

## 72

Which of these is a character in 'EastEnders'?

- A: Hilda Ogden
- B: Sinbad Sweeney
- C: Dot Branning
- D: Amos Brearly

## 73

What type of invisible animal was 'Harvey'
in the James Stewart film of the same name?

- A: Dog
- B: Cat
- C: Rabbit
- D: Guinea pig

## 74

Which character appeared in the 1970s
police drama, 'Starsky and Hutch'?

- A: Yogi Bear
- B: Huggy Bear
- C: Paddington Bear
- D: Boo-Boo

## 75

In which type of stress-filled
institution is the TV drama 'ER' set?

- A: Police station
- B: Hospital
- C: Fire station
- D: TV studio

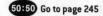 50:50 Go to page 245     Go to page 257     ? Answers on page 267

# 4 ◆ £500

Which of these is a method of casting
a play in which actors compete for parts?

A: Apparition

B: Altercation

C: Authorisation

D: Audition

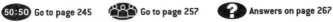

50:50 Go to page 245    Go to page 257    ? Answers on page 267

| 50:50 | | |
|---|---|---|
| **15** | **£1 MILLION** | |
| 14 | £500,000 | |
| 13 | £250,000 | |
| 12 | £125,000 | |
| 11 | £64,000 | |
| **10** | **£32,000** | |
| 9 | £16,000 | |
| 8 | £8,000 | |
| 7 | £4,000 | |
| 6 | £2,000 | |
| **5 ♦** | **£1,000** | |
| 4 ♦ | £500 | |
| 3 ♦ | £300 | |
| 2 ♦ | £200 | |
| 1 ♦ | £100 | |

# 5 ◆ £1,000

### 1

**Which of the following was decribed as 'full of eastern promise' in a television advertising campaign?**

- A: Turkish Delight
- B: Nissan Micra
- C: Thailand
- D: Pot Noodle

### 2

**In the 1977 film 'Star Wars', by what other first name is Obi-Wan Kenobi known?**

- A: Bin
- B: Ban
- C: Bon
- D: Ben

### 3

**Which of these is a traditional Japanese form of drama?**

- A: Yep
- B: Noh
- C: O-kay
- D: May-bee

### 4

**With which of the following did Oasis have a No 1 single in 2002?**

- A: Hindu Times
- B: Sikh Telegraph
- C: Buddhism Mirror
- D: Muslim Mail

### 5

**Which of the following are George Clooney and Brad Pitt planning to rob in the film 'Ocean's Eleven'?**

- A: Banks
- B: Casinos
- C: Payroll vans
- D: Sea chests

50:50 Go to page 245    Go to page 257    Answers on page 267

# 5 ◆ £1,000

## 6

**The actress Wendy Richard plays which character in the TV soap 'EastEnders'?**

A: Kat Slater

B: Peggy Butcher

C: Pauline Fowler

D: Sharon Watts

## 7

**Which of these British actors was named after the opening line of a Beatles' song?**

A: Sean Pertwee

B: Ewan McGregor

C: Jude Law

D: Tim Roth

## 8

**In September 1990, which 24-hour dance-music radio station became the first to legally broadcast in the UK?**

A: Cuddle FM

B: Hug FM

C: Kiss FM

D: Embrace FM

## 9

**Which musical was the longest-running Broadway show until 'Cats'?**

A: A Straight Line

B: A Fine Line

C: A Chorus Line

D: A Long Line

## 10

**Who plays Lovejoy in the TV series of the same name?**

A: Ian McShane

B: Michael Elphick

C: Albert Finney

D: Roger Moore

 50:50 Go to page 245    Go to page 257    ? Answers on page 267

# 5 ◆ £1,000

## 11

Which area of a theatre is specifically
reserved for the use of the cast?

A: Blue room      B: Green room

C: Red room       D: Black room

## 12

Complete Corporal Jones' catch-phrase
in 'Dad's Army', 'They don't like it...'?

A: Twice          B: In a hurry

C: Indoors        D: Up 'em

## 13

Which of the following phrases would you associate
with the films of Arnold Schwarzenegger?

A: Play it again, Sam      B: Shaken, not stirred

C: I'll be back            D: I'm terribly sorry about the mess

## 14

With which instrument is the Indian
musician Ravi Shankar chiefly associated?

A: Ukelele        B: Piano

C: Sitar          D: Xylophone

## 15

Around which of the following workplaces
is the TV drama series 'Cutting It' set?

A: Paper factory      B: Hospital

C: Garden centre      D: Hairdresser

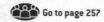 
50:50 Go to page 245      Go to page 257      ? Answers on page 267

# 5 ◆ £1,000

## 16

What is the name of Lady Penelope's butler
and chauffeur in the TV series 'Thunderbirds'?

A: Harker     B: Parker

C: Packer     D: Barker

## 17

In which popular musical, set in a 1950s US high school,
are Sandy and Danny the principal romantic leads?

A: Pomade     B: Grease

C: Gel     D: Brylcreem

## 18

Which Hollywood legend was nicknamed 'The Duke'?

A: John Wayne     B: Rock Hudson

C: James Dean     D: Steve McQueen

## 19

What is the name of the killer in the
'A Nightmare on Elm Street' series of films?

A: Rod     B: Jane

C: Freddy     D: Bungle

## 20

Paul Merton and Ian Hislop are regular
team captains on which quiz show?

A: A Question of Sport     B: Have I Got News For You

C: Does Doug Know?     D: They Think It's All Over

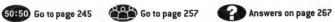

50:50 Go to page 245     Go to page 257     ? Answers on page 267

# 5 ◆ £1,000

## 21

What is the first name of the fictional serial killer played by Anthony Hopkins in two films?

A: Hannibal

B: Genghis

C: Attila

D: Caesar

## 22

What is the surname of the British acting brothers Ralph and Joseph?

A: Fiennes

B: Day-Lewis

C: Pertwee

D: Eccleston

## 23

For which film did Denzel Washington win an Oscar in 2002?

A: Painting Day

B: Raining Day

C: Training Day

D: Complaining Day

## 24

What was the name of the rabbit in the cult children's TV show 'The Magic Roundabout'?

A: David

B: Dylan

C: Donald

D: Dirk

## 25

Which band's final UK No 1 single was a cover of the Bee Gees' 'How Deep Is Your Love'?

A: Motörhead

B: Take That

C: East 17

D: Beatles

50:50 Go to page 245　　Go to page 257　　Answers on page 267

# 5 ◆ £1,000

## 26

Who starred as Rab C Nesbitt in the TV series of that name?

**A: Gregor Fisher**  **B: Robert Carlyle**

**C: Rowan Atkinson**  **D: Paul Shane**

## 27

Which of these is a 1940s/50s genre
of film, usually with a bleak storyline?

**A: Film gris**  **B: Film noir**

**C: Film vert**  **D: Film bleu**

## 28

With whom has Tony Hatch written
and produced many hit songs?

page
111

**A: Jackie Trent**  **B: Sammy Thames**

**C: Billy Derwent**  **D: Angi Amazon**

## 29

What is 'The Rock' in the film of the
same name starring Nicolas Cage?

**A: Mount Everest**  **B: Gibraltar**

**C: Koh-i-Noor diamond**  **D: Alcatraz**

## 30

In which TV series of the late 1970s and early 80s did Joanna
Lumley and David McCallum play aliens with special powers?

**A: Ruby and Nickel**  **B: Emerald and Silver**

**C: Diamond and Gold**  **D: Sapphire and Steel**

 50:50 Go to page 245    Go to page 257    Answers on page 267

# 5 ◆ £1,000

## 31

Who is Bob Mortimer's regular comedy partner?

- A: Vic Reeves
- B: Tommy Cannon
- C: Des O'Connor
- D: Kenny Lynch

## 32

What colour completes the title of the Rolling Stones 1964 hit single, 'Little... Rooster'?

- A: Red
- B: Blue
- C: Orange
- D: Purple

## 33

In Elizabethan theatre, what name was given to the central un-roofed area of the auditorium?

- A: Snare
- B: Pit
- C: Vault
- D: Crypt

## 34

Which actor reacted angrily when his acceptance speech was cut short at the 2002 BAFTA award ceremony?

- A: Kevin Spacey
- B: Russell Crowe
- C: Jim Broadbent
- D: Ian McKellen

## 35

Justin Hayward is best known for fronting which British group?

- A: The Thoughtful Reds
- B: The Pensive Greens
- C: The Contemplative Yellows
- D: The Moody Blues

50:50 Go to page 245    Go to page 257    ? Answers on page 267

# 5 ◆ £1,000

## 36

Which classic 1956 science fiction film
was loosely based on a Shakepeare play?

A: Comet of Errors

B: Twelfth Moon

C: Forbidden Planet

D: The Merchant of Venus

## 37

What can't 'White Men' do in the title of the 1992
film starring Wesley Snipes and Woody Harrelson?

A: Run

B: Jump

C: Play

D: Act

## 38

Which musical term means a slight
tremulous effect applied to a note?

A: Arabiato

B: Vibrato

C: Frascati

D: Largo

## 39

'Dangerous', 'Bad' and 'Thriller'
are albums by which singer?

A: Madonna

B: Michael Jackson

C: Bruce Springsteen

D: Cher

## 40

Which musical is adapted from
Prosper Mérimée's novel 'Carmen'?

A: Carmen Smith

B: Carmen Brown

C: Carmen Johnson

D: Carmen Jones

50:50 Go to page 245    Go to page 257    ? Answers on page 267

# 5 ◆ £1,000

## 41

In which fictional borough is 'Coronation Street' set?

A: Withenshawe

B: Walmington

C: Weatherfield

D: Westcliff

## 42

Which instrument does bandleader
Kenny Ball usually play?

A: Piano

B: Saxophone

C: Violin

D: Trumpet

## 43

The 1960s rock 'n' roll star Marty Wilde has an
equally famous daughter: what is her first name?

A: Kim

B: Kylie

C: Kathy

D: Kate

## 44

Which of these is a film biography
of the composer George Gershwin?

A: Rhapsody in Red

B: Rhapsody in Blue

C: Rhapsody in Green

D: Rhapsody in Yellow

## 45

Who collaborated with Richard Rodgers?

A: Arthur Sullivan

B: Stephen Sondheim

C: Oscar Hammerstein II

D: W S Gilbert

50:50 Go to page 245    Go to page 257    ? Answers on page 267

# 5 ◆ £1,000

## 46

**Which of the following was a famous Italian operatic tenor?**

- A: Enrico Caruso
- B: Rudolph Valentino
- C: Paolo di Canio
- D: Ahma Solauda

## 47

**What sort of 'room' appears in the title of a 2002 film starring Jodie Foster?**

- A: Panic
- B: Distress
- C: Sick
- D: Cutting

## 48

**Which northern playwright was responsible for the TV monologues 'Talking Heads'?**

- A: Hywel Bennett
- B: Alan Bennett
- C: Jill Bennett
- D: Gordon Bennett

## 49

**Complete the title of Smetana's opera, 'The Bartered...'?**

- A: Bride
- B: Usher
- C: Bridegroom
- D: Photographer

## 50

**Which independent television company has a franchise to broadcast to the North-East of England?**

- A: Severn Trent
- B: Mersey Avon
- C: Stour Ribble
- D: Tyne Tees

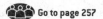 

# 5 ◆ £1,000

### 51

For which of these films did
Tom Hanks win a Best Actor Oscar?

- A: Seattle
- B: Philadelphia
- C: Sacramento
- D: Baltimore

### 52

Which of these composers' first names were Piotr Ilyich?

- A: Tchaikovsky
- B: Verdi
- C: Mozart
- D: Handel

### 53

Who is the star of the films 'An Officer and
a Gentleman' and 'Internal Affairs'?

- A: Richard Harris
- B: Richard Dreyfuss
- C: Richard Gere
- D: Richard Widmark

### 54

Which of these is a form of drama which
developed in the 16th and 17th centuries?

- A: Visor
- B: Screen
- C: Veil
- D: Masque

### 55

In which of these cities is the aptly-named
local radio station 96 Trent FM based?

- A: Plymouth
- B: Glasgow
- C: Swansea
- D: Nottingham

 50:50 Go to pages 245 & 246　　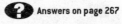 Go to page 257　　❓ Answers on page 267

# 5 ◆ £1,000

## 56

Which musical opened at the Shaftesbury
Theatre in London on 27th September 1968?

◆A: Teeth
◆B: Skin
◆C: Hair
◆D: Eyes

## 57

Who had a UK No 1 in 2000 with 'Rise'?

◆A: Gabrielle
◆B: Dido
◆C: Britney Spears
◆D: Kylie Minogue

## 58

Which of the following was not a
companion of the cartoon feline 'Top Cat'?

◆A: Benny the Ball
◆B: Brain
◆C: Choo Choo
◆D: Pluto

## 59

In which country was the actor Pierce Brosnan born?

◆A: USA
◆B: Australia
◆C: UK
◆D: Ireland

## 60

Which of these is a public musical
performance by one or a few musicians?

◆A: Rehearsal
◆B: Recital
◆C: Revival
◆D: Reversal

50:50 Go to pages 245 & 246　　Go to page 258　　? Answers on page 267

# 5 ♦ £1,000

## 61

What are the first names of the
comedy double act Hale and Pace?

A: Mike and Bernie
B: Syd and Eddie
C: Tommy and Bobby
D: Gareth and Norman

## 62

Which of the following is a 1969 western film musical?

A: Clean Your Saddle
B: Paint Your Wagon
C: Polish Your Boots
D: Shine Your Spurs

## 63

Complete the title of this Cole Porter
stage musical, 'Anything...'?

A: Does
B: Might
C: Goes
D: Else

## 64

Which character was played by Anne
Bancroft in the 1967 film 'The Graduate'?

A: Mrs Jones
B: Mrs Miniver
C: Mrs Doubtfire
D: Mrs Robinson

## 65

What did Tom Cruise's character 'feel the
need for' in the 1986 action film 'Top Gun'?

A: Greed
B: Tweed
C: Speed
D: Plot

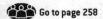 50:50 Go to page 246    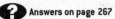 Go to page 258    ? Answers on page 267

# 5 ◆ £1,000

## 66

Which of these was a hit single
for 'Neighbours' actress Holly Valance?

A: Kiss Kiss
B: Hug Hug
C: Squeeze Squeeze
D: Mwah Mwah

## 67

In which 1990s TV series did Jimmy Nail play an
undercover detective in and around Newcastle-upon-Tyne?

A: Miser
B: Saver
C: Splasher
D: Spender

## 68

What kind of exclamation was the
title of a 1985 hit for Billy Idol?

A: Rebel Scream
B: Rebel Yell
C: Rebel Cry
D: Rebel Shout

## 69

Which breed of dog is the cartoon
crime-solving Scooby Doo?

A: German Shepherd
B: Chihuahua
C: Great Dane
D: Jack Russell

## 70

How were Tony Curtis and Roger Moore
known in a TV series of the 1970s?

A: The Tempters
B: The Attracters
C: The Persuaders
D: The Seducers

**50:50** Go to page 246 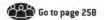 Go to page 258 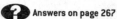 Answers on page 267

# 5 ◆ £1,000

## 71

Which ballet company is based in Moscow?

A: Ballet Russes
B: Bolshoi
C: Metropolitan Opera Ballet
D: Batsheva Dance Company

## 72

According to the title of the 1988 film comedy, 'Earth Girls Are...'?

A: Easy
B: Friendly
C: Aliens
D: High maintenance

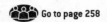 50:50 Go to page 246     Go to page 258     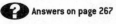 ? Answers on page 267

| 15 | £1 MILLION |
|----|------------|
| 14 | £500,000 |
| 13 | £250,000 |
| 12 | £125,000 |
| 11 | £64,000 |
| 10 | £32,000 |
| 9 | £16,000 |
| 8 | £8,000 |
| 7 | £4,000 |
| 6 ◆ | £2,000 |
| 5 ◆ | £1,000 |
| 4 ◆ | £500 |
| 3 ◆ | £300 |
| 2 ◆ | £200 |
| 1 ◆ | £100 |

# 6 ◆ £2,000

## 1
**Which of these was a regular character in 'EastEnders'?**

A: Dr Foot
B: Dr Legg
C: Dr Arm
D: Dr Shinn

## 2
**What name is given to the series of Italian westerns made in the 1960s starring Clint Eastwood?**

A: Macaroni
B: Spaghetti
C: Penne
D: Tagliatelli

## 3
**Which of the following is a character in the ITV drama 'Footballer's Wives'?**

A: Chablis
B: Shiraz
C: Chardonnay
D: Champagne

## 4
**Traditionally, how many strings are there on a ukulele?**

A: Two
B: Four
C: Six
D: Eight

## 5
**Which rock group went to No 1 in 2000 with 'Beautiful Day'?**

A: Status Quo
B: U2
C: Rolling Stones
D: Dire Straits

50:50 Go to page 246    Go to page 258    Answers on page 267

# 6 ◆ £2,000

**6**

How was Darth Vader actor Dave Prowse better known to millions of schoolchildren in the 1970s and 1980s?

- A: Jolly Green Giant
- B: Green Hornet
- C: Green Cross Code Man
- D: Incredible Hulk

**7**

Which group had a No 1 hit single in 2000 with 'Breathless'?

- A: The Fabbs
- B: The Wowws
- C: The Brills
- D: The Corrs

**8**

As which of the following is William Shakespeare popularly known?

- A: Bard of Avon
- B: Poet of Purfleet
- C: Minstrel of Merseyside
- D: Rhymer of Rhyl

**9**

What name is given to a usually humorous song performed very rapidly, as exemplified in the works of Gilbert and Sullivan?

- A: Natter
- B: Patter
- C: Splatter
- D: Mutter

**10**

Once married to a rock 'n' roll legend, who played opposite Leslie Nielsen in the 'Naked Gun' films?

- A: Loretta Lee Lewis
- B: Priscilla Presley
- C: Harriet Holly
- D: Hayley-Hazel Haley

**50:50** Go to page 246 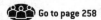 Go to page 258  Answers on page 267

# 6 ◆ £2,000

## 11

**Which of these names is often used to refer to the rock singer Bruce Springsteen?**

A: The Guv'nor
B: The Boss
C: The Gaffer
D: The Supervisor

## 12

**What was the first name of the composer Debussy?**

A: Francois
B: Jules
C: Maurice
D: Claude

## 13

**Which former newsreader began presenting Radio 4's 'Desert Island Discs' in 1988?**

A: Angela Rippon
B: Sue Lawley
C: Anna Ford
D: Moira Stewart

## 14

**In which decade was the sitcom 'Are You Being Served?' first broadcast?**

A: 1940s
B: 1950s
C: 1970s
D: 1980s

## 15

**The title of Maria McKee's 1990 UK No 1 single was 'Show Me...'?**

A: The Door
B: The Money
C: The Way To Go Home
D: Heaven

50:50 Go to page 246    Go to page 258    ? Answers on page 267

## 16

What was the name of the Cartwright family ranch in the western TV series 'Bonanza'?

◆A: Wonderosa

◆B: Dreamarosa

◆C: Ponderosa

◆D: Thinkerosa

## 17

Who is the star of the films 'The Shipping News' and 'The Usual Suspects'?

◆A: Al Pacino

◆B: Kevin Spacey

◆C: Ben Stiller

◆D: Matt Damon

## 18

Which surname is shared by Andy, Danny, Deniece and Robbie, all of whom have had UK No 1 singles?

◆A: Williams

◆B: Jones

◆C: Morgan

◆D: Evans

## 19

What is the name of Cambridge University's theatre group, renowned for its annual revue?

◆A: Footlights

◆B: Spotlights

◆C: Limelights

◆D: Floodlights

## 20

Which of the following is a popular children's satellite television channel?

◆A: Jukebox

◆B: Kaleidoscope

◆C: Nickelodeon

◆D: Piggybank

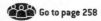 50:50 Go to page 246     Go to page 258      ? Answers on page 267

# 6 ◆ £2,000

## 21

Who starred as the DJ Adrian Cronauer in the 1987 film 'Good Morning Vietnam'?

A: Gene Wilder
B: Steve Martin
C: Robin Williams
D: Dustin Hoffman

## 22

Which of these was a character in the children's TV favourite 'The Clangers'?

A: Broth Griffin
B: Sauce Serpent
C: Soup Dragon
D: Salad Salamander

## 23

As what did Jelly Roll Morton become a famous figure?

A: Opera singer
B: Actor
C: TV chef
D: Jazz musician

## 24

In the production of which musical instrument was Leo Fender a pioneer?

A: Drums
B: Trumpet
C: Synthesizer
D: Electric guitar

## 25

Which of the following was a famous Manchester nightclub which closed in 1997?

A: Hacienda
B: Gazebo
C: Alhambra
D: Palazzo

50:50 Go to page 246    Go to page 258    ? Answers on page 267

# 6 ◆ £2,000

## 26

What is the first name of the famous ballerina, Ms Bussell?

- A: Margot
- B: Isadora
- C: Darcey
- D: Beryl

## 27

Which of the following took place 'On the Dancefloor', according to the title of the 2002 Sophie Ellis Bextor single?

- A: Murder
- B: Fisticuffs
- C: Assault
- D: GBH

## 28

In TV's 'Absolutely Fabulous', what is the name of Edina's daughter?

- A: Saffron
- B: Sadie
- C: Susan
- D: Selina

## 29

What is the name of the BBC's new digital radio station, launched in 2002?

- A: 5 Live
- B: talkSPORT
- C: 6 Music
- D: News 24

## 30

The action of which Hitchcock film centres on the Bates Motel?

- A: Rear Window
- B: The Birds
- C: Vertigo
- D: Psycho

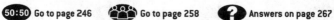

50:50 Go to page 246    Go to page 258    ? Answers on page 267

# 6 ◆ £2,000

## 31

In the action series 'The A-Team', for what did the 'BA' stand in the name of team member BA Baracus?

A: Bad Arthur

B: Bad Accent

C: Bad Attitude

D: Bad Acting

## 32

Which actor plays Mr Bean?

A: Nicholas Lyndhurst

B: David Jason

C: Rowan Atkinson

D: Rik Mayall

## 33

Dolly Parton starred in which of these films?

A: The Bridges of Madison County

B: Pale Rider

C: Nine to Five

D: Blazing Saddles

## 34

Which of these instruments is traditionally played using a pair of light hammers?

A: Harp

B: Cello

C: French horn

D: Dulcimer

## 35

What is the first name of the film star Charlie Sheen's actor father?

A: Malcolm

B: Michael

C: Marcus

D: Martin

50:50 Go to page 246 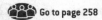 Go to page 258 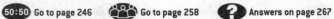 Answers on page 267

# 6 ◆ £2,000

## 36

Norman Clegg, Foggy Dewhurst and Truly Truelove are characters in which TV sitcom?

◆A: Last of the Summer Wine  ◆B: Dad's Army

◆C: Are You Being Served?  ◆D: Hi-De-Hi!

## 37

Which group had a No 1 hit in 1999 with 'Bring It All Back'?

◆A: S Club 7  ◆B: Savage Garden

◆C: Shamen  ◆D: Status Quo

## 38

In ballet, which of these is a term meaning a step?

◆A: Non  ◆B: Pas

◆C: Mais oui  ◆D: Rien

## 39

Which ITV company holds the franchise to broadcast to south and south-east England?

◆A: HTV  ◆B: Carlton

◆C: Central  ◆D: Meridian

## 40

With which film genre is the director John Ford particularly associated?

◆A: Horror  ◆B: Westerns

◆C: Romantic comedies  ◆D: Thrillers

50:50 Go to page 246    Go to page 258    ? Answers on page 267

## 41

Which London-based radio station broadcasts on 95.8 FM?

- A: City
- B: Metropolis
- C: Capital
- D: Conurbation

## 42

In which European city is the opera 'La Bohème' set?

- A: Rome
- B: Vienna
- C: Berlin
- D: Paris

## 43

According to the title of the sitcom, how many children did Bill and Ben Porter, played by Belinda Lang and Gary Olsen, have?

- A: 1.8
- B: 2.4
- C: 3.3
- D: 5.9

## 44

Which of these is the title of the 1997 chart-topper by family boy-band Hanson?

- A: Mmmbop
- B: Oohshop
- C: Wooplop
- D: Urghslop

## 45

What was the name of Martha Reeves' backing group?

- A: Ronnettes
- B: Vandellas
- C: Crystals
- D: Pips

50:50 Go to page 246      Go to page 258      ? Answers on page 267

# 6 ◆ £2,000

## 46
Which of these was a popular 1999 science-fiction thriller film starring Keanu Reeves?

- A: The Equation
- B: The Algorithm
- C: The Matrix
- D: The Vertex

## 47
Who played Richard Sharpe in the 1990s TV drama series 'Sharpe'?

- A: Nigel Havers
- B: Sean Bean
- C: Charles Dance
- D: Dennis Waterman

## 48
Which city is the setting for the Willy Russell musical 'Blood Brothers'?

- A: London
- B: Glasgow
- C: Liverpool
- D: Newcastle

## 49
What nationality is the singer Nana Mouskouri?

- A: Turkish
- B: Australian
- C: Italian
- D: Greek

## 50
Which Andrew Lloyd-Webber musical features the characters Greaseball, Rusty, Buffy and CB?

- A: Godspell
- B: Cats
- C: Evita
- D: Starlight Express

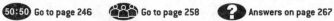 50:50 Go to page 246     Go to page 258    ? Answers on page 267

# 6 ◆ £2,000

## 51

**Of which of these musical forms is bebop a derivation?**

- A: Rock
- B: Pop
- C: Heavy metal
- D: Jazz

## 52

**Which Scottish city does TV's Rab C Nesbitt come from?**

- A: Edinburgh
- B: Aberdeen
- C: Dundee
- D: Glasgow

page
132

## 53

**Who did the character Daddy Warbucks adopt in a musical?**

- A: Annie
- B: Oliver
- C: Evita
- D: Sally

## 54

**Which TV puppet was originally operated by Harry Corbett?**

- A: Miss Piggy
- B: Basil Brush
- C: Kermit
- D: Sooty

## 55

**What nickname was given to the US actor and singer Jimmy Durante?**

- A: Hooter
- B: Conk
- C: Beak
- D: Schnozzle

**50:50** Go to page 246     Go to page 258     **?** Answers on page 267

# 6 ◆ £2,000

## 56

### Which of these quiz shows is hosted by Vic Reeves and Bob Mortimer?

- A: Celebrity Squares
- B: Shooting Stars
- C: Wipeout
- D: Wheel of Fortune

## 57

### In which British city is 'Taggart' chiefly set?

- A: Liverpool
- B: Manchester
- C: London
- D: Glasgow

## 58

### Which ex-Spice Girl has had hits with 'Bag It Up' and 'Lift Me Up'?

- A: Mel C
- B: Victoria Beckham
- C: Emma Bunton
- D: Geri Halliwell

## 59

### In which 2000 film did Clint Eastwood, Tommy Lee Jones, Donald Sutherland and James Garner play four geriatric astronauts who come out of retirement?

- A: Space Apaches
- B: Space Cavalry
- C: Space Pioneers
- D: Space Cowboys

## 60

### With which field of the arts is Dame Ninette de Valois famously associated?

- A: Ballet
- B: Film
- C: Jazz
- D: Opera

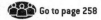 50:50 Go to page 246    Go to page 258   ? Answers on page 267

# 6 ◆ £2,000

## 61

Which creatures feature in the 1970s cult horror film 'Dawn of the Dead'?

- A: Werewolves
- B: Vampires
- C: Zombies
- D: Tube passengers

## 62

Which BBC national radio network began broadcasting on Monday 27th August 1990?

- A: Radio 2
- B: Radio 3
- C: Radio 4
- D: Radio 5 Live

## 63

In which European city is the opera 'Tosca' set?

- A: Berlin
- B: Oslo
- C: London
- D: Rome

## 64

Who topped the UK singles chart in 1991 with 'Should I Stay Or Should I Go'?

- A: The Bang
- B: The Clash
- C: The Wallop
- D: The Crash

## 65

Which of these did not play Batman on the big screen in the 1980s and 1990s?

- A: Val Kilmer
- B: Danny DeVito
- C: George Clooney
- D: Michael Keaton

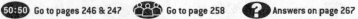

50:50 Go to pages 246 & 247    Go to page 258    ? Answers on page 267

# 6 ◆ £2,000

## 66

In which country is the TV series
'It Ain't Half Hot Mum' set?

A: China
B: Vietnam
C: Japan
D: India

## 67

The theme tune to which popular western series
included the words 'Rollin', rollin', rollin'...'?

A: Bonanza
B: The High Chaparral
C: Rawhide
D: Wagon Train

## 68

Which of these was a 1962 hit film starring Cliff Richard?

A: Blue Lagoon
B: Summer Holiday
C: The Next Time
D: Bachelor Boy

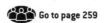 50:50 Go to page 247   Go to page 259    Answers on page 267

| 50:50 | | |
|---|---|---|
| 15 | £1 MILLION | |
| 14 | £500,000 | |
| 13 | £250,000 | |
| 12 | £125,000 | |
| 11 | £64,000 | |
| 10 | £32,000 | |
| 9 | £16,000 | |
| 8 | £8,000 | |
| 7 ◆ | £4,000 | |
| 6 ◆ | £2,000 | |
| 5 ◆ | £1,000 | |
| 4 ◆ | £500 | |
| 3 ◆ | £300 | |
| 2 ◆ | £200 | |
| 1 ◆ | £100 | |

# 7 ◆ £4,000

## 1

Gomez, Morticia and Lurch are characters
in which classic American sitcom?

- A: The Phil Silvers Show
- B: I Love Lucy
- C: The Addams Family
- D: Car 54 Where Are You?

## 2

What is the first name of the infamous 'Blackadder',
in the comedy series of the same name?

- A: Egbert
- B: Ethelred
- C: Edmund
- D: Edward

## 3

Which of these men was not married to Elizabeth Taylor?

- A: Jason Robards
- B: Michael Todd
- C: Eddie Fisher
- D: Richard Burton

## 4

Who was not one of the performing Osmond brothers?

- A: Alan
- B: Steve
- C: Wayne
- D: Merrill

## 5

Which of the following starred as
Jack Bauer in the TV drama '24'?

- A: Charlie Sheen
- B: Emilio Estevez
- C: Keanu Reeves
- D: Kiefer Sutherland

50:50 Go to page 247     Go to page 259     Answers on page 268

# 7 ◆ £4,000

**6**

### What is the name of Tom Petty's backing group?

- A: The Heartbreakers
- B: The Mindbenders
- C: The Soulsearchers
- D: The Headbangers

**7**

### Which body is responsible for regulating commercial television in the UK?

- A: IBM
- B: ITV
- C: ITC
- D: IMF

**8**

### Who wrote the music and lyrics for the hit musical 'Oliver!'?

page **139**

- A: Lionel Bart
- B: George Gershwin
- C: Irving Berlin
- D: Stephen Sondheim

**9**

### What was the name of the baddie played by Sean Connery in the 1998 film 'The Avengers'?

- A: Sir August de Wynter
- B: Sir April de Spryng
- C: Sir July d'Autumn
- D: Sir October de Summer

**10**

### In which UK city are the BBC Pebble Mill studios located?

- A: Bristol
- B: Glasgow
- C: Manchester
- D: Birmingham

**50:50** Go to page 247 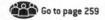 Go to page 259  Answers on page 268

# 7 ◆ £4,000

## 11

What is the surname of the film-making brothers Joel and Ethan, makers of 'O Brother, Where Art Thou' and 'Raising Arizona'?

A: Farrelly
B: Wayans
C: Coen
D: Hughes

## 12

Complete the name of the pioneering rap group, Grandmaster Flash and the...?

A: Irate Eight
B: Spitting Six
C: Furious Five
D: Tantrum Two

## 13

Which famous ballerina was born Lillian Alice Marks?

A: Margot Fonteyn
B: Anna Pavlova
C: Marie Rambert
D: Alicia Markova

## 14

In ballet, an 'entrechat' is a jump involving rapid crossings of which part of the body?

A: Legs
B: Arms
C: Fingers
D: Eyes

## 15

Which TV crime fighters reported to their commander George Cowley?

A: Crockett and Tubbs
B: Cagney and Lacey
C: Bodie and Doyle
D: Starsky and Hutch

50:50 Go to page 247     Go to page 259     Answers on page 268

# 7 ◆ £4,000

## 16

In the film industry, what name is given to a wheeled platform on which the camera is mounted for travelling shots?

- A: Dolly
- B: Patsy
- C: Janis
- D: Dusty

## 17

Which television duo sang England's official 2002 World Cup song, 'We're On The Ball'?

- A: Ant and Dec
- B: Baddiel and Skinner
- C: Eamon and Fiona
- D: Johnny and Denise

## 18

Where in London would you find the Theatre Royal?

page 141

- A: The Strand
- B: Shaftesbury Avenue
- C: Regent Street
- D: Drury Lane

## 19

Which British actor won an Oscar for his portrayal of John Bayley in 'Iris'?

- A: Tom Wilkinson
- B: Jim Broadbent
- C: Ian McKellen
- D: Ben Kingsley

## 20

The American actor Sam Wanamaker was influential in the reconstruction of which famous London theatre?

- A: Mermaid
- B: Shaftesbury
- C: Adelphi
- D: Globe

50:50 Go to page 247  Go to page 259  Answers on page 268

# 7 ◆ £4,000

## 21

Which group was formed during a break
in the career of the band Genesis?

- A: Dave and the Diggers
- B: Phil and the Firemen
- C: Peter and the Paperboys
- D: Mike and the Mechanics

## 22

What was the name of the character played
by Ewen Bremner in the cult film 'Trainspotting'?

- A: Mash
- B: Chip
- C: Spud
- D: Wedge

## 23

Which city provided the dramatic backdrop
for the 1968 Steve McQueen film 'Bullitt'?

- A: New York
- B: San Francisco
- C: Chicago
- D: Los Angeles

## 24

Who announces the moves in a barn dance?

- A: Namer
- B: Caller
- C: Shouter
- D: Yeller

## 25

Which part of an opera is referred to as the libretto?

- A: Text
- B: Music
- C: Introduction
- D: Interval

50:50 Go to page 247    Go to page 259    ? Answers on page 268

# 7 ◆ £4,000

## 26

Who is Chief Inspector Morse's sidekick?

- A: Regis
- B: Lewis
- C: Geddes
- D: Purves

## 27

'The Movie In My Mind' and 'The American Dream' are songs from which musical, based on the opera 'Madame Butterfly'?

- A: South Pacific
- B: Grease
- C: Miss Saigon
- D: Cats

## 28

Which breakfast show replaced the 'Big Breakfast' on Channel 4 in 2002?

- A: WKE
- B: RI:SE
- C: GET:UP
- D: DO:ZE

## 29

What were X-Press 2 and David Byrne according to the title of their 2002 UK Top 10 hit?

- A: Idle
- B: Workshy
- C: Sluggish
- D: Lazy

## 30

Which musician is famous for his Tijuana Brass?

- A: Acker Bilk
- B: Humphrey Lyttelton
- C: James Last
- D: Herb Alpert

 50:50 Go to page 247     Go to page 259     ? Answers on page 268

# 7 ◆ £4,000

## 31

In the children's TV cartoon,
who led the 'Three Muskehounds'?

◆A: Afox
◆B: Poochos
◆C: Dogtanian
◆D: Aramutt

## 32

Which of these is the title of a 1999 film
starring Brad Pitt and Edward Norton?

◆A: Scrap Club
◆B: Punch Club
◆C: Fist Club
◆D: Fight Club

## 33

Of which long-running sci-fi saga
is the film 'Attack of the Clones' a part?

◆A: Aliens
◆B: Star Trek
◆C: Planet of the Apes
◆D: Star Wars

## 34

Who are described as 'a pair of
star-crossed lovers' by William Shakespeare?

◆A: Antony and Cleopatra
◆B: Romeo and Juliet
◆C: Hamlet and Ophelia
◆D: Troilus and Cressida

## 35

What did Musical Youth tell you to pass
in the title of their 1982 UK No 1 single?

◆A: The Frenchie
◆B: The Aussie
◆C: The Dutchie
◆D: The Scottie

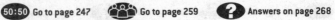
50:50 Go to page 247     Go to page 259     ❓ Answers on page 268

## 36

Which of the following was a character
in the BBC sci-fi series 'Blake's 7'?

A: Avon

B: Rimmel

C: Nivea

D: Max Factor

## 37

The bassoon belongs to which section of an orchestra?

A: Woodwind

B: Brass

C: Strings

D: Percussion

## 38

Who played Alf Garnett's son-in-law
in the TV series 'Till Death Us Do Part'?

A: Ian Lavender

B: James Beck

C: Anthony Booth

D: Reg Varney

## 39

What is the 'Black Hawk Down' in
the title of the Ridley Scott film?

A: Fighter plane

B: Helicopter

C: Submarine

D: Spacecraft

## 40

From which of the following areas does
Sacha Baron Cohen character Ali G claim to be?

A: Bronx

B: South Central

C: Hackney

D: Staines

50:50 Go to page 247     Go to page 259     Answers on page 268

# 7 ♦ £4,000

## 41

Fran Healy is the lead singer with which pop band?

A: Boyzone
B: Backstreet Boys
C: Travis
D: Green Day

## 42

Who played the lead role in the 1960s TV series 'The Fugitive'?

A: David Janssen
B: Roger Moore
C: Robert Vaughn
D: Patrick McGoohan

## 43

Which 1992 sci-fi film, starring Jeff Fahey and Pierce Brosnan, is based on a short story by Stephen King?

A: The Sprinkler Man
B: The Lawnmower Man
C: The Strimmer Man
D: The Secateurs Man

## 44

Who played the title role in the 1980 film 'The Jazz Singer'?

A: David Bowie
B: Bob Dylan
C: Roy Orbison
D: Neil Diamond

## 45

Steve Tyler and Joe Perry are the principal members of which rock group?

A: Westlife
B: The Police
C: Madness
D: Aerosmith

 50:50 Go to page 247    Go to page 259    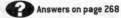 Answers on page 268

# 7 ◆ £4,000

## 46

Who was the lead singer with Herman's Hermits?

- A: Philip Afternoone
- B: Percy Duske
- C: Peter Noone
- D: Paul Eveninge

## 47

Which of these was a popular children's animated film in 2001?

- A: Monsters, Inc
- B: Ghosts Ltd
- C: Fiends Plc
- D: Ogres & Co

## 48

Who played Peter Mayle in the TV dramatisation of his book 'A Year in Provence'?

page
**147**

- A: David Jason
- B: John Thaw
- C: Richard Wilson
- D: David Suchet

## 49

From whom was Madonna divorced in 1989?

- A: Richard Gere
- B: Charlie Sheen
- C: Sean Penn
- D: Brad Pitt

## 50

Which of these was not one of the original members of the TV series 'Not The Nine O'Clock News'?

- A: Rowan Atkinson
- B: Mel Smith
- C: Pamela Stephenson
- D: John Cleese

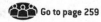 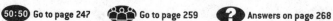
**50:50** Go to page 247　　Go to page 259　　? Answers on page 268

# 7 ◆ £4,000

## 51

With what sort of music would
you associate Garth Brooks?

A: Heavy metal
B: Punk
C: Glam rock
D: Country & Western

## 52

Which ballet by Delibes tells the story
of a mechanical doll brought to life?

A: Coppélia
B: Sleeping Beauty
C: Swan Lake
D: Nutcracker

## 53

'If music be the food of love, play on', is the
opening line of which Shakespeare play?

A: Hamlet
B: Twelfth Night
C: The Taming of the Shrew
D: The Tempest

## 54

Which 1939 classic western made a star of John Wayne?

A: Wagon Train
B: Pony Express
C: Railroad
D: Stagecoach

## 55

Where is the local radio station BRMB 96.4FM based?

A: Birmingham
B: Bolton
C: Brighton
D: Bournemouth

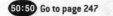 50:50 Go to page 247    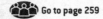 Go to page 259     ? Answers on page 268

# 7 ◆ £4,000

## 56

**Which sportsman is the title of a hit single by Simon and Garfunkel?**

- A: The Boxer
- B: The Wrestler
- C: The Footballer
- D: The Cricketer

## 57

**Background music to a film or play is known as what?**

- A: Accidental
- B: Incidental
- C: Nonessential
- D: Environmental

## 58

**Which former 'Starsky and Hutch' actor guest-starred in the BBC TV series 'Holby City'?**

page **149**

- A: Paul Michael Glaser
- B: David Soul
- C: Bernie Hamilton
- D: Antonio Fargas

## 59

**What is the name of the holiday camp in the TV sitcom 'Hi-Di-Hi!'?**

- A: Maplins
- B: Chaplins
- C: Pontins
- D: Butlins

## 60

**Which song has provided a UK No 1 for Jimmy Young, The Righteous Brothers, Robson & Jerome and Gareth Gates?**

- A: Up On The Roof
- B: Unchained Melody
- C: You've Lost That Loving Feeling
- D: Under The Boardwalk

 50:50 Go to page 247    Go to page 259     Answers on page 268

## 61

**What is the name of the son adopted by Barney and Betty Rubble in 'The Flintstones'?**

A: Bamm Bamm
B: Wamm Wamm
C: Ramm Ramm
D: Jamm Jamm

## 62

**Which Gilbert and Sullivan operetta features the characters Nanki-Poo and Ko-Ko?**

A: The Mikado
B: HMS Pinafore
C: The Pirates of Penzance
D: The Gondoliers

## 63

**Who played the title role in the 2000 film 'Erin Brokovich'?**

A: Helen Mirren
B: Kate Winslet
C: Julia Roberts
D: Maggie Smith

## 64

**Which 'Memoirs' feature in a stage comedy by Neil Simon?**

A: Brighton Beach
B: Portland Bill
C: Firth of Forth
D: Whitley Bay

50:50 Go to page 247    Go to page 259    ? Answers on page 268

| 50:50 | | |
|---|---|---|
| **15** | **£1 MILLION** | |
| 14 | £500,000 | |
| 13 | £250,000 | |
| 12 | £125,000 | |
| 11 | £64,000 | |
| **10** | **£32,000** | |
| 9 | £16,000 | |
| **8** ◆ | **£8,000** | |
| 7 ◆ | £4,000 | |
| 6 ◆ | £2,000 | |
| **5** ◆ | **£1,000** | |
| 4 ◆ | £500 | |
| 3 ◆ | £300 | |
| 2 ◆ | £200 | |
| 1 ◆ | £100 | |

# 8 ◆ £8,000

## 1

**Who has played Roger Murtaugh to Mel Gibson's Martin Riggs in the 'Lethal Weapon' series of films?**

- A: Danny Glover
- B: Denzil Washington
- C: Samuel L Jackson
- D: Eddie Murphy

## 2

**Cyd Charisse is best known as which of the following?**

- A: Film director
- B: Dancer
- C: Poet
- D: Playwright

## 3

**For which items of clothing was the Irish singer Val Doonican particularly noted on his TV series?**

- A: Socks
- B: Jumpers
- C: Hats
- D: Scarves

## 4

**Which of these is not one of the colours used to make up a colour TV picture?**

- A: Blue
- B: Green
- C: Red
- D: Yellow

## 5

**'Ars Gratia Artis' is the motto of which Hollywood film studio?**

- A: MGM
- B: Universal
- C: Warner Brothers
- D: 20th Century Fox

50:50 Go to page 248    Go to page 260    ? Answers on page 268

# 8 ◆ £8,000

## 6

Which of these took a cover of Don McLean's song
'American Pie' to the top of the UK charts in 2000?

- A: Mel C
- B: Billie Piper
- C: Madonna
- D: Gabrielle

## 7

John Ravenscroft is the real name
of which well known radio DJ?

- A: Johnny Walker
- B: Jimmy Young
- C: John Peel
- D: Steve Wright

## 8

Which televison personality made her
West End debut in the musical 'Chicago'?

- A: Denise van Outen
- B: Zoe Ball
- C: Kelly Brook
- D: Gail Porter

## 9

Country music legend Waylon Jennings
sang the theme song for which TV series?

- A: The A-Team
- B: The Six Million Dollar Man
- C: The Dukes of Hazzard
- D: Magnum, PI

## 10

For which film did Geoffrey Rush
win the Best Actor Oscar in 1996?

- A: Fargo
- B: Jerry Maguire
- C: Shine
- D: Dead Man Walking

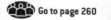 50:50 Go to page 248    Go to page 260   ? Answers on page 268

# 8 ◆ £8,000

## 11

Which character from the TV comedy
'Father Ted' is often heard to demand 'Drink!'?

A: Father Jack
B: Bishop Brennan
C: Father Dougal
D: Mrs Doyle

## 12

What is the correct spelling of the
first name of Kylie Minogue's sister?

A: Dannie
B: Dannii
C: Danny
D: Danney

## 13

Which theatrical term applies to a role in
which an actress plays a male character?

A: Garters part
B: Breeches part
C: Tights part
D: Codpiece part

## 14

What was the full title of the third 'Die Hard' movie?

A: Die Hard With a Bullet
B: Die Hard With a Gun
C: Die Hard Without a Care
D: Die Hard With a Vengeance

## 15

Which of these is an appropriately named
local radio station broadcasting from Portsmouth?

A: Cutty Sark 101.4
B: Victory 107.4
C: Titanic 98.3
D: Mary Celeste 101.3

50:50 Go to page 248        Go to page 260        Answers on page 268

# 8 ♦ £8,000

## 16

Who played Caligula in the historical TV drama 'I, Claudius'?

A: Derek Jacobi

B: John Hurt

C: Brian Blessed

D: Stratford Johns

## 17

Complete the name of the British pop group, The Jesus and Mary...?

A: Chain

B: Bracelet

C: Link

D: Brooch

## 18

Who played Daniel Hillard in the 1993 film 'Mrs Doubtfire'?

A: Dustin Hoffman

B: Tom Hanks

C: Gene Wilder

D: Robin Williams

## 19

Which character in 'EastEnders' owned a dog named Willy?

A: Nigel Bates

B: Dot Cotton

C: Pauline Fowler

D: Ethel Skinner

## 20

Who was the bass player with the rock group Queen?

A: John Bishop

B: John Deacon

C: John Pope

D: John Cardinal

**50:50** Go to page 248    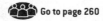 Go to page 260     Answers on page 268

**21**

In which city was the 'Waltz King' Johann Strauss the Younger born?

- A: Paris
- B: Brussels
- C: Berlin
- D: Vienna

**22**

Where is Stanley Kubrick's film 'The Shining' set?

- A: Cemetery
- B: Hotel
- C: Spaceship
- D: School

**23**

What is the name of BBC Radio 5 Live's evening football phone-in chat show?

- A: 321
- B: 909
- C: 606
- D: 442

**24**

Complete the title of the play written by Dario Fo, 'Accidental Death of...'?

- A: An Anarchist
- B: A Revolutionary
- C: A Bolshevik
- D: A Nihilist

**25**

Which comedy duo starred in a 2002 BBC remake of a classic 'Likely Lads' episode?

- A: Reeves and Mortimer
- B: Baddiel and Skinner
- C: Adam and Joe
- D: Ant and Dec

50:50 Go to page 248    Go to page 260    ? Answers on page 268

# 8 ◆ £8,000

## 26

### Who starred as Calvin Clifford Baxter in the 1960 film 'The Apartment'?

A: Walter Matthau

B: Tony Curtis

C: Sterling Hayden

D: Jack Lemmon

## 27

### Which city did Freddie Mercury and Montserrat Caballé sing about in their 1987 UK Top 10 single?

A: Vienna

B: Barcelona

C: Amsterdam

D: Lisbon

## 28

### Who played the title role in the 1999 remake of the film 'The Thomas Crown Affair'?

A: Robert Redford

B: Bruce Willis

C: Tom Cruise

D: Pierce Brosnan

page **157**

## 29

### Which of these entertainment venues is situated in Kensington Gore, London?

A: Royal Festival Hall

B: Royal Opera House

C: Theatre Royal

D: Royal Albert Hall

## 30

### According to the title of Tom Stoppard's famous play, 'Rosencrantz and Guildenstern Are...' what?

A: Alive

B: Sleeping

C: Unwell

D: Dead

 **50:50** Go to page 248  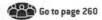 Go to page 260   Answers on page 268

# 8 ◆ £8,000

## 31

What was the name of the Harts' friend, butler and chauffeur in the 1980s US crime drama 'Hart to Hart'?

◆A: Max
◆B: Rocky
◆C: Herman
◆D: Jeeves

## 32

Who composed the ballet 'The Sleeping Beauty'?

◆A: Stravinsky
◆B: Mendelssohn
◆C: Prokofiev
◆D: Tchaikovsky

## 33

Which James Bond star played opposite Tippi Hedren in the Hitchcock film 'Marnie'?

◆A: Sean Connery
◆B: Pierce Brosnan
◆C: Roger Moore
◆D: George Lazenby

## 34

The actress Jane Wyman was once married to which former US president?

◆A: Gerald Ford
◆B: Jimmy Carter
◆C: Ronald Reagan
◆D: Bill Clinton

## 35

What is the name of the pet mogwai owned by Zach Galligan in the 1984 film 'Gremlins' and its 1990 sequel?

◆A: Gadget
◆B: Gizmo
◆C: Thingy
◆D: Zapper

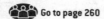 50:50 Go to page 248     Go to page 260    ? Answers on page 268

# 8 ◆ £8,000

## 36

Which 1961 film turned out to be the last appearance in front of the camera for both Clark Gable and Marilyn Monroe?

- **A: The Misfits**
- **B: The Foreigners**
- **C: The Outsiders**
- **D: The Odd Ones Out**

## 37

Who played Ma Larkin in the TV series 'The Darling Buds of May'?

- **A: Patricia Routledge**
- **B: Stephanie Cole**
- **C: Annette Crosbie**
- **D: Pam Ferris**

## 38

Which of these actors has starred in both 'EastEnders' and 'Heartbeat'?

- **A: Mike Reid**
- **B: Leslie Grantham**
- **C: Nick Berry**
- **D: Derek Fowlds**

## 39

In the 19th century, what name was given to itinerant rural theatre companies?

- **A: Farmfillers**
- **B: Barnstormers**
- **C: Haymakers**
- **D: Stablestokers**

## 40

Which Star Trek actor also played the title role in the TV crime series 'TJ Hooker'?

- **A: William Shatner**
- **B: DeForest Kelly**
- **C: Leonard Nimoy**
- **D: James Doohan**

 **50:50** Go to page 248    **Go to page 260**    **?** Answers on page 268

# 8 ◆ £8,000

## 41

Who played paramedic Frank Pierce
in the 1999 film 'Bringing Out the Dead'?

A: Bruce Willis
B: Nick Nolte
C: Mickey Rourke
D: Nicolas Cage

## 42

Which children's TV characters possess
a vacuum cleaner called 'The Noo-noo'?

A: The Tweenies
B: The Flumps
C: The Teletubbies
D: The Tots

## 43

In which county is the local
radio station Invicta FM based?

A: Cornwall
B: Cumbria
C: Hertfordshire
D: Kent

## 44

Which British actor played camp commandant Amon
Goeth in the Steven Spielberg film 'Schindler's List'?

A: Liam Neeson
B: Ralph Fiennes
C: Ben Kingsley
D: Alan Rickman

## 45

Who was the British member of the Monkees?

A: Peter Tork
B: Davy Jones
C: Mickey Dolenz
D: Michael Nesmith

 50:50 Go to page 248    Go to page 260     ? Answers on page 268

# 8 ◆ £8,000

## 46

Which of the following actors made a 'Journey to the Center of the Earth' in the 1959 film adaptation of the Jules Verne novel?

- A: James Mason
- B: Richard Burton
- C: Peter O'Toole
- D: Richard Harris

## 47

Who played Dr Wilbur Larch in the 1999 film 'The Cider House Rules'?

- A: Albert Finney
- B: Sean Connery
- C: Richard Harris
- D: Michael Caine

## 48

Which TV series is filmed in and around the Yorkshire village of Holmfirth?

- A: Heartbeat
- B: Last of the Summer Wine
- C: Peak Practice
- D: Lovejoy

## 49

Who played Dr Frank-N-Furter in the 1975 film 'The Rocky Horror Picture Show'?

- A: Charles Gray
- B: John Travolta
- C: Tim Curry
- D: Jon Finch

## 50

Which of these is a character in 'The Importance of Being Earnest'?

- A: Lady Bracknell
- B: Lady Bedford
- C: Lady Barking
- D: Lady Brighton

50:50 Go to page 248　　 Go to page 260　　? Answers on page 268

# 8 ◆ £8,000

## 51

Roscoe was the real first name of which silent screen comedy star?

- A: Harold Lloyd
- B: Ben Turpin
- C: Charlie Chaplin
- D: Fatty Arbuckle

## 52

To whom is the phrase 'There's a sucker born every minute' attributed?

- A: P T Barnum
- B: Sam Goldwyn
- C: D W Griffith
- D: Joseph Grimaldi

## 53

With which field of the arts was Sergei Diaghilev chiefly associated?

- A: Film
- B: Pop music
- C: Ballet
- D: Opera

## 54

In which TV sitcom were Mr and Mrs Roper the main characters?

- A: George and Mildred
- B: Bless This House
- C: Love Thy Neighbour
- D: Terry and June

## 55

With which field of entertainment would you associate the nationwide Jongleurs clubs?

- A: Comedy
- B: Music
- C: Film
- D: Opera

50:50 Go to page 248     Go to page 260     Answers on page 268

# 8 ◆ £8,000

## 56

Which British rock star appeared in the films 'Labyrinth', 'Absolute Beginners' and 'Merry Christmas Mister Lawrence'?

- A: Mick Jagger
- B: Sting
- C: David Bowie
- D: Phil Collins

## 57

In which city was Sean Connery born?

- A: Glasgow
- B: Aberdeen
- C: Dundee
- D: Edinburgh

## 58

What is the first name of James Gandolfini's character in the TV Mafia series 'The Sopranos'?

- A: Bugsy
- B: Joey
- C: Tony
- D: Micky

## 59

Which 1999 film is based on the relationship between lyricist W S Gilbert and composer Arthur Sullivan?

- A: Helter-Skelter
- B: Higgledy-Piggledy
- C: Topsy-Turvy
- D: Hunky-Dory

## 60

With which quiz programme is the phrase 'I've started so I'll finish' associated?

- A: Mastermind
- B: The People Versus
- C: Fifteen To One
- D: Countdown

50:50 Go to page 248    Go to page 260    ? Answers on page 268

| 50:50 | | |
|---|---|---|
| **15** | **£1 MILLION** | |
| 14 | £500,000 | |
| 13 | £250,000 | |
| 12 | £125,000 | |
| 11 | £64,000 | |
| **10** | **£32,000** | |
| **9** ◆ | **£16,000** | |
| 8 ◆ | £8,000 | |
| 7 ◆ | £4,000 | |
| 6 ◆ | £2,000 | |
| **5** ◆ | **£1,000** | |
| 4 ◆ | £500 | |
| 3 ◆ | £300 | |
| 2 ◆ | £200 | |
| 1 ◆ | £100 | |

# 9 ◆ £16,000

**1**

Which cinema classic ends with the
line 'It was Beauty killed the Beast'?

A: Alien
B: Frankenstein
C: King Kong
D: Hunchback of Notre Dame

**2**

Ethel, Lionel and John were members of
which famous American theatrical family?

A: Sondheim
B: Barrymore
C: Redgrave
D: Sutherland

**3**

Which TV cartoon character lived in 'Wheelie World'?

A: Chorlton
B: Didsbury
C: Eccles
D: Wigan

**4**

Who is the long-running chairman
of Radio 4's 'Just A Minute'?

A: Clement Freud
B: Nicholas Parsons
C: Humphrey Lyttleton
D: James Naughtie

**5**

Which popular singer shares her
name with a queen of Carthage?

A: Björk
B: Sade
C: Dido
D: Cher

50:50 Go to page 248      Go to page 260      Answers on page 268

# 9 ◆ £16,000

## 6

Who performed at both the London and
Philadelphia venues of Live Aid in 1985?

A: Mick Jagger
B: Whitney Houston
C: Cher
D: Phil Collins

## 7

Which popular US 1970s sitcom starred
the future film director Ron Howard?

A: Happy Days
B: The Partridge Family
C: The Brady Bunch
D: Soap

## 8

What is the literal translation of 'Nessun dorma', the aria
from 'Turandot' made famous by Luciano Pavarotti?

A: No-one dies
B: Love never sleeps
C: Nothing stirs
D: No-one shall sleep

## 9

Which 'Star Trek' icon plays the
Big Giant Head in '3rd Rock from the Sun'?

A: Patrick Stewart
B: William Shatner
C: Leonard Nimoy
D: Jonathan Frakes

## 10

The Oscar-winning documentary film 'One Day in
September' depicts events at which Olympic Games?

A: 1968
B: 1972
C: 1976
D: 1980

 **50:50** Go to page 248    Go to page 260    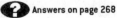 **?** Answers on page 268

# 9 ◆ £16,000

### 11

**Which of Steve Coogan's comic creations lived at the Linton Travel Tavern?**

- A: Alan Partridge
- B: Tony Ferrino
- C: Gareth Cheeseman
- D: Paul Calf

### 12

**In which county is the local radio station Orchard FM based?**

- A: East Sussex
- B: Devon
- C: Somerset
- D: Cornwall

### 13

**Which of the following are Cuban percussion instruments consisting of round sticks?**

- A: Clavichords
- B: Claves
- C: Claviers
- D: Clavicles

### 14

**The German town of Bayreuth is particularly associated with which composer?**

- A: Liszt
- B: Brahms
- C: Handel
- D: Wagner

### 15

**Which of these is the title of a ballet by Fokine and Stravinsky?**

- A: The Firebird
- B: The Thunderbird
- C: The Waterbird
- D: The Windbird

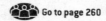  50:50 Go to page 248    Go to page 260    ? Answers on page 268

# 9 ◆ £16,000

## 16

Who is the famous actress daughter
of the film star Maureen O'Sullivan?

- A: Mia Farrow
- B: Meg Ryan
- C: Tatum O'Neal
- D: Jessica Lange

## 17

Which star of Hollywood westerns was
born Walter Palanuik in 1919?

- A: Yul Brynner
- B: Charles Bronson
- C: Jack Palance
- D: Robert Vaughn

## 18

Who played the part of 'The Engineer', in both the London
and New York original casts of the musical 'Miss Saigon'?

- A: Simon Bowman
- B: Michael Crawford
- C: Jonathan Pryce
- D: Michael Ball

## 19

Which country's social problems do the works
of the playwright Athol Fugard mainly portray?

- A: Albania
- B: South Africa
- C: Ireland
- D: India

## 20

In which Puccini opera do the characters
Ping, Pang and Pong appear?

- A: Madame Butterfly
- B: La Rondine
- C: Turandot
- D: Tosca

**50:50** Go to pages 248 & 249　 Go to page 261　**?** Answers on page 268

# 9 ◆ £16,000

## 21

Which games console manufacturer
launched the GameCube in the UK in 2002?

A: Sony
B: Microsoft
C: Sega
D: Nintendo

## 22

Which of the following did award-winning presenter
Louis Theroux memorably meet in his BBC series?

A: The Thatchers
B: The Blairs
C: The Bushes
D: The Hamiltons

## 23

By what stage name is the rapper
Sean Combs better known?

A: B Daddy
B: P Diddy
C: D Deddy
D: K Doddy

## 24

Who won a BAFTA for his performance as
David Brent in the comedy series 'The Office'?

A: Mackenzie Crook
B: Oliver Chris
C: Ricky Gervais
D: Martin Freeman

## 25

Which British city's music scene was the
subject of the 2002 film '24 Hour Party People'?

A: London
B: Glasgow
C: Bristol
D: Manchester

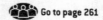 **50:50** Go to page 249     Go to page 261    **?** Answers on page 268

# 9 ◆ £16,000

## 26

**What is the English translation of the title of the Mozart opera 'Cosi fan tutte'?**

- A: Women are fickle
- B: Without a woman
- C: Women are all like that
- D: Women in love

## 27

**Which actor described kissing Marilyn Monroe on screen as 'like kissing Hitler'?**

- A: Tony Curtis
- B: Jack Lemmon
- C: Bob Hope
- D: Walter Matthau

## 28

**The 1993 film 'Cool Runnings' told the story of which unlikely country's four-man bobsleigh team at the 1988 Winter Olympics?**

- A: Jamaica
- B: Kenya
- C: Papua New Guinea
- D: Algeria

## 29

**Which ballet term describes a spring forward that takes off on one leg and lands on the other?**

- A: Fouetté
- B: Chassé
- C: Pirouette
- D: Jeté

## 30

**Which British comedian made his breakthrough as 'The Joan Collins Fan Club'?**

- A: Eddie Izzard
- B: Julian Clary
- C: Harry Hill
- D: Vic Reeves

**50:50** Go to page 249  Go to page 261  Answers on page 268

# 9 ◆ £16,000

## 31

Apart from London, in which British city would you find the Old Vic theatre?

- A: Bristol
- B: Oxford
- C: Sheffield
- D: York

## 32

Which 1988 film starred Michael Caine and Ben Kingsley as Sherlock Holmes and Doctor Watson?

- A: Clueless
- B: Give Us a Clue
- C: Haven't a Clue
- D: Without a Clue

## 33

In which TV drama does Martin Sheen play President Josiah Bartlet?

- A: The White House
- B: The Oval Office
- C: The Blue Room
- D: The West Wing

## 34

Which star of the silver screen was born Michael Shalhoub?

- A: Omar Sharif
- B: Charles Bronson
- C: Kirk Douglas
- D: Walter Matthau

## 35

In which UK city is there an international piano competition which was founded in 1963?

- A: Bristol
- B: Manchester
- C: Leeds
- D: Brighton

 50:50 Go to page 249   Go to page 261   ? Answers on page 268
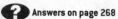

# 9 ◆ £16,000

## 36

Which 2002 TV drama centred
on an MI5 counter-terrorism unit?

- A: Ghouls
- B: Spooks
- C: Ghosts
- D: Spectres

## 37

Who played the Bond girl
Honey Ryder in the 1962 film 'Dr No'?

- A: Diana Rigg
- B: Linda Thorsen
- C: Ursula Andress
- D: Honor Blackman

## 38

Which musical, written by Boy George, opened in 2002?

page
173

- A: Veto
- B: Embargo
- C: Curfew
- D: Taboo

## 39

In which decade was the Sydney Opera House completed?

- A: 1950s
- B: 1960s
- C: 1970s
- D: 1980s

## 40

Which of the following letters are used to refer to someone
who scouts for new talent for a record company?

- A: A & M
- B: A & C
- C: A & R
- D: A & A

50:50 Go to page 249      Go to page 261      Answers on page 268

# 9 ◆ £16,000

## 41

Who plays the role of Professor
Charles Xavier in the 2000 film 'X-Men'?

A: Patrick Stewart     B: Ian McKellen

C: Ian Holm     D: Hugh Jackman

## 42

Which cult cartoon was 'Bigger, Longer
and Uncut' for cinema release in 1999?

A: The Simpsons     B: Beavis and Butthead

C: South Park     D: Futurama

## 43

By what name are the boy band members
Antony, Lee, Duncan and Simon better known?

A: Blue     B: *NSYNC

C: 911     D: Backstreet Boys

## 44

Which musical term describes the electronic method of
isolating certain sounds from a recording and playing them back?

A: Testing     B: Trying

C: Savouring     D: Sampling

## 45

What nickname was given to the
music hall entertainer Sir George Robey?

A: King of Comedy     B: Emperor of Elation

C: Kaiser of Conviviality     D: Prime Minister of Mirth

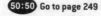 50:50 Go to page 249    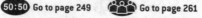 Go to page 261    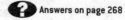 Answers on page 268

# 9 ◆ £16,000

## 46

Which TV cartoon hero was
accompanied by the Teen Angels?

A: Scooby Doo
B: Hong Kong Phooey
C: Danger Mouse
D: Captain Caveman

## 47

The 2002 film 'Crossroads' is the
feature debut of which singing star?

A: Janet Jackson
B: Britney Spears
C: Christina Aguilera
D: Whitney Houston

## 48

Which 'Coronation Street' character
was played by Peter Adamson?

A: Alf Roberts
B: Albert Tatlock
C: Jack Walker
D: Len Fairclough

## 49

A tabla is a form of which musical instrument?

A: Piano
B: Guitar
C: Flute
D: Drum

## 50

Which famous film director formed the
company Amblin Entertainment in 1984?

A: James Cameron
B: Ron Howard
C: Steven Spielberg
D: Robert Altman

50:50 Go to page 249     Go to page 261     Answers on page 268

# 9 ◆ £16,000

## 51

With which field of the arts are Britain's Adam Cooper and Jonathan Cope chiefly associated?

- A: Theatre
- B: Comedy
- C: Opera
- D: Ballet

## 52

Which Scottish actor played Private Mick Hopper in the Dennis Potter drama 'Lipstick on Your Collar'?

- A: Ewan McGregor
- B: Robert Carlyle
- C: Douglas Henshall
- D: Dougray Scott

## 53

What is the occupation of Billy Budd in Benjamin Britten's opera of that name?

- A: Soldier
- B: Policeman
- C: Sailor
- D: Blacksmith

## 54

Which comedy series features the character Bob Fleming, the coughing gardener?

- A: Absolutely
- B: The Fast Show
- C: The Adam & Joe Show
- D: Smack the Pony

## 55

Who or what was 'The Mexican' in the 2001 film of the same name starring Brad Pitt and Julia Roberts?

- A: Gold bar
- B: Spy
- C: Antique pistol
- D: Hitman

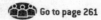 **50:50** Go to page 249     Go to page 261     **?** Answers on page 268

## 56

What is the first name of Victor Meldrew's
wife in TV's 'One Foot In The Grave'?

A: Ann
B: Sheila

C: Pat
D: Margaret

50:50 Go to page 249    Go to page 261    Answers on page 268

50:50

| 15 | £1 MILLION |
|----|------------|
| 14 | £500,000 |
| 13 | £250,000 |
| 12 | £125,000 |
| 11 | £64,000 |
| 10 ◆ | £32,000 |
| 9 ◆ | £16,000 |
| 8 ◆ | £8,000 |
| 7 ◆ | £4,000 |
| 6 ◆ | £2,000 |
| 5 ◆ | £1,000 |
| 4 ◆ | £500 |
| 3 ◆ | £300 |
| 2 ◆ | £200 |
| 1 ◆ | £100 |

**1**

**Which comedian co-presented the 2002 Brit Awards with Zoe Ball?**

A: Steve Coogan
B: Frank Skinner
C: Eddie Izzard
D: Sacha Baron Cohen

**2**

**What role did Susan Sarandon play in the 1995 film 'Dead Man Walking'?**

A: Police officer
B: Nun
C: Prison warden
D: Prostitute

**3**

**Which of these Hollywood stars was originally named Ruby Stevens?**

A: Lana Turner
B: Joan Crawford
C: Bette Davis
D: Barbara Stanwyck

**4**

**What was the name of Joan Jett's backing group on her 1982 hit 'I Love Rock 'n' Roll'?**

A: Blackheads
B: Blackhearts
C: Blackbeards
D: Blackeyes

**5**

**In which of these musicals is Lorelei Lee a principal character?**

A: Funny Girl
B: Cabaret
C: Gentlemen Prefer Blondes
D: Guys and Dolls

50:50 Go to page 249 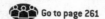 Go to page 261  Answers on page 269

### 6

**Which of these venues would you find on Argyll Street in London?**

- A: London Coliseum
- B: London Amphitheatre
- C: London Hippodrome
- D: London Palladium

### 7

**In which imaginary south coast town is 'Dad's Army' set?**

- A: Hitcham
- B: Kenwell-Super-Mare
- C: Easton
- D: Walmington-on-Sea

### 8

**Which 'Star Trek' film features both Captain James T Kirk and Captain Jean-Luc Picard?**

- A: Generations
- B: The Undiscovered Country
- C: Insurrection
- D: First Contact

### 9

**In musical terms, what is a madrigal?**

- A: Stringed instrument
- B: Musical poem
- C: High note
- D: Female singer

### 10

**Which TV soap was originally given the working title 'Florizel Street'?**

- A: Neighbours
- B: Crossroads
- C: Brookside
- D: Coronation Street

50:50 Go to page 249     Go to page 261     ? Answers on page 269

# 10 ◆ £32,000

## 11

**In which of these films does Dustin Hoffman play the part of Benjamin Braddock?**

A: Rain Man      B: The Graduate

C: Marathon Man      D: Straw Dogs

## 12

**Which of these performers was born David Albert Cook?**

A: David Cassidy      B: David Soul

C: David Jason      D: David Essex

## 13

**Coleman Hawkins is most closely associated with which form of music?**

A: Jazz      B: Opera

C: Heavy Metal      D: Skiffle

## 14

**In which city is the musical 'Les Miserables' set?**

A: Lyon      B: Paris

C: Marseille      D: Bordeaux

## 15

**Who played 'The Man Who Wasn't There' in the 2001 film of the same name?**

A: George Clooney      B: John Cusack

C: Billy Bob Thornton      D: Nicolas Cage

50:50 Go to page 249      Go to page 261      Answers on page 269

# 10 ◆ £32,000

## 16

In which of the following films does Robert Duvall utter the line 'I love the smell of napalm in the morning'?

- A: Platoon
- B: Apocalypse Now
- C: The Deerhunter
- D: Hamburger Hill

## 17

Who played Martin Clunes' flatmate in the first series of the TV sitcom, 'Men Behaving Badly'?

- A: Paul Whitehouse
- B: Nicholas Lyndhurst
- C: Nigel Planer
- D: Harry Enfield

## 18

In which British city is the West Yorkshire Playhouse?

- A: Bradford
- B: Leeds
- C: Sheffield
- D: York

## 19

Larry Hagman plays astronaut Tony Nelson in which classic US sitcom?

- A: Barney Miller
- B: Benson
- C: Soap
- D: I Dream Of Jeannie

## 20

In 1973, 'Eye Level' by the Simon Park Orchestra became the first TV theme music to top the UK singles chart: from which programme did it come?

- A: Z Cars
- B: Van Der Valk
- C: Softly Softly
- D: The Sweeney

 50:50 Go to page 249   Go to page 261   ? Answers on page 269

# 10 ◆ £32,000

## 21

Who was the second TV Doctor Who?

A: Patrick Troughton
B: Jon Pertwee
C: Tom Baker
D: William Hartnell

## 22

Which of these Swiss cities is known for its annual jazz festival?

A: Geneva
B: Zurich
C: Berne
D: Montreux

## 23

Who directed the 'Scream' series of films?

A: Sam Raimi
B: George Romero
C: Wes Craven
D: David Cronenberg

## 24

Which of the following is not a character in the superhero cartoon the 'X-Men'?

A: Cyclops
B: Gambit
C: Magneto
D: Gorgon

## 25

In which 007 film could you hear the line 'No, Mr Bond, I expect you to die!'?

A: Goldfinger
B: Dr No
C: Thunderball
D: From Russia With Love

 50:50 Go to page 249     Go to page 261    ? Answers on page 269

## 26

**Which funnyman played the characters CU Jimmy and Basildon Bond in his own TV sketch show?**

- A: Kenny Everett
- B: Les Dawson
- C: Bob Carolgees
- D: Russ Abbot

## 27

**Who released the album 'The Hour of Bewilderbeast' in 2000?**

- A: Beck
- B: Gorillaz
- C: Chemical Brothers
- D: Badly Drawn Boy

## 28

**Which future Hollywood star made his name as the bounty hunter Josh Randall in the TV series 'Wanted: Dead or Alive'?**

- A: Paul Newman
- B: Clint Eastwood
- C: James Garner
- D: Steve McQueen

## 29

**In which town did Spencer Tracy have a 'Bad Day' in the title of the 1955 film?**

- A: Black Rock
- B: Red Stone
- C: Yellow River
- D: Blue Water

## 30

**What is the first name of Hyacinth's henpecked husband in the TV series 'Keeping Up Appearances'?**

- A: Richard
- B: George
- C: Freddie
- D: Henry

**50:50** Go to page 249   Go to page 261   **?** Answers on page 269

# 10 ◆ £32,000

## 31

Which actor played the part of Soames
in the 2002 TV version of 'The Forsyte Saga'?

- A: Ioan Gruffud
- B: Damian Lewis
- C: Rupert Graves
- D: Ben Miles

## 32

In the 1974 film 'Young Frankenstein', what is
the name of the hunchbacked assistant?

- A: Boris
- B: Igor
- C: Ludwig
- D: Dimitri

## 33

Which London Underground station has given its name to a favourite
game on the BBC Radio 4 programme 'I'm Sorry I Haven't A Clue'?

- A: Mornington Crescent
- B: Wembley Central
- C: Shepherd's Bush
- D: Parsons Green

## 34

Who wrote the play 'The Admirable Crichton'?

- A: J M Barrie
- B: T S Eliot
- C: Christopher Fry
- D: J B Priestly

## 35

The cult TV series 'The Prisoner', starring
Patrick McGoohan, was filmed in which Welsh village?

- A: Dolgellau
- B: Tywyn
- C: Portmeirion
- D: Ffestiniog

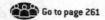 50:50 Go to page 249    Go to page 261     ? Answers on page 269

# 10 ◆ £32,000

## 36

Which of these is the title of a
2000 hit single by David Grey?

A: Babel
B: Byzantium
C: Bethlehem
D: Babylon

## 37

From which island did Steve McQueen
eventually escape in the 1973 film 'Papillon'?

A: St Helena
B: Elba
C: Devil's Island
D: Alcatraz

## 38

Which of these singers was shot and killed by his father?

A: James Brown
B: Marvin Gaye
C: Chuck Berry
D: Sam Cooke

## 39

Who composed the operas 'Il Trovatore' and 'Rigoletto'?

A: Puccini
B: Rossini
C: Stravinsky
D: Verdi

## 40

What was the first name of Beeblebrox, the two-headed
character in 'The Hitch-Hiker's Guide to the Galaxy'?

A: Deebram
B: Zaphod
C: Q-Nax
D: Trillian

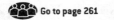 50:50 Go to page 249     Go to page 261      ? Answers on page 269

**41**

Who plays the title role in the 2002 film 'Spider-Man'?

A: Samuel L Jackson
B: Ben Affleck
C: Tobey Maguire
D: Josh Hartnett

**42**

Which of these composers' first name was Giacomo?

A: Verdi
B: Puccini
C: Monteverdi
D: Bellini

**43**

Who was the master of ceremonies in the early days of BBC TV's 'This is Your Life'?

A: Jimmy Young
B: Bruce Forsyth
C: Michael Aspel
D: Eamon Andrews

**44**

Which Hollywood actor and comedian was born Joe Yule Jr?

A: Jerry Lewis
B: Mickey Rooney
C: Oliver Hardy
D: Harold Lloyd

**45**

Where does the cartoon character Homer Simpson work?

A: Bar
B: DIY store
C: Nuclear power plant
D: Post office

50:50 Go to page 250    Go to page 262    ? Answers on page 269

# 10 ◆ £32,000

## 46

In which country was the actress Julie Christie born?

◆A: India
◆B: Thailand

◆C: Pakistan
◆D: Indonesia

## 47

Which classic 1960 British film was based on John Wyndham's book 'The Midwich Cuckoos'?

◆A: The Day of the Triffids
◆B: Village of the Damned

◆C: The Day the Earth Stood Still
◆D: The Danger Within

## 48

Who was not a member of the legendary rock band 'Cream'?

◆A: Ginger Baker
◆B: Jeff Beck

◆C: Eric Clapton
◆D: Jack Bruce

## 49

Which of these radio broadcasters was particularly famous for his commentaries on the Oxford and Cambridge University boat race?

◆A: Alistair Cooke
◆B: Kenneth Wolstenholme

◆C: Murray Walker
◆D: John Snagge

## 50

What was the name of Jeff and Beau Bridges' actor father?

◆A: Rufus Bridges
◆B: Lloyd Bridges

◆C: Francis Bridges
◆D: Armand Bridges

**50:50** Go to page 250    Go to page 262    **?** Answers on page 269

# 10 ◆ £32,000

### Which of Wagner's operas is also known as 'The Twilight of the Gods'?

**A: Das Rheingold**

**B: Die Walküre**

**C: Siegfried**

**D: Götterdammerung**

**52**

### Vince Clarke and Andy Bell formed which pop group in 1985?

**A: Pet Shop Boys**

**B: Erasure**

**C: Eurythmics**

**D: Tears for Fears**

 **50:50** Go to page 250   Go to page 262    **?** Answers on page 269

| 50:50 | | |
|---|---|---|
| **15** | **£1 MILLION** | |
| 14 | £500,000 | |
| 13 | £250,000 | |
| 12 | £125,000 | |
| **11 ◆** | **£64,000** | |
| 10 ◆ | £32,000 | |
| 9 ◆ | £16,000 | |
| 8 ◆ | £8,000 | |
| 7 ◆ | £4,000 | |
| 6 ◆ | £2,000 | |
| 5 ◆ | £1,000 | |
| 4 ◆ | £500 | |
| 3 ◆ | £300 | |
| 2 ◆ | £200 | |
| 1 ◆ | £100 | |

# 11 ◆ £64,000

### 1

**In which decade was the long-running radio series 'The Archers' first broadcast?**

- A: 1940s
- B: 1950s
- C: 1960s
- D: 1970s

### 2

**What is the name of the lead singer of the Fun Lovin' Criminals?**

- A: Joey
- B: Louis
- C: Huey
- D: Jackie

### 3

**In which film does Michael Caine's character say, 'You're a big man, but you're out of shape. With me it's a full time job. Now behave yourself.'?**

- A: Get Carter
- B: The Italian Job
- C: Billion Dollar Brain
- D: The Man Who Would Be King

### 4

**Which Gilbert and Sullivan operetta is alternatively titled 'A Slave to Duty'?**

- A: HMS Pinafore
- B: The Mikado
- C: Pirates of Penzance
- D: The Yeomen of the Guard

### 5

**What is the fictional occupation of the character Para Handy, who featured in the BBC TV comedy series?**

- A: Policeman
- B: Fireman
- C: Blacksmith
- D: Sailor

50:50 Go to page 250　　Go to page 262　　? Answers on page 269

# 11 ◆ £64,000

## 6

In which Shakespeare play do the father and son, Old Gobbo and Launcelot Gobbo, appear?

- A: The Tempest
- B: The Merchant of Venice
- C: King Lear
- D: Hamlet

## 7

What is the name of the US naval officer who seduces Madame Butterfly in Puccini's opera?

- A: Redington
- B: Greenford
- C: Browning
- D: Pinkerton

## 8

Which film actor was the USA's most decorated soldier in WWII?

- A: Gary Cooper
- B: James Stewart
- C: Audie Murphy
- D: Kirk Douglas

## 9

For which of these films did Bob Fosse provide the choreography?

- A: Show Boat
- B: High Society
- C: Cabaret
- D: Grease

## 10

How are Tom Rowlands and Ed Simons collectively known in the music world?

- A: Chas & Dave
- B: The Charlatans
- C: Lightning Seeds
- D: The Chemical Brothers

50:50 Go to page 250     Go to page 262     ? Answers on page 269

# 11 ◆ £64,000

## 11

In which city is Bizet's opera 'Carmen' set?

- A: Madrid
- B: Granada
- C: Barcelona
- D: Seville

## 12

What was the rank of George Carter, played by Dennis Waterman, in the TV series 'The Sweeney'?

- A: Detective Constable
- B: Detective Sergeant
- C: Chief Inspector
- D: Detective Inspector

## 13

Which musical features the characters Rum Tum Tugger and Skimbleshanks?

- A: Barnum
- B: Cabaret
- C: The Lion King
- D: Cats

## 14

In which of the following films does Ben Stiller play the character of Gaylord Focker?

- A: There's Something About Mary
- B: The Royal Tenenbaums
- C: Meet the Parents
- D: Zoolander

## 15

Which sci-fi TV show began with the line, 'There is nothing wrong with your television set. Do not attempt to adjust the picture'?

- A: The Twilight Zone
- B: The Outer Limits
- C: War of the Worlds
- D: The X-Files

50:50 Go to page 250    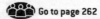 Go to page 262     Answers on page 269

# 11 ◆ £64,000

## 16

In which British city was the
superclub 'Cream' founded in 1992?

A: Glasgow
B: Liverpool
C: London
D: Manchester

## 17

Which singer's real surname is Panayiotou?

A: Vangelis
B: Demis Roussos
C: Nana Mouskouri
D: George Michael

## 18

What is the actress Angelina Jolie said to wear around her
neck to remind her of her second husband Billy Bob Thornton?

page
**195**

A: His photograph
B: Vial of his blood
C: One of his teeth
D: Lock of his hair

## 19

How many standard positions
are there in classical ballet?

A: Two
B: Five
C: Thirteen
D: Twenty-eight

## 20

In which sport was the operatic soprano
Dame Joan Hammond a championship winner?

A: Tennis
B: Skiing
C: Squash
D: Golf

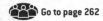 50:50 Go to page 250    Go to page 262    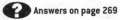 ? Answers on page 269

# 11 ◆ £64,000

## 21

Which British actor co-wrote and starred in
the musical, 'Stop the World, I Want to Get Off'?

A: Rex Harrison
B: Kenneth More
C: Anthony Newley
D: Ron Moody

## 22

'Luxury of Life', 'Silk and Steel' and 'Between the Lines'
are albums by which '80s pop sensations?

A: Level 42
B: Pat and Mick
C: Five Star
D: A-ha

## 23

Badly Drawn Boy provided songs for which 2002 hit film?

A: About A Boy
B: Jason X
C: Spider-Man
D: Show Time

## 24

Which of the following were the
subject of the 1999 film 'Pushing Tin'?

A: Car salesmen
B: Air traffic controllers
C: Astronauts
D: Aluminium salesmen

## 25

From a book by which author did the
group Marillion derive their name?

A: P D James
B: H G Wells
C: J R R Tolkien
D: D H Lawrence

50:50 Go to page 250    Go to page 262    ? Answers on page 269

# 11 ◆ £64,000

## 26

In which year was Britain's first
digital television programme broadcast?

A: 1991
B: 1995
C: 1998
D: 2001

## 27

From which city in Indiana do Michael, Janet
and the rest of the Jackson family come?

A: Steve
B: Gary
C: Ian
D: Shane

## 28

Which Frankie Goes To Hollywood video featured
caricatures of Reagan and Chernenko fighting each other?

page
**197**

A: Welcome to the Pleasuredome
B: Relax
C: Two Tribes
D: The Power of Love

## 29

The play 'Look Back In Anger' was
written by which English dramatist?

A: Nöel Coward
B: Harold Pinter
C: John Osborne
D: Tom Stoppard

## 30

Which renowned Scottish actor
is the uncle of Ewan McGregor?

A: Brian Cox
B: Sean Connery
C: Denis Lawson
D: Fulton Mackay

50:50 Go to page 250     Go to page 262     ? Answers on page 269

# 11 ◆ £64,000

## 31

In which city did the band Human League form?

- A: Manchester
- B: Birmingham
- C: Sheffield
- D: Nottingham

## 32

Who made her West End debut in 2002 in the play 'Up for Grabs'?

- A: Madonna
- B: Cher
- C: Jerry Hall
- D: Gwyneth Paltrow

## 33

Which of the following is a ballet step in which the dancer stands on one leg with the other leg stretched out behind?

- A: Pirouette
- B: Glissade
- C: Arabesque
- D: Capriole

## 34

Who plays Morpheus in the film 'The Matrix' and Ike Turner in the film 'What's Love Got To Do With It'?

- A: Denzel Washington
- B: Forrest Whittaker
- C: Laurence Fishburne
- D: Don Cheadle

## 35

In jazz, how are the flattened third and seventh notes of the scale sometimes described?

- A: White notes
- B: Black notes
- C: Red notes
- D: Blue notes

 50:50 Go to page 250     Go to page 262    ? Answers on page 269

# 11 ◆ £64,000

## 36

**Before playing James Bond, Pierce Brosnan was the star of which TV series?**

A: Moonlighting | B: Logan's Run
C: Remington Steele | D: Manimal

## 37

**'High Society' was a musical version of which film?**

A: Call Me Madam | B: The Philadelphia Story
C: Half a Sixpence | D: Meet Me in St Louis

## 38

**Who or what is Audrey II in 'The Little Shop of Horrors'?**

page **199**

A: A carnivorous plant | B: An evil dentist
C: A possessed car | D: A florist's shop

## 39

**The film 'Dr Strangelove' is subtitled 'or, How I Learned To Stop Worrying And Love...'?**

A: Myself | B: America
C: The Russkies | D: The Bomb

## 40

**Which Rod Stewart hit has the same title as a Lionel Bart musical?**

A: Sailing | B: Baby Jane
C: Ruby Tuesday | D: Maggie May

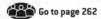 **50:50** Go to page 250    Go to page 262    **?** Answers on page 269

# 11 ◆ £64,000

## 41

Who directed the science-fiction films
'Robocop', 'Total Recall' and 'Starship Troopers'?

A: Joel Schumacher
B: Roland Emmerich
C: James Cameron
D: Paul Verhoeven

## 42

What was the rank of 'Hotlips' Houlihan
in the TV series 'M*A*S*H'?

A: Sergeant
B: Lieutenant
C: Captain
D: Major

## 43

Which ancient stringed instrument consisted
of a sound box with two symmetrical arms?

A: Mandolin
B: Lute
C: Lyre
D: Chitarrone

## 44

What is the nationality of the dancer and
choreographer Merce Cunningham?

A: Welsh
B: American
C: Swiss
D: Turkish

## 45

Which of these groups reached No 1 in the UK
with each of their first seven singles?

A: Beatles
B: Spice Girls
C: Boyzone
D: Westlife

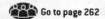 50:50 Go to page 250     Go to page 262    ? Answers on page 269

# 11 ◆ £64,000

## 46

What is the first name of the member of the Larkin family played by Catherine Zeta Jones in the TV series, 'The Darling Buds of May'?

- A: Marion
- B: Matilda
- C: Marlene
- D: Mariette

## 47

Based on the Brothers Grimm story, who wrote the opera 'Hansel and Gretel'?

- A: Johann Strauss
- B: Franz Schubert
- C: Engelbert Humperdink
- D: Gustav Holst

## 48

Who played the accident prone Brother Dominic in the TV sitcom, 'Oh Brother!'?

- A: Richard Briars
- B: Robert Lindsay
- C: Leslie Phillips
- D: Derek Nimmo

 50:50 Go to page 250     Go to page 262    ? Answers on page 269

50:50

| 15 | | **£1 MILLION** |
| 14 | | £500,000 |
| 13 | | £250,000 |
| **12** | ◆ | **£125,000** |
| 11 | ◆ | £64,000 |
| **10** | ◆ | **£32,000** |
| 9 | ◆ | £16,000 |
| 8 | ◆ | £8,000 |
| 7 | ◆ | £4,000 |
| 6 | ◆ | £2,000 |
| **5** | ◆ | **£1,000** |
| 4 | ◆ | £500 |
| 3 | ◆ | £300 |
| 2 | ◆ | £200 |
| 1 | ◆ | £100 |

# 12 ◆ £125,000

## 1

**Which of these film directors has a separate career as a jazz musician with his own group?**

- A: Steven Spielberg
- B: Ridley Scott
- C: Martin Scorsese
- D: Woody Allen

## 2

**In which Ingmar Bergman film is a knight challenged to a game of chess by Death?**

- A: Through a Glass Darkly
- B: The Seventh Seal
- C: Fanny and Alexander
- D: Wild Strawberries

## 3

**Which Gary Numan song provided the backing track for the Sugababes 2002 UK No 1 single 'Freak Like Me'?**

- A: Are 'Friends' Electric?
- B: Complex
- C: Cars
- D: We Are Glass

## 4

**What was the occupation of Maxwell Smart in the 1960s US sitcom 'Get Smart'?**

- A: Scuba diver
- B: Secret agent
- C: Baseball coach
- D: Air Force pilot

## 5

**Which comedian has an alter ego named 'Alan Parker, Urban Warrior'?**

- A: Phil Kaye
- B: Al Murray
- C: Ed Byrne
- D: Simon Munnery

50:50 Go to page 250    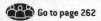 Go to page 262    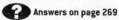 Answers on page 269

# 12 ◆ £125,000

**6**

**Who would use a 'fuzzbox'?**

A: Actress
B: Puppeteer
C: Guitarist
D: Make-up artist

**7**

**Which function does the 'best boy' carry out on the set of a feature film?**

A: Editor
B: Lighting technician
C: Focus puller
D: Wardrobe assistant

**8**

**In which year were the 'Proms', now held in the Royal Albert Hall, first performed?**

A: 1855
B: 1895
C: 1925
D: 1945

**9**

**Who is referred to in the film 'Wayne's World II' as the rock star who 'cannot be killed by conventional weapons'?**

A: Steven Tyler
B: Keith Richard
C: Ozzy Osbourne
D: Iggy Pop

**10**

**Which comedian collaborated with Queen in the production of the musical 'We Will Rock You'?**

A: Jack Dee
B: Ben Elton
C: John Cleese
D: Rowan Atkinson

 50:50 Go to page 250     Go to page 262     ? Answers on page 269

# 12 ◆ £125,000

## 11

According to the US press in 2001, which TV comedy actor became the highest-paid in history with a deal worth $1.6 million per episode?

- A: Jerry Seinfeld
- B: Jennifer Aniston
- C: Kelsey Grammer
- D: Sarah Jessica Parker

## 12

Which was the first British pop group to top the US singles chart?

- A: The Beatles
- B: The Rolling Stones
- C: The Shadows
- D: The Tornados

## 13

Where in Britain did the Barbican Theatre re-open in 1998?

- A: Brighton
- B: Bournemouth
- C: St Ives
- D: Plymouth

## 14

Starring Bette Midler, the 1979 film 'The Rose' was loosely based on the life and death of which singer?

- A: Billie Holliday
- B: Janis Joplin
- C: Judy Garland
- D: Alma Cogan

## 15

Which radio programme starring Spike Milligan, Peter Sellers, Harry Secombe and Michael Bentine was a forerunner of 'The Goon Show'?

- A: Those Crazy People
- B: The Wild Bunch
- C: The Mad Caps
- D: The Goofy Gang

50:50 Go to page 251     Go to page 263     ? Answers on page 269

# 12 ◆ £125,000

## 16

What type of musical instrument is a bible regal?

A: Drum
B: Flute
C: Harp
D: Organ

## 17

In how many of Shakespeare's plays
does Sir John Falstaff appear?

A: One
B: Two
C: Three
D: Four

## 18

Which of these is a famous
choreographer of modern dance?

A: Bridget Riley
B: Penelope Spheeris
C: Philip Glass
D: Twyla Tharp

## 19

Who won the Best Actor Oscar for his
role in the 1939 film 'Goodbye Mr Chips'?

A: James Stewart
B: Alec Guinness
C: Alastair Sim
D: Robert Donat

## 20

Which part was played by George, the brother
of Telly Savalas, in the TV series 'Kojak'?

A: Stavros
B: Saperstein
C: Rizzo
D: McNeil

50:50 Go to page 251      Go to page 263      ? Answers on page 269

## 21

**What was the name of James Bond's wife in the film 'On Her Majesty's Secret Service'?**

- A: Sharon
- B: Tracy
- C: Anna
- D: Sheila

## 22

**Which of the following leading ladies did actor Ryan Phillippe marry in 1999?**

- A: Kirsten Dunst
- B: Reese Witherspoon
- C: Alicia Silverstone
- D: Eliza Dushku

## 23

**Who were named Best British Group at the 2002 Brit Awards?**

- A: Travis
- B: Gorillaz
- C: Radiohead
- D: Stereophonics

## 24

**In which of these musicals do the characters Nathan Detroit and Harry the Horse appear?**

- A: Porgy and Bess
- B: 42nd Street
- C: Guys and Dolls
- D: Mack and Mabel

## 25

**Which of the following is the setting for the ballet 'Giselle'?**

- A: Left Bank of Paris
- B: Loire Valley
- C: Tuscany
- D: Rhine Valley

 50:50 Go to page 251     Go to page 263     ? Answers on page 269

# 12 ◆ £125,000

## 26

**What is unusual about the regular doctor in 'Star Trek - Voyager'?**

A: He is a hologram
B: He is a Romulan
C: He is blind
D: He is an android

## 27

**Who was the French singer responsible for the controversial '60s song 'Je T'Aime...Moi Non Plus'?**

A: Jacques Brel
B: Johnny Hallyday
C: Charles Aznavour
D: Serge Gainsbourg

## 28

**In which of the following did comedian Tommy Cooper serve before he became a full time entertainer?**

A: Army
B: Navy
C: RAF
D: Police

## 29

**Which city is the setting for Rossini's opera 'Otello'?**

A: Rome
B: Seville
C: Venice
D: Tangiers

## 30

**What is John Cusack's character's original occupation in the 1999 film 'Being John Malkovich'?**

A: Actor
B: Painter
C: Musician
D: Puppeteer

# 12 ◆ £125,000

## 31

Who sang the theme song to 'Dad's Army'?

A: Charlie Chester
B: Stanley Holloway
C: Billy Cotton
D: Bud Flanagan

## 32

Which part was played by
Carmen Silvera in TV's "Allo 'Allo!'?

A: Edith
B: Yvette
C: Maria
D: Mme Fanny

## 33

In which British city do The Lyceum and The Studio
form part of a large regional theatre complex?

A: Manchester
B: Birmingham
C: Sheffield
D: Newcastle

## 34

Which of the following was not a sequel
to the 1931 film 'Frankenstein'?

A: Son of Frankenstein
B: Daughter of Frankenstein
C: Bride of Frankenstein
D: The Ghost of Frankenstein

## 35

Who plays Dudley Moore's valet in the 1981 film 'Arthur'?

A: Denholm Elliott
B: Lawrence Olivier
C: John Gielgud
D: Ralph Richardson

50:50 Go to page 251    Go to page 263    ? Answers on page 269

# 12 ◆ £125,000

## 36

Which Hollywood actor made a West End stage appearance in 2002 in 'This Is Our Youth'?

- A: Ben Affleck
- B: Tobey Maguire
- C: Elijah Wood
- D: Matt Damon

## 37

During which conflict is the 2001 film 'Charlotte Gray' set?

- A: World War I
- B: World War II
- C: Crimean War
- D: American Civil War

## 38

Which UK synthesiser group was formed in the 1980s by Vince Clarke, Andy Fletcher, Dave Gahan and Martin Gore?

page
211

- A: Tears For Fears
- B: Landscape
- C: Depeche Mode
- D: Human League

## 39

Who plays TV presenter and record company boss Tony Wilson in the film '24 Hour Party People'?

- A: Charlie Higson
- B: Steve Coogan
- C: Simon Day
- D: John Thompson

## 40

Which Hollywood director was responsible for the films 'Ride the High Country', 'The Getaway' and 'Cross of Iron'?

- A: Billy Wilder
- B: Sam Peckinpah
- C: John Huston
- D: John Ford

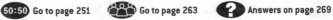 
50:50 Go to page 251     Go to page 263     ? Answers on page 269

# 12 ◆ £125,000

## 41

The name of the rap star LL Cool J is an abbreviation for 'Ladies Love Cool ...'?

- A: Joe
- B: Jeff
- C: Jazz
- D: James

## 42

Which cartoon cat and mouse duo appear on Krusty the Clown's show in 'The Simpsons'?

- A: Fidgety and Edgy
- B: Prickly and Tickly
- C: Itchy and Scratchy
- D: Tingly and Tetchy

## 43

What nationality is the orchestra leader James Last?

- A: Scottish
- B: South African
- C: German
- D: Mexican

## 44

Which rocker recorded the hit 'When You're Gone' with the Spice Girl, Mel C?

- A: Mick Jagger
- B: Bruce Dickinson
- C: Bryan Adams
- D: Jon Bon Jovi

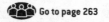 50:50 Go to page 251    Go to page 263     ? Answers on page 269

15 **£1 MILLION**

14 £500,000

13 ◆ **£250,000**

12 ◆ £125,000

11 ◆ £64,000

10 ◆ **£32,000**

9 ◆ £16,000

8 ◆ £8,000

7 ◆ £4,000

6 ◆ £2,000

5 ◆ **£1,000**

4 ◆ £500

3 ◆ £300

2 ◆ £200

1 ◆ £100

# 13 ◆ £250,000

## 1

Who created Kate Winslet's dress for her 1998 Oscar appearance, which later fetched $57,500 at auction?

A: Stella McCartney

B: Donna Karan

C: Alexander McQueen

D: Valentino

## 2

Which singer had the forenames William John Clifton?

A: Billy Fury

B: Bill Haley

C: Bill Brewster

D: Willy Nelson

## 3

In which TV sci-fi series does Ben Browder play John Crichton, an astronaut flung into a distant galaxy?

A: Farscape

B: Babylon 5

C: Sliders

D: Deep Space 9

## 4

Which pop star is the subject of the documentary feature 'Nobody Someday'?

A: Kylie Minogue

B: Robbie Williams

C: Britney Spears

D: Ricky Martin

## 5

Rollo and Sister Bliss are the two main members of which dance act?

A: The Prodigy

B: Faithless

C: The Orb

D: 2 Unlimited

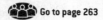 **50:50** Go to page 251   Go to page 263   **?** Answers on page 269

# 13 ◆ £250,000

## 6

Which Hollywood actor made an early film appearance in 'Return of the Killer Tomatoes!'?

- A: Matt Damon
- B: George Clooney
- C: Brad Pitt
- D: Billy Bob Thornton

## 7

From what occupation had Jack Nicholson's character retired in the 1983 film 'Terms of Endearment'?

- A: Lawyer
- B: Doctor
- C: Astronaut
- D: Architect

## 8

In which Verdi opera would you hear 'Va, pensiero', more commonly known as the 'Chorus of the Hebrew Slaves'?

- A: Rigoletto
- B: La Traviata
- C: Nabucco
- D: Otello

## 9

Which British actor is the brother of Laila Morse, who plays Mo Harris in 'EastEnders'?

- A: Tim Roth
- B: Ray Winstone
- C: Timothy Spall
- D: Gary Oldman

## 10

What is the name of the Royal Shakespeare Company's studio theatre, opened in Stratford-upon-Avon in 1974?

- A: The Other Stage
- B: The Other Lot
- C: The Other Place
- D: The Other Side

50:50 Go to page 251    Go to page 263    ? Answers on page 269

# 13 ◆ £250,000

## 11

Which US state is the setting for
Gershwin's opera 'Porgy and Bess'?

A: Alabama
B: South Carolina
C: Mississippi
D: Kentucky

## 12

In the classic 1954 sci-fi thriller
'Them!', what were 'Them'?

A: Mutant worms
B: Mutant bees
C: Mutant ants
D: Mutant apes

## 13

Which of the following was the very first
act to appear on 'Top of the Pops'?

A: Dusty Springfield
B: The Beatles
C: Freddie and the Dreamers
D: The Rolling Stones

## 14

Who is quoted as saying 'An actor is a guy who,
if you ain't talking about him, ain't listening'?

A: Tony Curtis
B: Kirk Douglas
C: Marlon Brando
D: Burt Lancaster

## 15

In which country was the actress Glynis Johns born?

A: Australia
B: New Zealand
C: USA
D: South Africa

 50:50 Go to page 251    Go to page 263    ? Answers on page 269

# 13 ◆ £250,000

## 16

Which Hollywood actor starred as Danny Zuko
in the original London cast of the musical 'Grease'?

A: Bruce Willis

B: John Travolta

C: Alec Baldwin

D: Richard Gere

## 17

In which region of Spain did the music
and dance called Flamenco originate?

A: Andalucìa

B: Cataluña

C: Aragón

D: Galicia

## 18

Which pop legend was made an honorary NYPD detective
at a Madison Square Gardens' concert in 2002?

A: Tom Jones

B: Paul McCartney

C: David Bowie

D: Bono

## 19

Who composed 'Carnival of the Animals'?

A: Rossini

B: Tchaikovsky

C: Saint-Saëns

D: Haydn

## 20

In 2002, the makers of 'The Simpsons' were forced to apologise to the
inhabitants of which city after portraying them in an unflattering light?

A: London

B: Paris

C: Rio de Janeiro

D: Mexico City

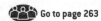 50:50 Go to page 251     Go to page 263     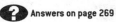 ? Answers on page 269

# 13 ◆ £250,000

## 21

**Sidney Poiter won the Best Actor Oscar for his role in which of these films?**

A: The Defiant Ones
B: The Blackboard Jungle
C: They Call Me Mr Tibbs
D: Lilies Of The Field

## 22

**Dave Grohl of the rock group Foo Fighters was previously the drummer in which of the following?**

A: Metallica
B: Europe
C: Nirvana
D: Oasis

## 23

**Which of these popular singers was born Frank Paul LoVecchio?**

A: Frankie Valli
B: Frankie Vaughan
C: Frankie Laine
D: Frankie Avalon

## 24

**Stan Getz is best known for playing which instrument?**

A: Drums
B: Bass guitar
C: Saxophone
D: Organ

## 25

**What is the name of the town where the TV series 'The League of Gentlemen' is set?**

A: Preston Brockhurst
B: Market Weighton
C: Royston Vasey
D: Hutton Cranswick

50:50 Go to page 251     Go to page 263     Answers on page 269

## 26

Which Italian island is the setting for Rossini's opera 'Tancredi'?

◆A: Capri
◆B: Sardinia
◆C: Sicily
◆D: Elba

## 27

By what nickname is Larry Crabbe, star of the early 'Flash Gordon' and 'Buck Rogers' film serials, better known?

◆A: Chopper
◆B: Buster
◆C: Crusher
◆D: Bruiser

## 28

What nationality was the orchestra leader Burt Kaempfert?

◆A: Dutch
◆B: Swiss
◆C: Austrian
◆D: German

## 29

Which of these musicals features the characters Christine Daae and Carlotta?

◆A: Sweet Charity
◆B: Gypsy
◆C: The Phantom of the Opera
◆D: Can-Can

## 30

Tracey Morrow is the real name of which US rapper turned film actor?

◆A: Vanilla Ice
◆B: Ice T
◆C: LL Cool J
◆D: Ice Cube

50:50 Go to page 251    Go to page 263    ? Answers on page 269

# 13 ◆ £250,000

## 31

What was the name of the submarine featured in the 1961 film 'Voyage to the Bottom of the Sea' and the subsequent TV series of the same name?

- A: Nautilus
- B: Discovery
- C: Voyager
- D: Seaview

## 32

Which legendary Hollywood actress was born Lucille Fay Le Sueur?

- A: Betty Grable
- B: Joan Crawford
- C: Rita Hayworth
- D: Katharine Hepburn

## 33

In which European city was the famous ballet dancer and teacher Marie Rambert born?

- A: Paris
- B: London
- C: Warsaw
- D: Rome

## 34

Which comedian was married to his long-time screen partner Gracie Allen?

- A: George Burns
- B: Bob Hope
- C: Ed Sullivan
- D: Desi Arnaz

## 35

Who resigned as artistic director of the Royal Shakespeare Company in 2002 after more than a decade in the job?

- A: Richard Eyre
- B: Peter Hall
- C: Adrian Noble
- D: Anthony Sher

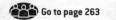 50:50 Go to page 251     Go to page 263      Answers on page 269

**36**

Which of these singers fronted the group
Vinegar Joe alongside Robert Palmer?

A: Kiki Dee
B: Marianne Faithfull
C: Elkie Brooks
D: Janis Joplin

**37**

Where is 'Einstein' in the title
of Philip Glass's 1976 opera?

A: In the Sea
B: On the Beach
C: In the Shade
D: On the Slopes

**38**

With which musical instrument is the radio
personality Sandy MacPherson associated?

A: Organ
B: Trumpet
C: Violin
D: Accordian

**39**

Which long-running police drama started
with a pilot episode called 'Woodentop'?

A: The Bill
B: Dixon of Dock Green
C: Z Cars
D: The Sweeney

**40**

In which country was the theatrical
company Cirque du Soleil founded?

A: France
B: USA
C: Canada
D: Switzerland

50:50 Go to page 251    Go to page 263    Answers on page 269

| 15 | | £1 MILLION |
|---|---|---|
| 14 | ♦ | **£500,000** |
| 13 | ♦ | £250,000 |
| 12 | ♦ | £125,000 |
| 11 | ♦ | £64,000 |
| 10 | ♦ | £32,000 |
| 9 | ♦ | £16,000 |
| 8 | ♦ | £8,000 |
| 7 | ♦ | £4,000 |
| 6 | ♦ | £2,000 |
| 5 | ♦ | £1,000 |
| 4 | ♦ | £500 |
| 3 | ♦ | £300 |
| 2 | ♦ | £200 |
| 1 | ♦ | £100 |

# 14 ◆ £500,000

**1**

Which Hollywood actress became
famous as the original 'Oomph Girl'?

A: Jane Russell
B: Rita Hayworth
C: Betty Grable
D: Ann Sheridan

**2**

In which 1960s sci-fi series did the first inter-racial
kiss reputedly take place on US television?

A: The Time Tunnel
B: Lost in Space
C: Star Trek
D: Voyage to the Bottom of the Sea

**3**

Which English architect was also a well-known Restoration playwright,
his works include 'The Relapse' and 'The Provok'd Wife'?

A: Inigo Jones
B: Christopher Wren
C: Nicholas Hawksmoor
D: John Vanbrugh

**4**

Who did not appear with Eric Clapton on the
1995 UK No 1 single 'Love Can Build A Bridge'?

A: Cher
B: Neneh Cherry
C: Tina Turner
D: Chrissie Hynde

**5**

Which surrealist artist created the
film 'Un Chien Andalou' with Luis Buñuel?

A: Tristan Tzara
B: Joan Miro
C: René Magritte
D: Salvador Dali

50:50 Go to page 252 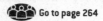 Go to page 264  Answers on page 270

page
224

## 6

**By what name is the musical instrument called the 'Jingling Johnny' also known?**

A: Chinese star

B: Greek cross

C: Russian hammer

D: Turkish crescent

## 7

**Which Irish actor numbers bullfighting among one of his previous jobs?**

A: Liam Neeson

B: Gabriel Byrne

C: Stephen Rea

D: Pierce Brosnan

## 8

**Who composed the one-act opera 'Cavalleria Rusticana'?**

A: Berio

B: Mascagni

C: Donizetti

D: Monteverdi

## 9

**Which British singer, who died in 1985, had the real name Terence Parsons?**

A: Billy Fury

B: Matt Monro

C: Ronnie Carroll

D: Michael Holliday

## 10

**What was the name of Britain's first public playhouse?**

A: Bankside

B: Rose

C: Globe

D: Theatre

50:50 Go to page 252      Go to page 264      ? Answers on page 270

# 14 ◆ £500,000

## 11

Which musical instrument does one play by moving one's hand closer or further away from its antenna?

A: Synthesiser
B: Electric guitar
C: Theremin
D: Celesta

## 12

Of which of these Spanish films is the Tom Cruise film 'Vanilla Sky' a remake?

A: Tie Me Up! Tie Me Down!
B: All About My Mother
C: Open Your Eyes
D: The Flower of My Secret

## 13

Which 1950s teen idol wrote the lyrics to Frank Sinatra's hit 'My Way'?

A: Paul Anka
B: Dion
C: Frankie Avalon
D: Del Shannon

## 14

Who became the first video game character to be signed by a Hollywood talent agency in 2002?

A: Mario
B: Lara Croft
C: Sonic the Hedgehog
D: Duke Nukem

## 15

Which of these films won Oliver Stone his second Best Director Oscar?

A: Platoon
B: JFK
C: Wall Street
D: Born on the Fourth of July

50:50 Go to page 252 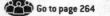 Go to page 264  Answers on page 270

# 14 ◆ £500,000

## 16

Formed in 1970, which legendary British rock band evolved from the group 'Smile'?

◆A: Status Quo ◆B: Queen

◆C: Slade ◆D: Genesis

## 17

Which French singer stars in François Truffaut's film 'Shoot The Pianist'?

◆A: Charles Aznavour ◆B: Sacha Distel

◆C: Johnny Hallyday ◆D: Jacques Brel

## 18

Who played TV's 'Flying Nun' in the 1960s?

◆A: Kate Jackson ◆B: Cheryl Ladd

◆C: Carrie Fisher ◆D: Sally Field

## 19

Which female singer was awarded an OBE for her services to music in 2002?

◆A: Sade ◆B: Kate Bush

◆C: Annie Lennox ◆D: Sinead O'Connor

## 20

In which country was comedian Eddie Izzard born?

◆A: Turkey ◆B: Egypt

◆C: Yemen ◆D: India

50:50 Go to page 252 Go to page 264 ? Answers on page 270

# 14 ◆ £500,000

## 21

### Which of these musicals was the first ever to win a Tony Award?

- A: 42nd Street
- B: Kiss Me Kate
- C: Annie Get Your Gun
- D: Show Boat

## 22

### From the works of which ancient playwright does the expression 'Cloud-Cuckoo-Land' come?

- A: Aristophanes
- B: Euripides
- C: Sophocles
- D: Aeschylus

## 23

### Which of these films received the most Oscar nominations?

- A: Forrest Gump
- B: The English Patient
- C: Dances With Wolves
- D: Schindler's List

## 24

### What was the middle name of the jazz legend Thelonius Monk?

- A: Sphere
- B: Orb
- C: Ball
- D: Ring

## 25

### Which character has been played on TV and the big screen by John Mills, André Morell, Andrew Keir, Reginald Tate and Brian Donlevy?

- A: Doctor Frankenstein
- B: Professor Quatermass
- C: Professor Van Helsing
- D: Big Brother

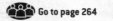 50:50 Go to page 252    Go to page 264     ? Answers on page 270

## 26

The Maly is reputedly the oldest surviving theatre in which city?

- A: Moscow
- B: Prague
- C: Paris
- D: Berlin

## 27

Which single was voted the UK's most favourite single ever, in a 2002 Guinness World Records poll?

- A: Imagine
- B: Hey Jude
- C: Bohemian Rhapsody
- D: Dancing Queen

## 28

Besides all appearing on 'A Question of Sport', what do Sue Barker, Ally McCoist and John Parrott have in common?

- A: All have twin sisters
- B: All left-handed
- C: All their fathers are vicars
- D: All been awarded the MBE

## 29

Which comedy duo starred in the 1967 film 'Bedazzled'?

- A: Mike and Bernie Winters
- B: Morecambe and Wise
- C: Peter Cook and Dudley Moore
- D: Dean Martin and Jerry Lewis

## 30

What did Lalo Schifrin contribute towards the TV series 'Mission: Impossible' and 'Starsky and Hutch'?

- A: Designed the clothes
- B: Composed the theme tunes
- C: Designed the sets
- D: Wrote the scripts

 50:50 Go to page 252  Go to page 264   Answers on page 270

# 14 ◆ £500,000

## 31

**Which of these was not one of the Russian composers known as 'The Five'?**

A: Shostakovich
B: Borodin
C: Mussorgsky
D: Rimsky-Korsakov

## 32

**Due to French copyright laws, which musical cannot be performed in that country without the permission of the descendants of Georges Bizet?**

A: Carmen Jones
B: Moulin Rouge
C: Martin Guerre
D: Les Miserables

## 33

**Which Hollywood actor is a founding member of the Steppenwolf Theatre in Chicago?**

A: John Malkovich
B: Edward Norton
C: John Cusack
D: Tom Hanks

## 34

**Who is the famous father-in-law of the film and pop video director Spike Jonze?**

A: Martin Scorsese
B: Ron Howard
C: Francis Ford Coppola
D: Ridley Scott

## 35

**Which prodigious composer wrote music for the films 'Planet of the Apes', 'The Omen' and 'Papillon'?**

A: Jerry Goldsmith
B: Henry Mancini
C: Mike Post
D: John Williams

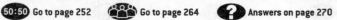

50:50 Go to page 252     Go to page 264     ? Answers on page 270

## 36

By what name is the singer
Clementina Dinah Campbell better known?

◆A: Cleo Laine ◆B: Nina Simone

◆C: Patti Labelle ◆D: Whitney Houston

| 15 | ◆ | **£1 MILLION** |
|----|---|----------------|
| 14 | ◆ | £500,000 |
| 13 | ◆ | £250,000 |
| 12 | ◆ | £125,000 |
| 11 | ◆ | £64,000 |
| **10** | ◆ | **£32,000** |
| 9 | ◆ | £16,000 |
| 8 | ◆ | £8,000 |
| 7 | ◆ | £4,000 |
| 6 | ◆ | £2,000 |
| **5** | ◆ | **£1,000** |
| 4 | ◆ | £500 |
| 3 | ◆ | £300 |
| 2 | ◆ | £200 |
| 1 | ◆ | £100 |

# 15 ◆ £1,000,000

## 1

**Which of these was a member of the Four Tops?**

- A: Tommy DeVito
- B: Levi Stubbs
- C: Al Alberts
- D: Bruce Belland

## 2

**The pilot show for which cult sci-fi TV series was entitled 'The Cage'?**

- A: Doctor Who
- B: Quatermass
- C: Star Trek
- D: The Time Tunnel

## 3

**Which of the following was a previous profession of the comedian Harry Hill?**

- A: Barrister
- B: Architect
- C: Surveyor
- D: Doctor

## 4

**From which country does the pattern of notes known as a raga originate?**

- A: China
- B: India
- C: Japan
- D: Brazil

## 5

**Which director established the film company 'American Zoetrope'?**

- A: Francis Ford Coppola
- B: Martin Scorsese
- C: Robert Altman
- D: Hal Ashby

**50:50** Go to page 252     Go to page 264     **?** Answers on page 270

# 15 ◆ £1,000,000

**6**

From which country did the 19th century
dance called the galop originate?

A: France
B: Ireland
C: Germany
D: Russia

**7**

Which sitcom, starring Bruce Forsyth, was a follow-on
from 'Tripper's Day' starring Leonard Rossiter?

A: Washer's Day
B: Slinger's Day
C: Leaver's Day
D: Coffer's Day

**8**

After Rolf Harris in 1969, who was the next
Australian act to have a UK No 1 single?

A: Men At Work
B: INXS
C: Jason Donovan
D: Kylie Minogue

**9**

Which performer received an ovation lasting one hour and
twenty minutes in 1991 after a performance in Vienna?

A: Kiri Te Kanawa
B: Placido Domingo
C: Luciano Pavarotti
D: Montserrat Caballé

**10**

In Shakespeare's 'Measure for Measure', who disguises himself
as a friar in order to move unnoticed amongst his people?

A: Vincentio
B: Claudio
C: Angelo
D: Elbow

**50:50** Go to page 252    Go to page 264    **?** Answers on page 270

# 15 ◆ £1,000,000

## 11

**Which of these is the name of the business correspondent on the spoof news show 'The Day Today'?**

A: Remedy Malahide

B: Collaterlie Sisters

C: Peter O'Hanraha'hanrahan

D: Sylvester Stuart

## 12

**Before finding fame as Alan Partridge, Steve Coogan appeared as various characters in one of the rounds of which TV quiz zhow?**

A: Don't Forget Your Toothbrush

B: 3-2-1

C: The Adventure Game

D: The Krypton Factor

## 13

**Which cast member from 'Happy Days' later turned up in his own sitcom playing Charles?**

A: Pat Morita

B: Donny Most

C: Scott Baio

D: Anson Williams

## 14

**Who played the part of the Turkish Bey in the 1962 film 'Lawrence of Arabia'?**

A: Alec Guinness

B: Anthony Quayle

C: Omar Sharif

D: José Ferrer

## 15

**Which indie band provided the music for the dancer Michael Clark's 1988 production, 'I Am Curious Orange'?**

A: The Soup Dragons

B: The Smiths

C: The Wedding Present

D: The Fall

**50:50** Go to page 252 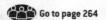 Go to page 264  Answers on page 270

# 15 ◆ £1,000,000

## 16

Harry Rule, Paul Buchet and Contessa di Contini were the three main characters in which TV action series?

- **A:** Target
- **B:** The Protectors
- **C:** Hunter's Walk
- **D:** Zodiac

## 17

Which of these operas by Puccini was left unfinished at his death?

- **A:** Madame Butterfly
- **B:** Tosca
- **C:** Turandot
- **D:** La Bohème

## 18

Which star wrote screenplays for his own films under the names Otis J Criblecoblis and Mahatma Kane Jeeves?

page
237

- **A:** W C Fields
- **B:** Groucho Marx
- **C:** Harold Lloyd
- **D:** Charlie Chaplin

## 19

What does Dougal name his pet rabbit in the episode of 'Father Ted' entitled 'The Plague'?

- **A:** Sampras
- **B:** Keegan
- **C:** Spitz
- **D:** Piggott

## 20

Which Sandy Wilson musical is set in Madame Dubonnet's Finishing School on the French Riviera in the 1920s?

- **A:** The Boy Friend
- **B:** Martin Guerre
- **C:** The Golden Apple
- **D:** Music in the Air

**50:50** Go to page 252　　Go to page 264　　**?** Answers on page 270

# 15 ◆ £1,000,000

## 21

What was the original name of Cliff Richard's backing band 'The Shadows'?

- A: The Miracles
- B: The Drifters
- C: The Crickets
- D: The Phantoms

## 22

Which of these is not a character in 'Reservoir Dogs'?

- A: Mr Orange
- B: Mr Red
- C: Mr White
- D: Mr Blue

## 23

Britt Reid is the alter ego of which superhero?

- A: Captain America
- B: Green Hornet
- C: The Thing
- D: Cyclops

## 24

Which of these is a 1953 ballet, with choreography by Jerome Robbins and music by Debussy?

- A: Primitive Mysteries
- B: Afternoon of a Faun
- C: Appalachian Spring
- D: Clytemnestra

## 25

Which was Benjamin Britten's last opera?

- A: Death in Venice
- B: Billy Budd
- C: The Turn of the Screw
- D: A Midsummer Night's Dream

 50:50 Go to page 252     Go to page 264     ? Answers on page 270

# 15 ◆ £1,000,000

## 26

What was the name of the camp commander
in the classic US sitcom 'Hogan's Heroes'?

A: Colonel Klink
B: Lieutenant Putsch
C: Marshall Schtirr
D: Commandant Ersatz

## 27

Who is Aida's lover in Verdi's opera of the same name?

A: Radames
B: Ramfis
C: Amneris
D: Amonasro

## 28

Which 'Carry On' actor had a Top 10
UK hit with 'Mad Passionate Love' in 1958?

A: Bernard Bresslaw
B: Kenneth Williams
C: Kenneth Connor
D: Sid James

## 29

What is the name of the Russian decoding device
central to the plot of 'From Russia With Love'?

A: Markon
B: Lektor
C: Textron
D: Skipole

## 30

Which Hollywood legend appeared in both the 1961
and the 1991 versions of the film 'Cape Fear'?

A: Burt Lancaster
B: Telly Savalas
C: Robert Mitchum
D: Rod Steiger

 50:50 Go to page 252      Go to page 264      ? Answers on page 270

# 15 ◆ £1,000,000

## 31

What is the actress Faye Dunaway's real first name?

A: Daisy

B: Daphne

C: Dawn

D: Dorothy

## 32

Which of these is not one of
Bob Geldof's real first names?

A: Frederick

B: Haughton

C: Robert

D: Zenon

# 50:50

## £100

| | | | |
|---|---|---|---|
| 1 | Options remaining are B and C | 38 | Options remaining are A and B |
| 2 | Options remaining are B and C | 39 | Options remaining are B and D |
| 3 | Options remaining are A and B | 40 | Options remaining are A and D |
| 4 | Options remaining are B and D | 41 | Options remaining are B and D |
| 5 | Options remaining are B and C | 42 | Options remaining are A and D |
| 6 | Options remaining are A and C | 43 | Options remaining are A and C |
| 7 | Options remaining are B and D | 44 | Options remaining are A and D |
| 8 | Options remaining are B and D | 45 | Options remaining are B and C |
| 9 | Options remaining are A and B | 46 | Options remaining are B and D |
| 10 | Options remaining are A and D | 47 | Options remaining are A and D |
| 11 | Options remaining are C and D | 48 | Options remaining are A and C |
| 12 | Options remaining are B and D | 49 | Options remaining are C and D |
| 13 | Options remaining are A and B | 50 | Options remaining are A and D |
| 14 | Options remaining are A and D | 51 | Options remaining are C and D |
| 15 | Options remaining are A and D | 52 | Options remaining are A and B |
| 16 | Options remaining are B and D | 53 | Options remaining are A and D |
| 17 | Options remaining are B and D | 54 | Options remaining are B and D |
| 18 | Options remaining are B and D | 55 | Options remaining are C and D |
| 19 | Options remaining are B and D | 56 | Options remaining are A and C |
| 20 | Options remaining are B and D | 57 | Options remaining are A and C |
| 21 | Options remaining are B and D | 58 | Options remaining are B and D |
| 22 | Options remaining are B and D | 59 | Options remaining are B and C |
| 23 | Options remaining are A and C | 60 | Options remaining are A and C |
| 24 | Options remaining are A and B | 61 | Options remaining are A and C |
| 25 | Options remaining are A and C | 62 | Options remaining are B and C |
| 26 | Options remaining are A and B | 63 | Options remaining are C and D |
| 27 | Options remaining are A and D | 64 | Options remaining are A and D |
| 28 | Options remaining are C and D | 65 | Options remaining are B and D |
| 29 | Options remaining are A and B | 66 | Options remaining are C and D |
| 30 | Options remaining are A and B | 67 | Options remaining are A and C |
| 31 | Options remaining are A and B | 68 | Options remaining are A and D |
| 32 | Options remaining are C and D | 69 | Options remaining are A and B |
| 33 | Options remaining are B and D | 70 | Options remaining are A and D |
| 34 | Options remaining are A and D | 71 | Options remaining are A and D |
| 35 | Options remaining are A and D | 72 | Options remaining are B and D |
| 36 | Options remaining are C and D | 73 | Options remaining are B and D |
| 37 | Options remaining are A and D | 74 | Options remaining are B and C |

# 50:50

75  Options remaining are A and C
76  Options remaining are B and D
77  Options remaining are C and D
78  Options remaining are A and C
79  Options remaining are A and B
80  Options remaining are A and C
81  Options remaining are B and D

82  Options remaining are C and D
83  Options remaining are A and C
84  Options remaining are A and C
85  Options remaining are B and D
86  Options remaining are B and C
87  Options remaining are A and D
88  Options remaining are A and C

## £200

1   Options remaining are B and C
2   Options remaining are A and D
3   Options remaining are B and D
4   Options remaining are A and D
5   Options remaining are A and D
6   Options remaining are A and B
7   Options remaining are C and D
8   Options remaining are A and B
9   Options remaining are C and D
10  Options remaining are A and D
11  Options remaining are A and C
12  Options remaining are B and D
13  Options remaining are A and B
14  Options remaining are B and D
15  Options remaining are B and D
16  Options remaining are A and C
17  Options remaining are A and C
18  Options remaining are C and D
19  Options remaining are A and B
20  Options remaining are A and B
21  Options remaining are B and D
22  Options remaining are A and C
23  Options remaining are C and D
24  Options remaining are C and D
25  Options remaining are A and C
26  Options remaining are B and C
27  Options remaining are A and D
28  Options remaining are C and D
29  Options remaining are B and C
30  Options remaining are B and C
31  Options remaining are C and D
32  Options remaining are A and C

33  Options remaining are A and D
34  Options remaining are B and D
35  Options remaining are A and D
36  Options remaining are C and D
37  Options remaining are B and C
38  Options remaining are A and D
39  Options remaining are B and D
40  Options remaining are A and C
41  Options remaining are A and D
42  Options remaining are A and B
43  Options remaining are A and C
44  Options remaining are A and C
45  Options remaining are C and D
46  Options remaining are A and B
47  Options remaining are A and C
48  Options remaining are C and D
49  Options remaining are B and D
50  Options remaining are B and C
51  Options remaining are B and D
52  Options remaining are A and D
53  Options remaining are B and D
54  Options remaining are A and B
55  Options remaining are A and D
56  Options remaining are A and D
57  Options remaining are A and C
58  Options remaining are A and B
59  Options remaining are B and D
60  Options remaining are A and B
61  Options remaining are B and C
62  Options remaining are B and C
63  Options remaining are A and C
64  Options remaining are A and C

# 50:50

| | | | |
|---|---|---|---|
| 65 | Options remaining are A and B | 75 | Options remaining are A and D |
| 66 | Options remaining are A and D | 76 | Options remaining are A and C |
| 67 | Options remaining are C and D | 77 | Options remaining are A and D |
| 68 | Options remaining are A and C | 78 | Options remaining are A and C |
| 69 | Options remaining are A and B | 79 | Options remaining are A and C |
| 70 | Options remaining are A and C | 80 | Options remaining are A and B |
| 71 | Options remaining are B and D | 81 | Options remaining are C and D |
| 72 | Options remaining are A and B | 82 | Options remaining are C and D |
| 73 | Options remaining are A and B | 83 | Options remaining are A and C |
| 74 | Options remaining are A and C | 84 | Options remaining are A and C |

## £300

| | | | |
|---|---|---|---|
| 1 | Options remaining are B and D | 30 | Options remaining are A and C |
| 2 | Options remaining are B and D | 31 | Options remaining are A and D |
| 3 | Options remaining are A and D | 32 | Options remaining are A and C |
| 4 | Options remaining are B and D | 33 | Options remaining are B and C |
| 5 | Options remaining are B and D | 34 | Options remaining are C and D |
| 6 | Options remaining are B and D | 35 | Options remaining are A and C |
| 7 | Options remaining are A and D | 36 | Options remaining are A and C |
| 8 | Options remaining are A and B | 37 | Options remaining are B and D |
| 9 | Options remaining are B and D | 38 | Options remaining are A and C |
| 10 | Options remaining are B and D | 39 | Options remaining are B and C |
| 11 | Options remaining are A and B | 40 | Options remaining are B and C |
| 12 | Options remaining are A and D | 41 | Options remaining are A and B |
| 13 | Options remaining are B and D | 42 | Options remaining are B and D |
| 14 | Options remaining are A and C | 43 | Options remaining are A and B |
| 15 | Options remaining are A and C | 44 | Options remaining are B and D |
| 16 | Options remaining are C and D | 45 | Options remaining are B and D |
| 17 | Options remaining are A and D | 46 | Options remaining are A and D |
| 18 | Options remaining are B and C | 47 | Options remaining are A and C |
| 19 | Options remaining are B and D | 48 | Options remaining are A and C |
| 20 | Options remaining are C and D | 49 | Options remaining are A and D |
| 21 | Options remaining are A and C | 50 | Options remaining are A and B |
| 22 | Options remaining are A and D | 51 | Options remaining are A and C |
| 23 | Options remaining are A and B | 52 | Options remaining are B and C |
| 24 | Options remaining are C and D | 53 | Options remaining are A and B |
| 25 | Options remaining are A and B | 54 | Options remaining are A and B |
| 26 | Options remaining are A and C | 55 | Options remaining are C and D |
| 27 | Options remaining are C and D | 56 | Options remaining are C and D |
| 28 | Options remaining are B and D | 57 | Options remaining are A and B |
| 29 | Options remaining are A and C | 58 | Options remaining are B and C |

# 50:50

| | | | |
|---|---|---|---|
| 59 | Options remaining are A and C | 70 | Options remaining are A and D |
| 60 | Options remaining are A and D | 71 | Options remaining are C and D |
| 61 | Options remaining are C and D | 72 | Options remaining are A and B |
| 62 | Options remaining are A and D | 73 | Options remaining are A and B |
| 63 | Options remaining are A and B | 74 | Options remaining are B and D |
| 64 | Options remaining are B and D | 75 | Options remaining are A and D |
| 65 | Options remaining are A and D | 76 | Options remaining are A and B |
| 66 | Options remaining are B and D | 77 | Options remaining are A and C |
| 67 | Options remaining are A and C | 78 | Options remaining are B and D |
| 68 | Options remaining are A and C | 79 | Options remaining are A and D |
| 69 | Options remaining are B and D | 80 | Options remaining are C and D |

## £500

| | | | |
|---|---|---|---|
| 1 | Options remaining are C and D | 29 | Options remaining are A and C |
| 2 | Options remaining are A and D | 30 | Options remaining are A and D |
| 3 | Options remaining are A and C | 31 | Options remaining are A and D |
| 4 | Options remaining are A and C | 32 | Options remaining are B and D |
| 5 | Options remaining are B and C | 33 | Options remaining are B and D |
| 6 | Options remaining are B and D | 34 | Options remaining are B and C |
| 7 | Options remaining are A and B | 35 | Options remaining are A and B |
| 8 | Options remaining are A and C | 36 | Options remaining are B and D |
| 9 | Options remaining are A and D | 37 | Options remaining are C and D |
| 10 | Options remaining are A and D | 38 | Options remaining are A and B |
| 11 | Options remaining are A and C | 39 | Options remaining are A and B |
| 12 | Options remaining are A and B | 40 | Options remaining are A and B |
| 13 | Options remaining are A and C | 41 | Options remaining are A and C |
| 14 | Options remaining are A and C | 42 | Options remaining are B and C |
| 15 | Options remaining are B and D | 43 | Options remaining are A and C |
| 16 | Options remaining are A and B | 44 | Options remaining are A and D |
| 17 | Options remaining are A and D | 45 | Options remaining are A and C |
| 18 | Options remaining are C and D | 46 | Options remaining are B and D |
| 19 | Options remaining are B and D | 47 | Options remaining are A and C |
| 20 | Options remaining are B and C | 48 | Options remaining are A and B |
| 21 | Options remaining are A and C | 49 | Options remaining are A and C |
| 22 | Options remaining are B and C | 50 | Options remaining are B and C |
| 23 | Options remaining are A and C | 51 | Options remaining are B and D |
| 24 | Options remaining are B and C | 52 | Options remaining are A and B |
| 25 | Options remaining are B and C | 53 | Options remaining are A and C |
| 26 | Options remaining are A and D | 54 | Options remaining are A and B |
| 27 | Options remaining are A and C | 55 | Options remaining are B and D |
| 28 | Options remaining are A and C | 56 | Options remaining are B and C |

# 50:50

| | | | |
|---|---|---|---|
| 57 | Options remaining are A and D | 67 | Options remaining are A and C |
| 58 | Options remaining are C and D | 68 | Options remaining are B and D |
| 59 | Options remaining are A and D | 69 | Options remaining are A and B |
| 60 | Options remaining are A and B | 70 | Options remaining are A and B |
| 61 | Options remaining are A and B | 71 | Options remaining are B and D |
| 62 | Options remaining are A and B | 72 | Options remaining are C and D |
| 63 | Options remaining are A and B | 73 | Options remaining are B and C |
| 64 | Options remaining are A and D | 74 | Options remaining are B and D |
| 65 | Options remaining are A and D | 75 | Options remaining are A and B |
| 66 | Options remaining are A and B | 76 | Options remaining are A and D |

## £1,000

| | | | |
|---|---|---|---|
| 1 | Options remaining are A and D | 30 | Options remaining are B and D |
| 2 | Options remaining are A and D | 31 | Options remaining are A and D |
| 3 | Options remaining are B and C | 32 | Options remaining are A and C |
| 4 | Options remaining are A and C | 33 | Options remaining are B and C |
| 5 | Options remaining are A and B | 34 | Options remaining are A and B |
| 6 | Options remaining are C and D | 35 | Options remaining are B and D |
| 7 | Options remaining are A and C | 36 | Options remaining are B and C |
| 8 | Options remaining are B and C | 37 | Options remaining are A and D |
| 9 | Options remaining are C and D | 38 | Options remaining are A and B |
| 10 | Options remaining are A and D | 39 | Options remaining are B and C |
| 11 | Options remaining are A and B | 40 | Options remaining are A and D |
| 12 | Options remaining are A and D | 41 | Options remaining are B and C |
| 13 | Options remaining are B and C | 42 | Options remaining are B and D |
| 14 | Options remaining are C and D | 43 | Options remaining are A and C |
| 15 | Options remaining are A and D | 44 | Options remaining are A and B |
| 16 | Options remaining are B and C | 45 | Options remaining are A and C |
| 17 | Options remaining are B and D | 46 | Options remaining are A and B |
| 18 | Options remaining are A and D | 47 | Options remaining are A and D |
| 19 | Options remaining are C and D | 48 | Options remaining are A and B |
| 20 | Options remaining are B and D | 49 | Options remaining are A and B |
| 21 | Options remaining are A and D | 50 | Options remaining are A and D |
| 22 | Options remaining are A and C | 51 | Options remaining are A and B |
| 23 | Options remaining are B and C | 52 | Options remaining are A and D |
| 24 | Options remaining are B and D | 53 | Options remaining are A and C |
| 25 | Options remaining are B and C | 54 | Options remaining are C and D |
| 26 | Options remaining are A and B | 55 | Options remaining are C and D |
| 27 | Options remaining are A and B | 56 | Options remaining are A and C |
| 28 | Options remaining are A and C | 57 | Options remaining are A and C |
| 29 | Options remaining are C and D | 58 | Options remaining are B and D |

# 50:50

| | | | |
|---|---|---|---|
| 59 | Options remaining are C and D | 66 | Options remaining are A and C |
| 60 | Options remaining are B and C | 67 | Options remaining are B and D |
| 61 | Options remaining are A and D | 68 | Options remaining are B and C |
| 62 | Options remaining are B and D | 69 | Options remaining are A and C |
| 63 | Options remaining are B and C | 70 | Options remaining are A and C |
| 64 | Options remaining are B and D | 71 | Options remaining are A and B |
| 65 | Options remaining are A and C | 72 | Options remaining are A and C |

## £2,000

| | | | |
|---|---|---|---|
| 1 | Options remaining are B and D | 32 | Options remaining are C and D |
| 2 | Options remaining are A and B | 33 | Options remaining are A and C |
| 3 | Options remaining are A and C | 34 | Options remaining are A and D |
| 4 | Options remaining are B and C | 35 | Options remaining are B and D |
| 5 | Options remaining are B and C | 36 | Options remaining are A and D |
| 6 | Options remaining are A and C | 37 | Options remaining are A and B |
| 7 | Options remaining are B and D | 38 | Options remaining are B and D |
| 8 | Options remaining are A and B | 39 | Options remaining are B and D |
| 9 | Options remaining are A and B | 40 | Options remaining are B and C |
| 10 | Options remaining are B and D | 41 | Options remaining are A and C |
| 11 | Options remaining are A and B | 42 | Options remaining are A and D |
| 12 | Options remaining are B and D | 43 | Options remaining are B and C |
| 13 | Options remaining are A and B | 44 | Options remaining are A and B |
| 14 | Options remaining are B and C | 45 | Options remaining are B and C |
| 15 | Options remaining are B and D | 46 | Options remaining are B and C |
| 16 | Options remaining are A and C | 47 | Options remaining are A and B |
| 17 | Options remaining are A and B | 48 | Options remaining are B and C |
| 18 | Options remaining are A and C | 49 | Options remaining are B and D |
| 19 | Options remaining are A and B | 50 | Options remaining are B and D |
| 20 | Options remaining are C and D | 51 | Options remaining are A and D |
| 21 | Options remaining are A and C | 52 | Options remaining are A and D |
| 22 | Options remaining are B and C | 53 | Options remaining are A and D |
| 23 | Options remaining are C and D | 54 | Options remaining are B and D |
| 24 | Options remaining are C and D | 55 | Options remaining are A and D |
| 25 | Options remaining are A and C | 56 | Options remaining are A and B |
| 26 | Options remaining are B and C | 57 | Options remaining are A and D |
| 27 | Options remaining are A and D | 58 | Options remaining are B and D |
| 28 | Options remaining are A and D | 59 | Options remaining are B and D |
| 29 | Options remaining are C and D | 60 | Options remaining are A and C |
| 30 | Options remaining are A and D | 61 | Options remaining are B and C |
| 31 | Options remaining are A and C | 62 | Options remaining are C and D |

# 50:50

| | |
|---|---|
| 63 Options remaining are B and D | 66 Options remaining are B and D |
| 64 Options remaining are B and D | 67 Options remaining are C and D |
| 65 Options remaining are B and C | 68 Options remaining are A and B |

## £4,000

| | |
|---|---|
| 1 Options remaining are B and C | 33 Options remaining are A and D |
| 2 Options remaining are C and D | 34 Options remaining are B and D |
| 3 Options remaining are A and B | 35 Options remaining are C and D |
| 4 Options remaining are A and B | 36 Options remaining are A and B |
| 5 Options remaining are C and D | 37 Options remaining are A and B |
| 6 Options remaining are A and C | 38 Options remaining are A and C |
| 7 Options remaining are C and D | 39 Options remaining are A and B |
| 8 Options remaining are A and B | 40 Options remaining are A and D |
| 9 Options remaining are A and C | 41 Options remaining are C and D |
| 10 Options remaining are A and D | 42 Options remaining are A and C |
| 11 Options remaining are C and D | 43 Options remaining are B and C |
| 12 Options remaining are A and C | 44 Options remaining are B and D |
| 13 Options remaining are A and D | 45 Options remaining are A and D |
| 14 Options remaining are A and B | 46 Options remaining are B and C |
| 15 Options remaining are A and C | 47 Options remaining are A and D |
| 16 Options remaining are A and B | 48 Options remaining are B and D |
| 17 Options remaining are A and B | 49 Options remaining are B and C |
| 18 Options remaining are A and D | 50 Options remaining are C and D |
| 19 Options remaining are A and B | 51 Options remaining are A and D |
| 20 Options remaining are A and D | 52 Options remaining are A and C |
| 21 Options remaining are B and D | 53 Options remaining are B and C |
| 22 Options remaining are B and C | 54 Options remaining are A and D |
| 23 Options remaining are B and D | 55 Options remaining are A and D |
| 24 Options remaining are B and C | 56 Options remaining are A and B |
| 25 Options remaining are A and B | 57 Options remaining are B and C |
| 26 Options remaining are A and B | 58 Options remaining are B and D |
| 27 Options remaining are A and C | 59 Options remaining are A and B |
| 28 Options remaining are B and C | 60 Options remaining are B and C |
| 29 Options remaining are A and D | 61 Options remaining are A and B |
| 30 Options remaining are C and D | 62 Options remaining are A and B |
| 31 Options remaining are B and C | 63 Options remaining are B and C |
| 32 Options remaining are A and D | 64 Options remaining are A and D |

# 50:50

## £8,000

| | | | |
|---|---|---|---|
| 1 | Options remaining are A and C | 31 | Options remaining are A and D |
| 2 | Options remaining are B and D | 32 | Options remaining are B and D |
| 3 | Options remaining are B and C | 33 | Options remaining are A and C |
| 4 | Options remaining are B and D | 34 | Options remaining are A and C |
| 5 | Options remaining are A and C | 35 | Options remaining are B and C |
| 6 | Options remaining are C and D | 36 | Options remaining are A and C |
| 7 | Options remaining are A and C | 37 | Options remaining are C and D |
| 8 | Options remaining are A and C | 38 | Options remaining are A and C |
| 9 | Options remaining are B and C | 39 | Options remaining are B and C |
| 10 | Options remaining are A and C | 40 | Options remaining are A and C |
| 11 | Options remaining are A and D | 41 | Options remaining are B and D |
| 12 | Options remaining are A and B | 42 | Options remaining are A and C |
| 13 | Options remaining are A and B | 43 | Options remaining are A and D |
| 14 | Options remaining are A and D | 44 | Options remaining are A and B |
| 15 | Options remaining are B and D | 45 | Options remaining are B and D |
| 16 | Options remaining are B and D | 46 | Options remaining are A and C |
| 17 | Options remaining are A and C | 47 | Options remaining are A and D |
| 18 | Options remaining are C and D | 48 | Options remaining are A and B |
| 19 | Options remaining are B and D | 49 | Options remaining are C and D |
| 20 | Options remaining are A and B | 50 | Options remaining are A and D |
| 21 | Options remaining are B and D | 51 | Options remaining are B and D |
| 22 | Options remaining are B and D | 52 | Options remaining are A and B |
| 23 | Options remaining are B and C | 53 | Options remaining are A and C |
| 24 | Options remaining are A and D | 54 | Options remaining are A and B |
| 25 | Options remaining are A and D | 55 | Options remaining are A and D |
| 26 | Options remaining are A and D | 56 | Options remaining are C and D |
| 27 | Options remaining are A and B | 57 | Options remaining are A and D |
| 28 | Options remaining are A and D | 58 | Options remaining are B and C |
| 29 | Options remaining are B and D | 59 | Options remaining are C and D |
| 30 | Options remaining are C and D | 60 | Options remaining are A and C |

## £16,000

| | | | |
|---|---|---|---|
| 1 | Options remaining are B and C | 10 | Options remaining are B and C |
| 2 | Options remaining are B and D | 11 | Options remaining are A and C |
| 3 | Options remaining are A and C | 12 | Options remaining are A and C |
| 4 | Options remaining are B and C | 13 | Options remaining are B and C |
| 5 | Options remaining are B and C | 14 | Options remaining are B and D |
| 6 | Options remaining are B and D | 15 | Options remaining are A and B |
| 7 | Options remaining are A and C | 16 | Options remaining are A and D |
| 8 | Options remaining are C and D | 17 | Options remaining are B and C |
| 9 | Options remaining are A and B | 18 | Options remaining are A and C |

# 50:50

| | | | |
|---|---|---|---|
| 19 | Options remaining are B and C | 38 | Options remaining are C and D |
| 20 | Options remaining are A and C | 39 | Options remaining are B and C |
| 21 | Options remaining are B and D | 40 | Options remaining are B and C |
| 22 | Options remaining are B and D | 41 | Options remaining are A and B |
| 23 | Options remaining are A and B | 42 | Options remaining are B and C |
| 24 | Options remaining are A and C | 43 | Options remaining are A and C |
| 25 | Options remaining are A and D | 44 | Options remaining are C and D |
| 26 | Options remaining are A and C | 45 | Options remaining are C and D |
| 27 | Options remaining are A and C | 46 | Options remaining are A and D |
| 28 | Options remaining are A and B | 47 | Options remaining are B and C |
| 29 | Options remaining are A and D | 48 | Options remaining are A and D |
| 30 | Options remaining are B and C | 49 | Options remaining are C and D |
| 31 | Options remaining are A and B | 50 | Options remaining are C and D |
| 32 | Options remaining are A and D | 51 | Options remaining are A and D |
| 33 | Options remaining are B and D | 52 | Options remaining are A and C |
| 34 | Options remaining are A and C | 53 | Options remaining are B and C |
| 35 | Options remaining are C and D | 54 | Options remaining are B and C |
| 36 | Options remaining are B and D | 55 | Options remaining are C and D |
| 37 | Options remaining are C and D | 56 | Options remaining are A and D |

## £32,000

| | | | |
|---|---|---|---|
| 1 | Options remaining are B and C | 21 | Options remaining are A and C |
| 2 | Options remaining are B and C | 22 | Options remaining are B and D |
| 3 | Options remaining are B and D | 23 | Options remaining are A and C |
| 4 | Options remaining are B and C | 24 | Options remaining are B and D |
| 5 | Options remaining are C and D | 25 | Options remaining are A and C |
| 6 | Options remaining are C and D | 26 | Options remaining are A and D |
| 7 | Options remaining are C and D | 27 | Options remaining are A and D |
| 8 | Options remaining are A and D | 28 | Options remaining are B and D |
| 9 | Options remaining are A and B | 29 | Options remaining are A and C |
| 10 | Options remaining are C and D | 30 | Options remaining are A and B |
| 11 | Options remaining are B and C | 31 | Options remaining are A and B |
| 12 | Options remaining are A and D | 32 | Options remaining are A and B |
| 13 | Options remaining are A and B | 33 | Options remaining are A and D |
| 14 | Options remaining are B and C | 34 | Options remaining are A and C |
| 15 | Options remaining are B and C | 35 | Options remaining are A and C |
| 16 | Options remaining are B and D | 36 | Options remaining are C and D |
| 17 | Options remaining are C and D | 37 | Options remaining are B and C |
| 18 | Options remaining are B and D | 38 | Options remaining are B and D |
| 19 | Options remaining are B and D | 39 | Options remaining are A and D |
| 20 | Options remaining are B and C | 40 | Options remaining are B and C |

# 50:50

| | | | |
|---|---|---|---|
| 41 | Options remaining are C and D | 47 | Options remaining are A and B |
| 42 | Options remaining are A and B | 48 | Options remaining are B and D |
| 43 | Options remaining are A and D | 49 | Options remaining are B and D |
| 44 | Options remaining are A and B | 50 | Options remaining are B and C |
| 45 | Options remaining are A and C | 51 | Options remaining are B and D |
| 46 | Options remaining are A and B | 52 | Options remaining are A and B |

## £64,000

| | | | |
|---|---|---|---|
| 1 | Options remaining are A and B | 25 | Options remaining are C and D |
| 2 | Options remaining are A and C | 26 | Options remaining are A and C |
| 3 | Options remaining are A and C | 27 | Options remaining are B and D |
| 4 | Options remaining are A and C | 28 | Options remaining are B and C |
| 5 | Options remaining are A and D | 29 | Options remaining are A and C |
| 6 | Options remaining are A and B | 30 | Options remaining are A and C |
| 7 | Options remaining are C and D | 31 | Options remaining are A and C |
| 8 | Options remaining are A and C | 32 | Options remaining are A and B |
| 9 | Options remaining are C and D | 33 | Options remaining are A and C |
| 10 | Options remaining are B and D | 34 | Options remaining are B and C |
| 11 | Options remaining are B and D | 35 | Options remaining are A and D |
| 12 | Options remaining are A and B | 36 | Options remaining are A and C |
| 13 | Options remaining are C and D | 37 | Options remaining are A and B |
| 14 | Options remaining are A and C | 38 | Options remaining are A and C |
| 15 | Options remaining are A and B | 39 | Options remaining are A and D |
| 16 | Options remaining are B and D | 40 | Options remaining are A and D |
| 17 | Options remaining are B and D | 41 | Options remaining are A and D |
| 18 | Options remaining are B and D | 42 | Options remaining are B and D |
| 19 | Options remaining are B and D | 43 | Options remaining are B and C |
| 20 | Options remaining are A and D | 44 | Options remaining are B and C |
| 21 | Options remaining are A and C | 45 | Options remaining are B and D |
| 22 | Options remaining are A and C | 46 | Options remaining are C and D |
| 23 | Options remaining are A and C | 47 | Options remaining are A and C |
| 24 | Options remaining are A and B | 48 | Options remaining are A and D |

## £125,000

| | | | |
|---|---|---|---|
| 1 | Options remaining are C and D | 6 | Options remaining are C and D |
| 2 | Options remaining are A and B | 7 | Options remaining are B and C |
| 3 | Options remaining are A and C | 8 | Options remaining are B and C |
| 4 | Options remaining are B and C | 9 | Options remaining are B and C |
| 5 | Options remaining are A and D | 10 | Options remaining are B and D |

# 50:50

| | | | |
|---|---|---|---|
| 11 | Options remaining are A and C | 28 | Options remaining are A and D |
| 12 | Options remaining are A and D | 29 | Options remaining are B and C |
| 13 | Options remaining are B and D | 30 | Options remaining are C and D |
| 14 | Options remaining are B and D | 31 | Options remaining are B and D |
| 15 | Options remaining are A and C | 32 | Options remaining are A and D |
| 16 | Options remaining are A and D | 33 | Options remaining are B and C |
| 17 | Options remaining are A and D | 34 | Options remaining are B and D |
| 18 | Options remaining are C and D | 35 | Options remaining are C and D |
| 19 | Options remaining are B and D | 36 | Options remaining are B and D |
| 20 | Options remaining are A and C | 37 | Options remaining are B and D |
| 21 | Options remaining are A and B | 38 | Options remaining are B and C |
| 22 | Options remaining are B and C | 39 | Options remaining are A and B |
| 23 | Options remaining are A and B | 40 | Options remaining are B and C |
| 24 | Options remaining are A and C | 41 | Options remaining are B and D |
| 25 | Options remaining are B and D | 42 | Options remaining are A and C |
| 26 | Options remaining are A and D | 43 | Options remaining are B and C |
| 27 | Options remaining are B and D | 44 | Options remaining are B and C |

## £250,000

| | | | |
|---|---|---|---|
| 1 | Options remaining are A and C | 21 | Options remaining are C and D |
| 2 | Options remaining are B and D | 22 | Options remaining are A and C |
| 3 | Options remaining are A and C | 23 | Options remaining are A and C |
| 4 | Options remaining are B and D | 24 | Options remaining are C and D |
| 5 | Options remaining are B and D | 25 | Options remaining are C and D |
| 6 | Options remaining are B and D | 26 | Options remaining are B and C |
| 7 | Options remaining are A and C | 27 | Options remaining are A and B |
| 8 | Options remaining are C and D | 28 | Options remaining are B and D |
| 9 | Options remaining are B and D | 29 | Options remaining are C and D |
| 10 | Options remaining are C and D | 30 | Options remaining are B and D |
| 11 | Options remaining are B and C | 31 | Options remaining are C and D |
| 12 | Options remaining are C and D | 32 | Options remaining are B and D |
| 13 | Options remaining are A and D | 33 | Options remaining are A and C |
| 14 | Options remaining are A and C | 34 | Options remaining are A and D |
| 15 | Options remaining are A and D | 35 | Options remaining are A and C |
| 16 | Options remaining are B and D | 36 | Options remaining are A and C |
| 17 | Options remaining are A and D | 37 | Options remaining are B and C |
| 18 | Options remaining are B and D | 38 | Options remaining are A and C |
| 19 | Options remaining are A and C | 39 | Options remaining are A and C |
| 20 | Options remaining are B and C | 40 | Options remaining are A and C |

# 50:50

## £500,000

| | |
|---|---|
| 1 Options remaining are A and D | 19 Options remaining are A and D |
| 2 Options remaining are B and C | 20 Options remaining are C and D |
| 3 Options remaining are A and D | 21 Options remaining are A and B |
| 4 Options remaining are A and C | 22 Options remaining are A and C |
| 5 Options remaining are C and D | 23 Options remaining are A and D |
| 6 Options remaining are B and D | 24 Options remaining are A and B |
| 7 Options remaining are B and D | 25 Options remaining are B and C |
| 8 Options remaining are B and C | 26 Options remaining are A and B |
| 9 Options remaining are B and C | 27 Options remaining are B and C |
| 10 Options remaining are B and D | 28 Options remaining are C and D |
| 11 Options remaining are C and D | 29 Options remaining are C and D |
| 12 Options remaining are C and D | 30 Options remaining are A and B |
| 13 Options remaining are A and D | 31 Options remaining are A and C |
| 14 Options remaining are A and B | 32 Options remaining are A and B |
| 15 Options remaining are A and D | 33 Options remaining are A and C |
| 16 Options remaining are B and D | 34 Options remaining are C and D |
| 17 Options remaining are A and B | 35 Options remaining are A and D |
| 18 Options remaining are C and D | 36 Options remaining are A and C |

## £1,000,000

| | |
|---|---|
| 1 Options remaining are A and B | 17 Options remaining are B and C |
| 2 Options remaining are A and C | 18 Options remaining are A and B |
| 3 Options remaining are A and D | 19 Options remaining are A and D |
| 4 Options remaining are A and B | 20 Options remaining are A and C |
| 5 Options remaining are A and D | 21 Options remaining are B and D |
| 6 Options remaining are A and C | 22 Options remaining are B and D |
| 7 Options remaining are B and D | 23 Options remaining are B and D |
| 8 Options remaining are A and D | 24 Options remaining are B and D |
| 9 Options remaining are B and C | 25 Options remaining are A and D |
| 10 Options remaining are A and D | 26 Options remaining are A and D |
| 11 Options remaining are A and B | 27 Options remaining are A and B |
| 12 Options remaining are A and D | 28 Options remaining are A and C |
| 13 Options remaining are A and C | 29 Options remaining are B and C |
| 14 Options remaining are C and D | 30 Options remaining are B and C |
| 15 Options remaining are B and D | 31 Options remaining are B and D |
| 16 Options remaining are B and C | 32 Options remaining are A and B |

# Ask The Audience

## £100

| | | | | | | | | | |
|---|---|---|---|---|---|---|---|---|---|
| 1 | A:0% | B:100% | C:0% | D:0% | 38 | A:0% | B:100% | C:0% | D:0% |
| 2 | A:0% | B:100% | C:0% | D:0% | 39 | A:0% | B:0% | C:0% | D:100% |
| 3 | A:0% | B:100% | C:0% | D:0% | 40 | A:100% | B:0% | C:0% | D:0% |
| 4 | A:0% | B:0% | C:0% | D:100% | 41 | A:0% | B:0% | C:0% | D:100% |
| 5 | A:0% | B:100% | C:0% | D:0% | 42 | A:94% | B:6% | C:0% | D:0% |
| 6 | A:6% | B:0% | C:94% | D:0% | 43 | A:100% | B:0% | C:0% | D:0% |
| 7 | A:0% | B:100% | C:0% | D:0% | 44 | A:0% | B:0% | C:0% | D:100% |
| 8 | A:0% | B:0% | C:0% | D:100% | 45 | A:0% | B:0% | C:100% | D:0% |
| 9 | A:100% | B:0% | C:0% | D:0% | 46 | A:0% | B:94% | C:6% | D:0% |
| 10 | A:0% | B:0% | C:0% | D:100% | 47 | A:0% | B:0% | C:0% | D:100% |
| 11 | A:0% | B:0% | C:0% | D:100% | 48 | A:0% | B:0% | C:100% | D:0% |
| 12 | A:0% | B:100% | C:0% | D:0% | 49 | A:0% | B:0% | C:0% | D:100% |
| 13 | A:0% | B:100% | C:0% | D:0% | 50 | A:0% | B:0% | C:0% | D:100% |
| 14 | A:0% | B:0% | C:0% | D:100% | 51 | A:0% | B:0% | C:0% | D:100% |
| 15 | A:0% | B:0% | C:6% | D:94% | 52 | A:0% | B:100% | C:0% | D:0% |
| 16 | A:0% | B:100% | C:0% | D:0% | 53 | A:0% | B:0% | C:0% | D:100% |
| 17 | A:0% | B:100% | C:0% | D:0% | 54 | A:0% | B:100% | C:0% | D:0% |
| 18 | A:0% | B:0% | C:0% | D:100% | 55 | A:0% | B:0% | C:100% | D:0% |
| 19 | A:0% | B:6% | C:0% | D:94% | 56 | A:0% | B:0% | C:100% | D:0% |
| 20 | A:0% | B:0% | C:0% | D:100% | 57 | A:0% | B:0% | C:100% | D:0% |
| 21 | A:0% | B:0% | C:0% | D:100% | 58 | A:0% | B:100% | C:0% | D:0% |
| 22 | A:0% | B:100% | C:0% | D:0% | 59 | A:0% | B:0% | C:100% | D:0% |
| 23 | A:0% | B:0% | C:100% | D:0% | 60 | A:0% | B:0% | C:100% | D:0% |
| 24 | A:100% | B:0% | C:0% | D:0% | 61 | A:0% | B:0% | C:100% | D:0% |
| 25 | A:88% | B:6% | C:0% | D:6% | 62 | A:0% | B:12% | C:88% | D:0% |
| 26 | A:0% | B:94% | C:0% | D:6% | 63 | A:0% | B:0% | C:100% | D:0% |
| 27 | A:0% | B:0% | C:0% | D:100% | 64 | A:100% | B:0% | C:0% | D:0% |
| 28 | A:0% | B:0% | C:100% | D:0% | 65 | A:0% | B:0% | C:100% | D:0% |
| 29 | A:0% | B:100% | C:0% | D:0% | 66 | A:0% | B:0% | C:100% | D:0% |
| 30 | A:0% | B:100% | C:0% | D:0% | 67 | A:0% | B:0% | C:100% | D:0% |
| 31 | A:0% | B:100% | C:0% | D:0% | 68 | A:6% | B:0% | C:0% | D:94% |
| 32 | A:0% | B:0% | C:100% | D:0% | 69 | A:100% | B:0% | C:0% | D:0% |
| 33 | A:0% | B:100% | C:0% | D:0% | 70 | A:0% | B:0% | C:0% | D:100% |
| 34 | A:100% | B:0% | C:0% | D:0% | 71 | A:0% | B:0% | C:0% | D:100% |
| 35 | A:0% | B:0% | C:0% | D:100% | 72 | A:0% | B:100% | C:0% | D:0% |
| 36 | A:0% | B:0% | C:100% | D:0% | 73 | A:0% | B:0% | C:0% | D:100% |
| 37 | A:6% | B:0% | C:0% | D:94% | 74 | A:0% | B:94% | C:0% | D:6% |

# ASK THE AUDIENCE

| | | | | | | | | |
|---|---|---|---|---|---|---|---|---|
| 75 | A:0% | B:0% | C:100% | D:0% | 82 | A:0% | B:0% | C:0% | D:100% |
| 76 | A:0% | B:12% | C:0% | D:88% | 83 | A:100% | B:0% | C:0% | D:0% |
| 77 | A:0% | B:0% | C:0% | D:100% | 84 | A:0% | B:0% | C:100% | D:0% |
| 78 | A:100% | B:0% | C:0% | D:0% | 85 | A:0% | B:0% | C:12% | D:88% |
| 79 | A:100% | B:0% | C:0% | D:0% | 86 | A:0% | B:0% | C:100% | D:0% |
| 80 | A:100% | B:0% | C:0% | D:0% | 87 | A:0% | B:0% | C:0% | D:100% |
| 81 | A:0% | B:100% | C:0% | D:0% | 88 | A:0% | B:0% | C:100% | D:0% |

## £200

| | | | | | | | | | |
|---|---|---|---|---|---|---|---|---|---|
| 1 | A:0% | B:100% | C:0% | D:0% | 33 | A:0% | B:0% | C:0% | D:100% |
| 2 | A:100% | B:0% | C:0% | D:0% | 34 | A:0% | B:6% | C:0% | D:94% |
| 3 | A:0% | B:100% | C:0% | D:0% | 35 | A:0% | B:0% | C:6% | D:94% |
| 4 | A:100% | B:0% | C:0% | D:0% | 36 | A:0% | B:6% | C:0% | D:94% |
| 5 | A:100% | B:0% | C:0% | D:0% | 37 | A:0% | B:0% | C:100% | D:0% |
| 6 | A:0% | B:100% | C:0% | D:0% | 38 | A:0% | B:0% | C:0% | D:100% |
| 7 | A:0% | B:0% | C:0% | D:100% | 39 | A:6% | B:6% | C:0% | D:88% |
| 8 | A:0% | B:100% | C:0% | D:0% | 40 | A:94% | B:0% | C:0% | D:6% |
| 9 | A:0% | B:0% | C:100% | D:0% | 41 | A:18% | B:0% | C:0% | D:82% |
| 10 | A:0% | B:0% | C:0% | D:100% | 42 | A:94% | B:0% | C:6% | D:0% |
| 11 | A:0% | B:0% | C:100% | D:0% | 43 | A:0% | B:0% | C:94% | D:6% |
| 12 | A:0% | B:0% | C:0% | D:100% | 44 | A:0% | B:6% | C:88% | D:6% |
| 13 | A:0% | B:100% | C:0% | D:0% | 45 | A:6% | B:0% | C:0% | D:94% |
| 14 | A:0% | B:94% | C:6% | D:0% | 46 | A:88% | B:0% | C:6% | D:6% |
| 15 | A:0% | B:0% | C:0% | D:100% | 47 | A:100% | B:0% | C:0% | D:0% |
| 16 | A:0% | B:100% | C:0% | D:0% | 48 | A:0% | B:0% | C:6% | D:94% |
| 17 | A:94% | B:6% | C:0% | D:0% | 49 | A:6% | B:0% | C:6% | D:88% |
| 18 | A:0% | B:0% | C:0% | D:100% | 50 | A:0% | B:94% | C:0% | D:6% |
| 19 | A:0% | B:94% | C:6% | D:0% | 51 | A:0% | B:100% | C:0% | D:0% |
| 20 | A:0% | B:100% | C:0% | D:0% | 52 | A:17% | B:12% | C:0% | D:71% |
| 21 | A:0% | B:0% | C:0% | D:100% | 53 | A:0% | B:100% | C:0% | D:0% |
| 22 | A:100% | B:0% | C:0% | D:0% | 54 | A:100% | B:0% | C:0% | D:0% |
| 23 | A:0% | B:0% | C:100% | D:0% | 55 | A:100% | B:0% | C:0% | D:0% |
| 24 | A:0% | B:0% | C:100% | D:0% | 56 | A:0% | B:0% | C:0% | D:100% |
| 25 | A:100% | B:0% | C:0% | D:0% | 57 | A:100% | B:0% | C:0% | D:0% |
| 26 | A:0% | B:0% | C:100% | D:0% | 58 | A:100% | B:0% | C:0% | D:0% |
| 27 | A:0% | B:0% | C:0% | D:100% | 59 | A:0% | B:76% | C:0% | D:24% |
| 28 | A:0% | B:0% | C:0% | D:100% | 60 | A:0% | B:100% | C:0% | D:0% |
| 29 | A:0% | B:0% | C:100% | D:0% | 61 | A:0% | B:100% | C:0% | D:0% |
| 30 | A:0% | B:0% | C:100% | D:0% | 62 | A:0% | B:6% | C:94% | D:0% |
| 31 | A:18% | B:0% | C:59% | D:23% | 63 | A:6% | B:0% | C:94% | D:0% |
| 32 | A:0% | B:0% | C:100% | D:0% | 64 | A:0% | B:0% | C:100% | D:0% |

| | | | | |
|---|---|---|---|---|
| 65 | A:100% | B:0% | C:0% | D:0% |
| 66 | A:0% | B:0% | C:0% | D:100% |
| 67 | A:35% | B:0% | C:59% | D:6% |
| 68 | A:100% | B:0% | C:0% | D:0% |
| 69 | A:100% | B:0% | C:0% | D:0% |
| 70 | A:100% | B:0% | C:0% | D:0% |
| 71 | A:0% | B:0% | C:0% | D:100% |
| 72 | A:0% | B:100% | C:0% | D:0% |
| 73 | A:0% | B:100% | C:0% | D:0% |
| 74 | A:0% | B:0% | C:100% | D:0% |
| 75 | A:100% | B:0% | C:0% | D:0% |
| 76 | A:0% | B:0% | C:100% | D:0% |
| 77 | A:100% | B:0% | C:0% | D:0% |
| 78 | A:0% | B:0% | C:100% | D:0% |
| 79 | A:0% | B:0% | C:100% | D:0% |
| 80 | A:0% | B:100% | C:0% | D:0% |
| 81 | A:18% | B:0% | C:76% | D:6% |
| 82 | A:0% | B:0% | C:0% | D:100% |
| 83 | A:0% | B:0% | C:100% | D:0% |
| 84 | A:0% | B:0% | C:100% | D:0% |

## £300

| | | | | |
|---|---|---|---|---|
| 1 | A:0% | B:0% | C:0% | D:100% |
| 2 | A:0% | B:0% | C:12% | D:88% |
| 3 | A:0% | B:0% | C:0% | D:100% |
| 4 | A:0% | B:0% | C:0% | D:100% |
| 5 | A:0% | B:0% | C:0% | D:100% |
| 6 | A:0% | B:0% | C:0% | D:100% |
| 7 | A:0% | B:0% | C:0% | D:100% |
| 8 | A:100% | B:0% | C:0% | D:0% |
| 9 | A:0% | B:88% | C:6% | D:6% |
| 10 | A:0% | B:6% | C:0% | D:94% |
| 11 | A:0% | B:100% | C:0% | D:0% |
| 12 | A:94% | B:6% | C:0% | D:0% |
| 13 | A:0% | B:100% | C:0% | D:0% |
| 14 | A:94% | B:6% | C:0% | D:0% |
| 15 | A:0% | B:0% | C:100% | D:0% |
| 16 | A:0% | B:0% | C:0% | D:100% |
| 17 | A:94% | B:6% | C:0% | D:0% |
| 18 | A:0% | B:0% | C:100% | D:0% |
| 19 | A:6% | B:0% | C:6% | D:88% |
| 20 | A:0% | B:0% | C:0% | D:100% |
| 21 | A:0% | B:17% | C:71% | D:12% |
| 22 | A:100% | B:0% | C:0% | D:0% |
| 23 | A:41% | B:59% | C:0% | D:0% |
| 24 | A:6% | B:0% | C:0% | D:94% |
| 25 | A:0% | B:100% | C:0% | D:0% |
| 26 | A:47% | B:41% | C:6% | D:6% |
| 27 | A:0% | B:6% | C:0% | D:94% |
| 28 | A:0% | B:0% | C:0% | D:100% |
| 29 | A:0% | B:0% | C:100% | D:0% |
| 30 | A:100% | B:0% | C:0% | D:0% |
| 31 | A:18% | B:12% | C:0% | D:70% |
| 32 | A:0% | B:0% | C:100% | D:0% |
| 33 | A:0% | B:6% | C:94% | D:0% |
| 34 | A:0% | B:0% | C:100% | D:0% |
| 35 | A:0% | B:6% | C:94% | D:0% |
| 36 | A:100% | B:0% | C:0% | D:0% |
| 37 | A:0% | B:100% | C:0% | D:0% |
| 38 | A:0% | B:0% | C:100% | D:0% |
| 39 | A:6% | B:0% | C:94% | D:0% |
| 40 | A:0% | B:100% | C:0% | D:0% |
| 41 | A:100% | B:0% | C:0% | D:0% |
| 42 | A:0% | B:0% | C:0% | D:100% |
| 43 | A:94% | B:0% | C:0% | D:6% |
| 44 | A:6% | B:88% | C:6% | D:0% |
| 45 | A:0% | B:0% | C:0% | D:100% |
| 46 | A:100% | B:0% | C:0% | D:0% |
| 47 | A:0% | B:0% | C:100% | D:0% |
| 48 | A:0% | B:0% | C:100% | D:0% |
| 49 | A:0% | B:6% | C:18% | D:76% |
| 50 | A:0% | B:100% | C:0% | D:0% |
| 51 | A:100% | B:0% | C:0% | D:0% |
| 52 | A:0% | B:0% | C:100% | D:0% |
| 53 | A:100% | B:0% | C:0% | D:0% |
| 54 | A:0% | B:100% | C:0% | D:0% |
| 55 | A:0% | B:0% | C:0% | D:100% |
| 56 | A:0% | B:6% | C:82% | D:12% |
| 57 | A:0% | B:100% | C:0% | D:0% |
| 58 | A:0% | B:100% | C:0% | D:0% |

# ASK THE AUDIENCE

| | | | | | | | | | |
|---|---|---|---|---|---|---|---|---|---|
| 59 | A:0% | B:0% | C:100% | D:0% | 70 | A:0% | B:0% | C:0% | D:100% |
| 60 | A:94% | B:6% | C:0% | D:0% | 71 | A:0% | B:0% | C:100% | D:0% |
| 61 | A:0% | B:0% | C:100% | D:0% | 72 | A:100% | B:0% | C:0% | D:0% |
| 62 | A:100% | B:0% | C:0% | D:0% | 73 | A:100% | B:0% | C:0% | D:0% |
| 63 | A:29% | B:29% | C:42% | D:0% | 74 | A:6% | B:88% | C:0% | D:6% |
| 64 | A:0% | B:100% | C:0% | D:0% | 75 | A:0% | B:6% | C:0% | D:94% |
| 65 | A:0% | B:0% | C:0% | D:100% | 76 | A:94% | B:6% | C:0% | D:0% |
| 66 | A:0% | B:0% | C:0% | D:100% | 77 | A:100% | B:0% | C:0% | D:0% |
| 67 | A:0% | B:0% | C:100% | D:0% | 78 | A:0% | B:100% | C:0% | D:0% |
| 68 | A:0% | B:0% | C:100% | D:0% | 79 | A:88% | B:0% | C:6% | D:6% |
| 69 | A:0% | B:0% | C:0% | D:100% | 80 | A:0% | B:0% | C:0% | D:100% |

## £500

| | | | | | | | | | |
|---|---|---|---|---|---|---|---|---|---|
| 1 | A:0% | B:0% | C:0% | D:100% | 28 | A:0% | B:0% | C:95% | D:5% |
| 2 | A:100% | B:0% | C:0% | D:0% | 29 | A:0% | B:0% | C:100% | D:0% |
| 3 | A:0% | B:0% | C:100% | D:0% | 30 | A:90% | B:10% | C:0% | D:0% |
| 4 | A:0% | B:0% | C:100% | D:0% | 31 | A:0% | B:0% | C:0% | D:100% |
| 5 | A:0% | B:0% | C:100% | D:0% | 32 | A:0% | B:0% | C:0% | D:100% |
| 6 | A:0% | B:95% | C:0% | D:5% | 33 | A:0% | B:100% | C:0% | D:0% |
| 7 | A:5% | B:95% | C:0% | D:0% | 34 | A:0% | B:0% | C:100% | D:0% |
| 8 | A:0% | B:0% | C:100% | D:0% | 35 | A:0% | B:100% | C:0% | D:0% |
| 9 | A:0% | B:0% | C:0% | D:100% | 36 | A:0% | B:0% | C:0% | D:100% |
| 10 | A:0% | B:0% | C:0% | D:100% | 37 | A:0% | B:0% | C:100% | D:0% |
| 11 | A:10% | B:0% | C:90% | D:0% | 38 | A:100% | B:0% | C:0% | D:0% |
| 12 | A:95% | B:5% | C:0% | D:0% | 39 | A:80% | B:10% | C:10% | D:0% |
| 13 | A:0% | B:0% | C:100% | D:0% | 40 | A:35% | B:55% | C:0% | D:10% |
| 14 | A:0% | B:0% | C:100% | D:0% | 41 | A:100% | B:0% | C:0% | D:0% |
| 15 | A:25% | B:5% | C:0% | D:70% | 42 | A:5% | B:0% | C:95% | D:0% |
| 16 | A:0% | B:100% | C:0% | D:0% | 43 | A:0% | B:0% | C:100% | D:0% |
| 17 | A:0% | B:0% | C:5% | D:95% | 44 | A:0% | B:0% | C:0% | D:100% |
| 18 | A:0% | B:0% | C:0% | D:100% | 45 | A:85% | B:0% | C:15% | D:0% |
| 19 | A:0% | B:0% | C:0% | D:100% | 46 | A:0% | B:100% | C:0% | D:0% |
| 20 | A:0% | B:100% | C:0% | D:0% | 47 | A:5% | B:0% | C:95% | D:0% |
| 21 | A:100% | B:0% | C:0% | D:0% | 48 | A:100% | B:0% | C:0% | D:0% |
| 22 | A:0% | B:100% | C:0% | D:0% | 49 | A:0% | B:5% | C:95% | D:0% |
| 23 | A:0% | B:0% | C:100% | D:0% | 50 | A:0% | B:0% | C:100% | D:0% |
| 24 | A:0% | B:0% | C:100% | D:0% | 51 | A:0% | B:100% | C:0% | D:0% |
| 25 | A:0% | B:0% | C:100% | D:0% | 52 | A:0% | B:100% | C:0% | D:0% |
| 26 | A:5% | B:20% | C:5% | D:70% | 53 | A:100% | B:0% | C:0% | D:0% |
| 27 | A:0% | B:0% | C:100% | D:0% | 54 | A:0% | B:100% | C:0% | D:0% |

# ASK THE AUDIENCE

| | | | | | | | | |
|----|--------|----------|----------|----------|----|--------|----------|----------|----------|
| 55 | A:0% | B:0% | C:0% | D:100% | 66 | A:0% | B:70% | C:20% | D:10% |
| 56 | A:0% | B:100% | C:0% | D:0% | 67 | A:0% | B:0% | C:100% | D:0% |
| 57 | A:85% | B:0% | C:0% | D:15% | 68 | A:0% | B:0% | C:0% | D:100% |
| 58 | A:0% | B:0% | C:100% | D:0% | 69 | A:100% | B:0% | C:0% | D:0% |
| 59 | A:0% | B:0% | C:0% | D:100% | 70 | A:0% | B:100% | C:0% | D:0% |
| 60 | A:75% | B:5% | C:5% | D:15% | 71 | A:0% | B:100% | C:0% | D:0% |
| 61 | A:100% | B:0% | C:0% | D:0% | 72 | A:0% | B:0% | C:100% | D:0% |
| 62 | A:0% | B:100% | C:0% | D:0% | 73 | A:45% | B:0% | C:50% | D:5% |
| 63 | A:100% | B:0% | C:0% | D:0% | 74 | A:5% | B:80% | C:0% | D:15% |
| 64 | A:100% | B:0% | C:0% | D:0% | 75 | A:5% | B:95% | C:0% | D:0% |
| 65 | A:0% | B:0% | C:0% | D:100% | 76 | A:0% | B:0% | C:0% | D:100% |

## £1,000

| | | | | | | | | |
|----|--------|--------|--------|--------|----|--------|--------|--------|--------|
| 1 | A:95% | B:0% | C:5% | D:0% | 29 | A:0% | B:0% | C:0% | D:100% |
| 2 | A:5% | B:0% | C:0% | D:95% | 30 | A:0% | B:0% | C:10% | D:90% |
| 3 | A:10% | B:75% | C:15% | D:0% | 31 | A:100% | B:0% | C:0% | D:0% |
| 4 | A:95% | B:5% | C:0% | D:0% | 32 | A:100% | B:0% | C:0% | D:0% |
| 5 | A:5% | B:95% | C:0% | D:0% | 33 | A:0% | B:95% | C:0% | D:5% |
| 6 | A:0% | B:0% | C:100% | D:0% | 34 | A:5% | B:85% | C:5% | D:5% |
| 7 | A:0% | B:0% | C:100% | D:0% | 35 | A:0% | B:0% | C:0% | D:100% |
| 8 | A:0% | B:0% | C:95% | D:5% | 36 | A:0% | B:0% | C:100% | D:0% |
| 9 | A:5% | B:15% | C:80% | D:0% | 37 | A:0% | B:100% | C:0% | D:0% |
| 10 | A:95% | B:0% | C:5% | D:0% | 38 | A:5% | B:95% | C:0% | D:0% |
| 11 | A:0% | B:100% | C:0% | D:0% | 39 | A:0% | B:100% | C:0% | D:0% |
| 12 | A:5% | B:10% | C:20% | D:65% | 40 | A:0% | B:10% | C:5% | D:85% |
| 13 | A:0% | B:0% | C:100% | D:0% | 41 | A:0% | B:5% | C:95% | D:0% |
| 14 | A:0% | B:0% | C:100% | D:0% | 42 | A:5% | B:35% | C:5% | D:55% |
| 15 | A:0% | B:0% | C:0% | D:100% | 43 | A:100% | B:0% | C:0% | D:0% |
| 16 | A:0% | B:100% | C:0% | D:0% | 44 | A:5% | B:95% | C:0% | D:0% |
| 17 | A:0% | B:100% | C:0% | D:0% | 45 | A:0% | B:15% | C:75% | D:10% |
| 18 | A:70% | B:25% | C:5% | D:0% | 46 | A:65% | B:25% | C:10% | D:0% |
| 19 | A:0% | B:0% | C:100% | D:0% | 47 | A:100% | B:0% | C:0% | D:0% |
| 20 | A:0% | B:100% | C:0% | D:0% | 48 | A:0% | B:100% | C:0% | D:0% |
| 21 | A:100% | B:0% | C:0% | D:0% | 49 | A:100% | B:0% | C:0% | D:0% |
| 22 | A:0% | B:100% | C:0% | D:0% | 50 | A:0% | B:5% | C:0% | D:95% |
| 23 | A:0% | B:5% | C:95% | D:0% | 51 | A:0% | B:100% | C:0% | D:0% |
| 24 | A:0% | B:100% | C:0% | D:0% | 52 | A:90% | B:5% | C:0% | D:5% |
| 25 | A:0% | B:90% | C:10% | D:0% | 53 | A:0% | B:5% | C:95% | D:0% |
| 26 | A:80% | B:15% | C:0% | D:5% | 54 | A:0% | B:0% | C:0% | D:100% |
| 27 | A:0% | B:100% | C:0% | D:0% | 55 | A:0% | B:0% | C:5% | D:95% |
| 28 | A:75% | B:5% | C:20% | D:0% | 56 | A:0% | B:0% | C:100% | D:0% |

# ASK THE AUDIENCE

| # | A | B | C | D | | # | A | B | C | D |
|---|---|---|---|---|---|---|---|---|---|---|
| 57 | A:95% | B:5% | C:0% | D:0% | | 65 | A:0% | B:0% | C:100% | D:0% |
| 58 | A:5% | B:0% | C:5% | D:90% | | 66 | A:95% | B:0% | C:5% | D:0% |
| 59 | A:0% | B:0% | C:20% | D:80% | | 67 | A:0% | B:0% | C:0% | D:100% |
| 60 | A:5% | B:95% | C:0% | D:0% | | 68 | A:0% | B:70% | C:20% | D:10% |
| 61 | A:0% | B:0% | C:0% | D:100% | | 69 | A:0% | B:0% | C:100% | D:0% |
| 62 | A:0% | B:95% | C:0% | D:5% | | 70 | A:5% | B:0% | C:90% | D:5% |
| 63 | A:0% | B:0% | C:100% | D:0% | | 71 | A:0% | B:100% | C:0% | D:0% |
| 64 | A:10% | B:5% | C:0% | D:85% | | 72 | A:90% | B:5% | C:5% | D:0% |

## £2,000

| # | A | B | C | D | | # | A | B | C | D |
|---|---|---|---|---|---|---|---|---|---|---|
| 1 | A:5% | B:95% | C:0% | D:0% | | 32 | A:0% | B:0% | C:100% | D:0% |
| 2 | A:0% | B:100% | C:0% | D:0% | | 33 | A:20% | B:0% | C:70% | D:10% |
| 3 | A:0% | B:10% | C:90% | D:0% | | 34 | A:0% | B:0% | C:0% | D:100% |
| 4 | A:5% | B:75% | C:10% | D:10% | | 35 | A:0% | B:0% | C:0% | D:100% |
| 5 | A:0% | B:90% | C:10% | D:0% | | 36 | A:85% | B:10% | C:5% | D:0% |
| 6 | A:25% | B:0% | C:65% | D:10% | | 37 | A:90% | B:5% | C:5% | D:0% |
| 7 | A:0% | B:0% | C:0% | D:100% | | 38 | A:0% | B:85% | C:0% | D:15% |
| 8 | A:100% | B:0% | C:0% | D:0% | | 39 | A:0% | B:70% | C:0% | D:30% |
| 9 | A:15% | B:80% | C:0% | D:5% | | 40 | A:10% | B:80% | C:0% | D:10% |
| 10 | A:5% | B:95% | C:0% | D:0% | | 41 | A:0% | B:0% | C:100% | D:0% |
| 11 | A:5% | B:95% | C:0% | D:0% | | 42 | A:5% | B:30% | C:0% | D:65% |
| 12 | A:0% | B:0% | C:5% | D:95% | | 43 | A:5% | B:95% | C:0% | D:0% |
| 13 | A:15% | B:80% | C:0% | D:5% | | 44 | A:100% | B:0% | C:0% | D:0% |
| 14 | A:0% | B:20% | C:80% | D:0% | | 45 | A:5% | B:60% | C:0% | D:35% |
| 15 | A:0% | B:0% | C:0% | D:100% | | 46 | A:0% | B:0% | C:100% | D:0% |
| 16 | A:20% | B:5% | C:75% | D:0% | | 47 | A:5% | B:80% | C:0% | D:15% |
| 17 | A:0% | B:100% | C:0% | D:0% | | 48 | A:5% | B:15% | C:75% | D:5% |
| 18 | A:100% | B:0% | C:0% | D:0% | | 49 | A:5% | B:5% | C:0% | D:90% |
| 19 | A:80% | B:0% | C:5% | D:15% | | 50 | A:0% | B:35% | C:0% | D:65% |
| 20 | A:0% | B:0% | C:0% | D:100% | | 51 | A:0% | B:20% | C:0% | D:80% |
| 21 | A:0% | B:0% | C:100% | D:0% | | 52 | A:0% | B:20% | C:5% | D:75% |
| 22 | A:0% | B:0% | C:100% | D:0% | | 53 | A:100% | B:0% | C:0% | D:0% |
| 23 | A:0% | B:5% | C:0% | D:95% | | 54 | A:0% | B:5% | C:5% | D:90% |
| 24 | A:0% | B:0% | C:0% | D:100% | | 55 | A:40% | B:0% | C:25% | D:35% |
| 25 | A:5% | B:0% | C:5% | D:90% | | 56 | A:0% | B:100% | C:0% | D:0% |
| 26 | A:95% | B:5% | C:0% | D:0% | | 57 | A:5% | B:20% | C:5% | D:70% |
| 27 | A:95% | B:0% | C:0% | D:5% | | 58 | A:0% | B:0% | C:25% | D:75% |
| 28 | A:100% | B:0% | C:0% | D:0% | | 59 | A:5% | B:0% | C:0% | D:95% |
| 29 | A:25% | B:20% | C:30% | D:25% | | 60 | A:55% | B:0% | C:0% | D:45% |
| 30 | A:0% | B:5% | C:0% | D:95% | | 61 | A:5% | B:15% | C:75% | D:5% |
| 31 | A:10% | B:0% | C:90% | D:0% | | 62 | A:5% | B:0% | C:5% | D:90% |

# ASK THE AUDIENCE

| | | | | | | | | |
|---|---|---|---|---|---|---|---|---|
| 63 | A:0% | B:0% | C:0% | D:100% | 66 | A:0% | B:0% | C:15% | D:85% |
| 64 | A:0% | B:100% | C:0% | D:0% | 67 | A:5% | B:0% | C:90% | D:5% |
| 65 | A:0% | B:90% | C:10% | D:0% | 68 | A:0% | B:90% | C:0% | D:10% |

## £4,000

| 1 | A:0% | B:0% | C:100% | D:0% | 33 | A:5% | B:22% | C:5% | D:68% |
|---|---|---|---|---|---|---|---|---|---|
| 2 | A:5% | B:0% | C:95% | D:0% | 34 | A:0% | B:90% | C:0% | D:10% |
| 3 | A:53% | B:32% | C:10% | D:5% | 35 | A:16% | B:0% | C:84% | D:0% |
| 4 | A:16% | B:16% | C:21% | D:47% | 36 | A:58% | B:32% | C:5% | D:5% |
| 5 | A:16% | B:0% | C:0% | D:84% | 37 | A:74% | B:21% | C:0% | D:5% |
| 6 | A:84% | B:5% | C:11% | D:0% | 38 | A:0% | B:10% | C:53% | D:37% |
| 7 | A:0% | B:0% | C:100% | D:0% | 39 | A:47% | B:53% | C:0% | D:0% |
| 8 | A:58% | B:16% | C:10% | D:16% | 40 | A:0% | B:0% | C:5% | D:95% |
| 9 | A:89% | B:0% | C:0% | D:11% | 41 | A:5% | B:0% | C:95% | D:0% |
| 10 | A:11% | B:0% | C:21% | D:68% | 42 | A:32% | B:15% | C:32% | D:21% |
| 11 | A:0% | B:0% | C:100% | D:0% | 43 | A:5% | B:95% | C:0% | D:0% |
| 12 | A:5% | B:11% | C:84% | D:0% | 44 | A:10% | B:6% | C:10% | D:74% |
| 13 | A:42% | B:21% | C:5% | D:32% | 45 | A:0% | B:5% | C:0% | D:95% |
| 14 | A:95% | B:5% | C:0% | D:0% | 46 | A:0% | B:0% | C:95% | D:5% |
| 15 | A:16% | B:47% | C:21% | D:16% | 47 | A:100% | B:0% | C:0% | D:0% |
| 16 | A:100% | B:0% | C:0% | D:0% | 48 | A:0% | B:90% | C:5% | D:5% |
| 17 | A:90% | B:5% | C:0% | D:5% | 49 | A:0% | B:0% | C:100% | D:0% |
| 18 | A:16% | B:21% | C:5% | D:58% | 50 | A:11% | B:5% | C:5% | D:79% |
| 19 | A:5% | B:90% | C:5% | D:0% | 51 | A:0% | B:0% | C:0% | D:100% |
| 20 | A:0% | B:0% | C:5% | D:95% | 52 | A:42% | B:0% | C:0% | D:58% |
| 21 | A:0% | B:0% | C:0% | D:100% | 53 | A:0% | B:95% | C:0% | D:5% |
| 22 | A:0% | B:0% | C:95% | D:5% | 54 | A:32% | B:0% | C:0% | D:68% |
| 23 | A:5% | B:68% | C:27% | D:0% | 55 | A:84% | B:11% | C:5% | D:0% |
| 24 | A:0% | B:100% | C:0% | D:0% | 56 | A:90% | B:5% | C:5% | D:0% |
| 25 | A:42% | B:16% | C:26% | D:16% | 57 | A:0% | B:95% | C:0% | D:5% |
| 26 | A:5% | B:95% | C:0% | D:0% | 58 | A:5% | B:74% | C:16% | D:5% |
| 27 | A:5% | B:0% | C:95% | D:0% | 59 | A:69% | B:21% | C:5% | D:5% |
| 28 | A:0% | B:100% | C:0% | D:0% | 60 | A:0% | B:100% | C:0% | D:0% |
| 29 | A:5% | B:5% | C:0% | D:90% | 61 | A:100% | B:0% | C:0% | D:0% |
| 30 | A:16% | B:16% | C:36% | D:32% | 62 | A:100% | B:0% | C:0% | D:0% |
| 31 | A:0% | B:0% | C:95% | D:5% | 63 | A:0% | B:0% | C:100% | D:0% |
| 32 | A:0% | B:0% | C:0% | D:100% | 64 | A:85% | B:5% | C:5% | D:5% |

page
259

# ASK THE AUDIENCE

## £8,000

| 1 | A:95% | B:0% | C:5% | D:0% |
|---|---|---|---|---|
| 2 | A:5% | B:74% | C:5% | D:16% |
| 3 | A:5% | B:58% | C:16% | D:21% |
| 4 | A:11% | B:53% | C:5% | D:31% |
| 5 | A:47% | B:16% | C:16% | D:21% |
| 6 | A:0% | B:0% | C:100% | D:0% |
| 7 | A:37% | B:0% | C:58% | D:5% |
| 8 | A:100% | B:0% | C:0% | D:0% |
| 9 | A:0% | B:5% | C:90% | D:5% |
| 10 | A:10% | B:0% | C:90% | D:0% |
| 11 | A:74% | B:11% | C:11% | D:4% |
| 12 | A:0% | B:100% | C:0% | D:0% |
| 13 | A:5% | B:68% | C:22% | D:5% |
| 14 | A:0% | B:0% | C:0% | D:100% |
| 15 | A:0% | B:74% | C:10% | D:16% |
| 16 | A:79% | B:16% | C:0% | D:5% |
| 17 | A:100% | B:0% | C:0% | D:0% |
| 18 | A:5% | B:0% | C:0% | D:95% |
| 19 | A:0% | B:16% | C:0% | D:84% |
| 20 | A:16% | B:74% | C:5% | D:5% |
| 21 | A:0% | B:5% | C:0% | D:95% |
| 22 | A:5% | B:90% | C:0% | D:5% |
| 23 | A:10% | B:37% | C:16% | D:37% |
| 24 | A:79% | B:21% | C:0% | D:0% |
| 25 | A:10% | B:22% | C:0% | D:68% |
| 26 | A:21% | B:26% | C:0% | D:53% |
| 27 | A:5% | B:90% | C:5% | D:0% |
| 28 | A:16% | B:0% | C:0% | D:84% |
| 29 | A:0% | B:10% | C:4% | D:86% |
| 30 | A:0% | B:5% | C:5% | D:90% |
| 31 | A:68% | B:5% | C:16% | D:11% |
| 32 | A:16% | B:0% | C:10% | D:74% |
| 33 | A:47% | B:6% | C:21% | D:26% |
| 34 | A:21% | B:53% | C:26% | D:0% |
| 35 | A:5% | B:85% | C:5% | D:5% |
| 36 | A:74% | B:0% | C:21% | D:5% |
| 37 | A:5% | B:5% | C:0% | D:90% |
| 38 | A:0% | B:0% | C:100% | D:0% |
| 39 | A:0% | B:37% | C:58% | D:5% |
| 40 | A:84% | B:0% | C:5% | D:11% |
| 41 | A:0% | B:21% | C:5% | D:74% |
| 42 | A:37% | B:0% | C:63% | D:0% |
| 43 | A:16% | B:47% | C:11% | D:26% |
| 44 | A:37% | B:63% | C:0% | D:0% |
| 45 | A:21% | B:53% | C:21% | D:5% |
| 46 | A:21% | B:47% | C:21% | D:11% |
| 47 | A:16% | B:0% | C:5% | D:79% |
| 48 | A:42% | B:26% | C:32% | D:0% |
| 49 | A:0% | B:11% | C:84% | D:5% |
| 50 | A:80% | B:5% | C:5% | D:10% |
| 51 | A:5% | B:16% | C:21% | D:58% |
| 52 | A:32% | B:42% | C:16% | D:10% |
| 53 | A:0% | B:0% | C:84% | D:16% |
| 54 | A:68% | B:16% | C:5% | D:11% |
| 55 | A:90% | B:5% | C:0% | D:5% |
| 56 | A:0% | B:5% | C:95% | D:0% |
| 57 | A:16% | B:16% | C:16% | D:52% |
| 58 | A:0% | B:0% | C:95% | D:5% |
| 59 | A:26% | B:0% | C:74% | D:0% |
| 60 | A:74% | B:0% | C:16% | D:10% |

## £16,000

| 1 | A:0% | B:10% | C:43% | D:47% |
|---|---|---|---|---|
| 2 | A:47% | B:43% | C:5% | D:5% |
| 3 | A:32% | B:26% | C:37% | D:5% |
| 4 | A:6% | B:74% | C:10% | D:10% |
| 5 | A:5% | B:21% | C:53% | D:21% |
| 6 | A:16% | B:0% | C:0% | D:84% |
| 7 | A:100% | B:0% | C:0% | D:0% |
| 8 | A:5% | B:26% | C:21% | D:48% |
| 9 | A:47% | B:32% | C:21% | D:0% |
| 10 | A:16% | B:52% | C:16% | D:16% |
| 11 | A:78% | B:11% | C:0% | D:11% |
| 12 | A:0% | B:16% | C:68% | D:16% |
| 13 | A:42% | B:21% | C:32% | D:5% |
| 14 | A:11% | B:11% | C:4% | D:74% |
| 15 | A:63% | B:0% | C:37% | D:0% |
| 16 | A:26% | B:16% | C:26% | D:32% |

# ASK THE AUDIENCE

| # | A | B | C | D |
|---|---|---|---|---|
| 17 | A:21% | B:32% | C:26% | D:21% |
| 18 | A:5% | B:21% | C:63% | D:11% |
| 19 | A:21% | B:58% | C:16% | D:5% |
| 20 | A:68% | B:0% | C:11% | D:21% |
| 21 | A:10% | B:16% | C:16% | D:58% |
| 22 | A:5% | B:0% | C:0% | D:95% |
| 23 | A:11% | B:89% | C:0% | D:0% |
| 24 | A:5% | B:0% | C:95% | D:0% |
| 25 | A:5% | B:11% | C:0% | D:84% |
| 26 | A:26% | B:21% | C:16% | D:37% |
| 27 | A:43% | B:47% | C:5% | D:5% |
| 28 | A:100% | B:0% | C:0% | D:0% |
| 29 | A:5% | B:21% | C:11% | D:63% |
| 30 | A:21% | B:79% | C:0% | D:0% |
| 31 | A:79% | B:16% | C:5% | D:0% |
| 32 | A:37% | B:10% | C:0% | D:53% |
| 33 | A:0% | B:0% | C:0% | D:100% |
| 34 | A:63% | B:5% | C:16% | D:16% |
| 35 | A:11% | B:21% | C:63% | D:5% |
| 36 | A:0% | B:95% | C:0% | D:5% |
| 37 | A:15% | B:0% | C:53% | D:32% |
| 38 | A:0% | B:0% | C:0% | D:100% |
| 39 | A:26% | B:21% | C:42% | D:11% |
| 40 | A:0% | B:5% | C:90% | D:5% |
| 41 | A:32% | B:32% | C:21% | D:15% |
| 42 | A:0% | B:11% | C:89% | D:0% |
| 43 | A:68% | B:0% | C:11% | D:21% |
| 44 | A:5% | B:0% | C:0% | D:95% |
| 45 | A:84% | B:0% | C:0% | D:16% |
| 46 | A:16% | B:42% | C:11% | D:31% |
| 47 | A:0% | B:95% | C:5% | D:0% |
| 48 | A:42% | B:0% | C:21% | D:37% |
| 49 | A:16% | B:21% | C:5% | D:58% |
| 50 | A:11% | B:15% | C:63% | D:11% |
| 51 | A:32% | B:21% | C:15% | D:32% |
| 52 | A:32% | B:26% | C:42% | D:0% |
| 53 | A:16% | B:16% | C:53% | D:15% |
| 54 | A:11% | B:84% | C:5% | D:0% |
| 55 | A:10% | B:16% | C:53% | D:21% |
| 56 | A:11% | B:11% | C:4% | D:74% |

# £32,000

| # | A | B | C | D |
|---|---|---|---|---|
| 1 | A:0% | B:88% | C:6% | D:6% |
| 2 | A:24% | B:58% | C:12% | D:6% |
| 3 | A:41% | B:6% | C:29% | D:24% |
| 4 | A:0% | B:88% | C:0% | D:12% |
| 5 | A:12% | B:6% | C:29% | D:53% |
| 6 | A:12% | B:0% | C:17% | D:71% |
| 7 | A:0% | B:0% | C:6% | D:94% |
| 8 | A:47% | B:0% | C:6% | D:47% |
| 9 | A:47% | B:41% | C:6% | D:6% |
| 10 | A:23% | B:0% | C:18% | D:59% |
| 11 | A:29% | B:59% | C:0% | D:12% |
| 12 | A:8% | B:24% | C:8% | D:60% |
| 13 | A:65% | B:6% | C:0% | D:29% |
| 14 | A:0% | B:71% | C:18% | D:11% |
| 15 | A:6% | B:18% | C:70% | D:6% |
| 16 | A:12% | B:82% | C:0% | D:6% |
| 17 | A:17% | B:0% | C:24% | D:59% |
| 18 | A:17% | B:59% | C:6% | D:18% |
| 19 | A:6% | B:6% | C:18% | D:70% |
| 20 | A:18% | B:29% | C:6% | D:47% |
| 21 | A:17% | B:35% | C:24% | D:24% |
| 22 | A:17% | B:0% | C:12% | D:71% |
| 23 | A:0% | B:0% | C:88% | D:12% |
| 24 | A:18% | B:24% | C:18% | D:40% |
| 25 | A:47% | B:18% | C:11% | D:24% |
| 26 | A:0% | B:0% | C:0% | D:100% |
| 27 | A:11% | B:24% | C:18% | D:47% |
| 28 | A:17% | B:24% | C:35% | D:24% |
| 29 | A:64% | B:12% | C:12% | D:12% |
| 30 | A:65% | B:11% | C:0% | D:24% |
| 31 | A:29% | B:41% | C:6% | D:24% |
| 32 | A:12% | B:41% | C:29% | D:18% |
| 33 | A:65% | B:6% | C:6% | D:23% |
| 34 | A:24% | B:11% | C:18% | D:47% |
| 35 | A:0% | B:18% | C:76% | D:6% |
| 36 | A:6% | B:0% | C:0% | D:94% |
| 37 | A:6% | B:18% | C:29% | D:47% |
| 38 | A:5% | B:59% | C:12% | D:24% |

# ASK THE AUDIENCE

| | | | | | | | | |
|---|---|---|---|---|---|---|---|
| 39 | A:47% | B:24% | C:0% | D:29% | 46 | A:71% | B:6% | C:6% | D:17% |
| 40 | A:18% | B:47% | C:6% | D:29% | 47 | A:18% | B:41% | C:12% | D:29% |
| 41 | A:0% | B:0% | C:88% | D:12% | 48 | A:29% | B:41% | C:6% | D:24% |
| 42 | A:59% | B:24% | C:0% | D:17% | 49 | A:29% | B:29% | C:13% | D:29% |
| 43 | A:12% | B:0% | C:12% | D:76% | 50 | A:6% | B:82% | C:6% | D:6% |
| 44 | A:41% | B:41% | C:6% | D:12% | 51 | A:24% | B:5% | C:12% | D:59% |
| 45 | A:0% | B:6% | C:88% | D:6% | 52 | A:6% | B:88% | C:0% | D:6% |

## £64,000

| | | | | | | | | |
|---|---|---|---|---|---|---|---|
| 1 | A:18% | B:59% | C:23% | D:0% | 25 | A:6% | B:29% | C:41% | D:24% |
| 2 | A:12% | B:6% | C:76% | D:6% | 26 | A:0% | B:24% | C:41% | D:35% |
| 3 | A:76% | B:18% | C:6% | D:0% | 27 | A:6% | B:41% | C:0% | D:53% |
| 4 | A:29% | B:18% | C:6% | D:47% | 28 | A:6% | B:0% | C:88% | D:6% |
| 5 | A:35% | B:18% | C:18% | D:29% | 29 | A:12% | B:12% | C:41% | D:35% |
| 6 | A:29% | B:29% | C:18% | D:24% | 30 | A:12% | B:12% | C:35% | D:41% |
| 7 | A:12% | B:6% | C:47% | D:35% | 31 | A:29% | B:12% | C:53% | D:6% |
| 8 | A:35% | B:29% | C:24% | D:12% | 32 | A:76% | B:0% | C:6% | D:18% |
| 9 | A:12% | B:12% | C:52% | D:24% | 33 | A:0% | B:12% | C:76% | D:12% |
| 10 | A:24% | B:6% | C:6% | D:64% | 34 | A:0% | B:0% | C:100% | D:0% |
| 11 | A:18% | B:12% | C:29% | D:41% | 35 | A:12% | B:12% | C:5% | D:71% |
| 12 | A:12% | B:41% | C:0% | D:47% | 36 | A:0% | B:12% | C:88% | D:0% |
| 13 | A:12% | B:12% | C:12% | D:64% | 37 | A:18% | B:46% | C:18% | D:18% |
| 14 | A:6% | B:24% | C:41% | D:29% | 38 | A:82% | B:6% | C:6% | D:6% |
| 15 | A:71% | B:18% | C:11% | D:0% | 39 | A:41% | B:6% | C:12% | D:41% |
| 16 | A:6% | B:71% | C:6% | D:17% | 40 | A:5% | B:24% | C:24% | D:47% |
| 17 | A:11% | B:24% | C:0% | D:65% | 41 | A:18% | B:11% | C:24% | D:47% |
| 18 | A:6% | B:76% | C:12% | D:6% | 42 | A:18% | B:29% | C:12% | D:41% |
| 19 | A:6% | B:59% | C:35% | D:0% | 43 | A:18% | B:24% | C:47% | D:11% |
| 20 | A:24% | B:5% | C:24% | D:47% | 44 | A:24% | B:53% | C:23% | D:0% |
| 21 | A:18% | B:11% | C:53% | D:18% | 45 | A:12% | B:29% | C:6% | D:53% |
| 22 | A:47% | B:41% | C:0% | D:12% | 46 | A:24% | B:0% | C:17% | D:59% |
| 23 | A:88% | B:0% | C:12% | D:0% | 47 | A:53% | B:29% | C:12% | D:6% |
| 24 | A:47% | B:47% | C:0% | D:6% | 48 | A:17% | B:24% | C:18% | D:41% |

## £125,000

| | | | | | | | | |
|---|---|---|---|---|---|---|---|
| 1 | A:0% | B:29% | C:24% | D:47% | 5 | A:11% | B:24% | C:41% | D:24% |
| 2 | A:24% | B:47% | C:24% | D:5% | 6 | A:0% | B:24% | C:71% | D:5% |
| 3 | A:35% | B:18% | C:35% | D:12% | 7 | A:0% | B:29% | C:42% | D:29% |
| 4 | A:0% | B:65% | C:35% | D:0% | 8 | A:5% | B:47% | C:24% | D:24% |

# ASK THE AUDIENCE

| 9 | A:12% | B:12% | C:71% | D:5% | 27 | A:0% | B:6% | C:12% | D:82% |
|---|-------|-------|-------|------|----|------|------|-------|-------|
| 10 | A:0% | B:94% | C:6% | D:0% | 28 | A:24% | B:17% | C:47% | D:12% |
| 11 | A:41% | B:18% | C:41% | D:0% | 29 | A:29% | B:24% | C:41% | D:6% |
| 12 | A:41% | B:12% | C:41% | D:6% | 30 | A:5% | B:18% | C:5% | D:72% |
| 13 | A:41% | B:24% | C:24% | D:11% | 31 | A:24% | B:6% | C:29% | D:41% |
| 14 | A:35% | B:30% | C:35% | D:0% | 32 | A:53% | B:35% | C:12% | D:0% |
| 15 | A:12% | B:35% | C:35% | D:18% | 33 | A:24% | B:18% | C:47% | D:11% |
| 16 | A:12% | B:5% | C:24% | D:59% | 34 | A:29% | B:47% | C:6% | D:18% |
| 17 | A:0% | B:65% | C:29% | D:6% | 35 | A:18% | B:5% | C:59% | D:18% |
| 18 | A:24% | B:12% | C:47% | D:17% | 36 | A:6% | B:0% | C:18% | D:76% |
| 19 | A:35% | B:29% | C:12% | D:24% | 37 | A:5% | B:71% | C:12% | D:12% |
| 20 | A:53% | B:0% | C:29% | D:18% | 38 | A:6% | B:0% | C:82% | D:12% |
| 21 | A:0% | B:29% | C:42% | D:29% | 39 | A:0% | B:94% | C:6% | D:0% |
| 22 | A:6% | B:76% | C:18% | D:0% | 40 | A:18% | B:35% | C:29% | D:18% |
| 23 | A:41% | B:24% | C:11% | D:24% | 41 | A:12% | B:0% | C:41% | D:47% |
| 24 | A:12% | B:18% | C:53% | D:17% | 42 | A:0% | B:12% | C:88% | D:0% |
| 25 | A:41% | B:6% | C:35% | D:18% | 43 | A:53% | B:6% | C:41% | D:0% |
| 26 | A:35% | B:18% | C:29% | D:18% | 44 | A:0% | B:6% | C:94% | D:0% |

## £250,000

| 1 | A:30% | B:5% | C:35% | D:30% | 21 | A:5% | B:25% | C:50% | D:20% |
|---|-------|------|-------|-------|----|------|-------|-------|-------|
| 2 | A:15% | B:45% | C:0% | D:40% | 22 | A:15% | B:5% | C:80% | D:0% |
| 3 | A:45% | B:35% | C:0% | D:20% | 23 | A:55% | B:15% | C:5% | D:25% |
| 4 | A:0% | B:95% | C:0% | D:5% | 24 | A:15% | B:30% | C:55% | D:0% |
| 5 | A:5% | B:90% | C:5% | D:0% | 25 | A:5% | B:5% | C:70% | D:20% |
| 6 | A:5% | B:75% | C:5% | D:15% | 26 | A:15% | B:35% | C:45% | D:5% |
| 7 | A:35% | B:10% | C:45% | D:10% | 27 | A:10% | B:55% | C:25% | D:10% |
| 8 | A:5% | B:55% | C:30% | D:10% | 28 | A:30% | B:25% | C:20% | D:25% |
| 9 | A:0% | B:30% | C:30% | D:40% | 29 | A:15% | B:40% | C:20% | D:25% |
| 10 | A:25% | B:0% | C:40% | D:35% | 30 | A:15% | B:40% | C:15% | D:30% |
| 11 | A:25% | B:15% | C:40% | D:20% | 31 | A:40% | B:25% | C:35% | D:0% |
| 12 | A:15% | B:25% | C:45% | D:15% | 32 | A:5% | B:30% | C:65% | D:0% |
| 13 | A:20% | B:10% | C:65% | D:5% | 33 | A:65% | B:0% | C:25% | D:10% |
| 14 | A:40% | B:15% | C:25% | D:20% | 34 | A:40% | B:45% | C:10% | D:5% |
| 15 | A:5% | B:35% | C:15% | D:45% | 35 | A:25% | B:35% | C:30% | D:10% |
| 16 | A:60% | B:0% | C:30% | D:10% | 36 | A:10% | B:25% | C:45% | D:20% |
| 17 | A:70% | B:25% | C:5% | D:0% | 37 | A:10% | B:45% | C:30% | D:15% |
| 18 | A:10% | B:35% | C:20% | D:35% | 38 | A:20% | B:45% | C:15% | D:20% |
| 19 | A:15% | B:25% | C:50% | D:10% | 39 | A:10% | B:40% | C:30% | D:20% |
| 20 | A:5% | B:20% | C:25% | D:50% | 40 | A:35% | B:0% | C:60% | D:5% |

# ASK THE AUDIENCE

## £500,000

| # | A | B | C | D |
|---|---|---|---|---|
| 1 | A:55% | B:20% | C:20% | D:5% |
| 2 | A:15% | B:25% | C:60% | D:0% |
| 3 | A:5% | B:35% | C:20% | D:40% |
| 4 | A:15% | B:20% | C:55% | D:10% |
| 5 | A:0% | B:20% | C:20% | D:60% |
| 6 | A:25% | B:30% | C:25% | D:20% |
| 7 | A:30% | B:60% | C:10% | D:0% |
| 8 | A:5% | B:20% | C:15% | D:60% |
| 9 | A:50% | B:35% | C:10% | D:5% |
| 10 | A:0% | B:45% | C:45% | D:10% |
| 11 | A:25% | B:10% | C:35% | D:30% |
| 12 | A:5% | B:5% | C:75% | D:15% |
| 13 | A:40% | B:0% | C:50% | D:10% |
| 14 | A:5% | B:95% | C:0% | D:0% |
| 15 | A:10% | B:30% | C:15% | D:45% |
| 16 | A:25% | B:20% | C:35% | D:20% |
| 17 | A:25% | B:40% | C:20% | D:15% |
| 18 | A:30% | B:10% | C:5% | D:55% |
| 19 | A:0% | B:15% | C:85% | D:0% |
| 20 | A:10% | B:10% | C:55% | D:25% |
| 21 | A:40% | B:15% | C:25% | D:20% |
| 22 | A:35% | B:45% | C:20% | D:0% |
| 23 | A:10% | B:20% | C:15% | D:55% |
| 24 | A:25% | B:45% | C:30% | D:0% |
| 25 | A:50% | B:20% | C:20% | D:10% |
| 26 | A:35% | B:50% | C:10% | D:5% |
| 27 | A:15% | B:10% | C:75% | D:0% |
| 28 | A:10% | B:30% | C:20% | D:40% |
| 29 | A:15% | B:0% | C:60% | D:25% |
| 30 | A:0% | B:60% | C:10% | D:30% |
| 31 | A:15% | B:35% | C:35% | D:15% |
| 32 | A:30% | B:10% | C:30% | D:30% |
| 33 | A:70% | B:5% | C:15% | D:10% |
| 34 | A:30% | B:0% | C:50% | D:20% |
| 35 | A:20% | B:35% | C:15% | D:30% |
| 36 | A:40% | B:30% | C:20% | D:10% |

## £1,000,000

| # | A | B | C | D |
|---|---|---|---|---|
| 1 | A:15% | B:30% | C:35% | D:20% |
| 2 | A:40% | B:30% | C:20% | D:10% |
| 3 | A:10% | B:15% | C:20% | D:55% |
| 4 | A:5% | B:70% | C:5% | D:20% |
| 5 | A:45% | B:20% | C:30% | D:5% |
| 6 | A:30% | B:40% | C:10% | D:20% |
| 7 | A:20% | B:35% | C:15% | D:30% |
| 8 | A:50% | B:15% | C:10% | D:25% |
| 9 | A:15% | B:25% | C:55% | D:5% |
| 10 | A:25% | B:30% | C:35% | D:10% |
| 11 | A:30% | B:5% | C:45% | D:20% |
| 12 | A:40% | B:5% | C:45% | D:10% |
| 13 | A:15% | B:0% | C:75% | D:10% |
| 14 | A:25% | B:15% | C:55% | D:5% |
| 15 | A:15% | B:50% | C:15% | D:20% |
| 16 | A:5% | B:60% | C:10% | D:25% |
| 17 | A:5% | B:30% | C:45% | D:20% |
| 18 | A:5% | B:45% | C:15% | D:35% |
| 19 | A:25% | B:30% | C:20% | D:25% |
| 20 | A:60% | B:10% | C:0% | D:30% |
| 21 | A:30% | B:30% | C:20% | D:20% |
| 22 | A:40% | B:45% | C:0% | D:15% |
| 23 | A:60% | B:20% | C:10% | D:10% |
| 24 | A:15% | B:35% | C:30% | D:20% |
| 25 | A:35% | B:40% | C:10% | D:15% |
| 26 | A:75% | B:5% | C:5% | D:15% |
| 27 | A:35% | B:20% | C:20% | D:25% |
| 28 | A:20% | B:20% | C:40% | D:20% |
| 29 | A:30% | B:45% | C:25% | D:0% |
| 30 | A:20% | B:0% | C:60% | D:20% |
| 31 | A:10% | B:40% | C:20% | D:30% |
| 32 | A:10% | B:20% | C:15% | D:55% |

# Answers

## Fastest Finger First

| | | | | | | | | | |
|---|---|---|---|---|---|---|---|---|---|
| 1 | BCAD | 2 | BCAD | 3 | CABD | 4 | DACB | 5 | DBCA |
| 6 | DABC | 7 | CABD | 8 | CDAB | 9 | CBDA | 10 | CBDA |
| 11 | BADC | 12 | DCBA | 13 | CDAB | 14 | CBAD | 15 | DCAB |
| 16 | CBAD | 17 | DCBA | 18 | CABD | 19 | BCAD | 20 | CDBA |
| 21 | BDCA | 22 | CDBA | 23 | BADC | 24 | DACB | 25 | DBCA |
| 26 | BDAC | 27 | BADC | 28 | DBCA | 29 | BDAC | 30 | DACB |
| 31 | CADB | 32 | BCAD | 33 | BDAC | 34 | BADC | 35 | CBAD |
| 36 | CADB | 37 | DBCA | 38 | CBDA | 39 | CBDA | 40 | DBCA |
| 41 | BCDA | 42 | BCDA | 43 | BACD | 44 | CBDA | 45 | ACDB |
| 46 | BCAD | 47 | DBAC | 48 | CBDA | 49 | CBDA | 50 | ABCD |
| 51 | DBCA | 52 | BADC | 53 | CBDA | 54 | DCBA | 55 | BCAD |
| 56 | ADBC | 57 | BADC | 58 | CDAB | 59 | DACB | 60 | CBAD |
| 61 | DBCA | 62 | CADB | 63 | CBDA | 64 | CADB | 65 | BDAC |
| 66 | BDAC | 67 | DACB | 68 | DACB | 69 | BCDA | 70 | BDCA |
| 71 | DBCA | 72 | CDAB | 73 | CADB | 74 | CBDA | 75 | DBCA |
| 76 | CADB | 77 | CADB | 78 | CADB | 79 | DBCA | 80 | CBAD |
| 81 | CBAD | 82 | ABCD | 83 | ACDB | 84 | CDAB | 85 | DBAC |
| 86 | CDAB | 87 | CDBA | 88 | DACB | 89 | DBCA | 90 | BADC |
| 91 | CDBA | 92 | DACB | 93 | DACB | 94 | CDAB | 95 | ABDC |
| 96 | BDCA | 97 | DBCA | 98 | CBDA | 99 | BADC | 100 | CDAB |

If you answered correctly, well done! Turn to page 31 to play for £100!

## £100

| | | | | | | | | | | | | | |
|---|---|---|---|---|---|---|---|---|---|---|---|---|---|
| 1 | B | 2 | B | 3 | B | 4 | D | 5 | B | 6 | C | 7 | B |
| 8 | D | 9 | A | 10 | D | 11 | D | 12 | B | 13 | B | 14 | D |
| 15 | D | 16 | B | 17 | B | 18 | D | 19 | D | 20 | D | 21 | D |
| 22 | B | 23 | C | 24 | A | 25 | A | 26 | B | 27 | D | 28 | C |
| 29 | B | 30 | B | 31 | B | 32 | C | 33 | B | 34 | A | 35 | D |
| 36 | C | 37 | D | 38 | B | 39 | D | 40 | A | 41 | D | 42 | A |
| 43 | A | 44 | D | 45 | C | 46 | B | 47 | D | 48 | C | 49 | D |
| 50 | D | 51 | D | 52 | B | 53 | D | 54 | B | 55 | C | 56 | C |

# ANSWERS

| | | | | | | |
|---|---|---|---|---|---|---|
| 57 C | 58 B | 59 C | 60 C | 61 C | 62 C | 63 C |
| 64 A | 65 D | 66 C | 67 C | 68 D | 69 A | 70 D |
| 71 D | 72 B | 73 D | 74 B | 75 C | 76 D | 77 D |
| 78 A | 79 A | 80 A | 81 B | 82 D | 83 A | 84 C |
| 85 D | 86 C | 87 D | 88 C | | | |

If you have won £100, well done! Turn to page 51 to play for £200!

## £200

| | | | | | | |
|---|---|---|---|---|---|---|
| 1 B | 2 A | 3 B | 4 A | 5 A | 6 B | 7 D |
| 8 B | 9 C | 10 D | 11 C | 12 D | 13 B | 14 B |
| 15 D | 16 C | 17 A | 18 D | 19 B | 20 B | 21 D |
| 22 A | 23 C | 24 C | 25 A | 26 C | 27 D | 28 D |
| 29 C | 30 C | 31 C | 32 C | 33 D | 34 A | 35 D |
| 36 D | 37 C | 38 D | 39 D | 40 A | 41 D | 42 A |
| 43 C | 44 C | 45 D | 46 A | 47 A | 48 D | 49 D |
| 50 B | 51 B | 52 D | 53 B | 54 A | 55 A | 56 D |
| 57 A | 58 A | 59 B | 60 B | 61 B | 62 C | 63 C |
| 64 C | 65 A | 66 D | 67 C | 68 A | 69 A | 70 A |
| 71 D | 72 B | 73 B | 74 C | 75 A | 76 C | 77 A |
| 78 C | 79 C | 80 B | 81 C | 82 D | 83 C | 84 C |

If you have won £200, well done! Turn to page 69 to play for £300!

## £300

| | | | | | | |
|---|---|---|---|---|---|---|
| 1 D | 2 D | 3 D | 4 D | 5 D | 6 D | 7 D |
| 8 A | 9 B | 10 D | 11 B | 12 A | 13 B | 14 A |
| 15 C | 16 D | 17 A | 18 C | 19 D | 20 D | 21 C |
| 22 A | 23 B | 24 D | 25 B | 26 A | 27 D | 28 D |
| 29 C | 30 A | 31 D | 32 C | 33 C | 34 C | 35 C |
| 36 A | 37 B | 38 C | 39 C | 40 B | 41 A | 42 D |
| 43 A | 44 B | 45 D | 46 A | 47 C | 48 C | 49 D |
| 50 B | 51 A | 52 C | 53 A | 54 B | 55 D | 56 C |
| 57 B | 58 B | 59 C | 60 A | 61 C | 62 A | 63 B |
| 64 B | 65 D | 66 D | 67 C | 68 C | 69 D | 70 D |
| 71 C | 72 A | 73 A | 74 B | 75 D | 76 A | 77 A |
| 78 B | 79 A | 80 D | | | | |

If you have won £300, well done! Turn to page 87 to play for £500!

# ANSWERS

## £500

| | | | | | | | | | | | | | |
|---|---|---|---|---|---|---|---|---|---|---|---|---|---|
| 1 | D | 2 | A | 3 | C | 4 | C | 5 | C | 6 | B | 7 | B |
| 8 | C | 9 | D | 10 | D | 11 | C | 12 | A | 13 | C | 14 | C |
| 15 | D | 16 | B | 17 | D | 18 | D | 19 | D | 20 | B | 21 | A |
| 22 | B | 23 | C | 24 | C | 25 | C | 26 | D | 27 | C | 28 | C |
| 29 | C | 30 | A | 31 | D | 32 | D | 33 | B | 34 | C | 35 | B |
| 36 | D | 37 | C | 38 | A | 39 | A | 40 | B | 41 | A | 42 | C |
| 43 | C | 44 | D | 45 | A | 46 | B | 47 | C | 48 | A | 49 | C |
| 50 | C | 51 | B | 52 | B | 53 | A | 54 | B | 55 | D | 56 | B |
| 57 | A | 58 | C | 59 | D | 60 | A | 61 | A | 62 | B | 63 | A |
| 64 | A | 65 | D | 66 | B | 67 | C | 68 | D | 69 | A | 70 | B |
| 71 | B | 72 | C | 73 | C | 74 | B | 75 | B | 76 | D | | |

If you have won £500, well done! Turn to page 105 to play for £1,000!

## £1,000

| | | | | | | | | | | | | | |
|---|---|---|---|---|---|---|---|---|---|---|---|---|---|
| 1 | A | 2 | D | 3 | B | 4 | A | 5 | B | 6 | C | 7 | C |
| 8 | C | 9 | C | 10 | A | 11 | B | 12 | D | 13 | C | 14 | C |
| 15 | D | 16 | B | 17 | B | 18 | A | 19 | C | 20 | B | 21 | A |
| 22 | A | 23 | C | 24 | B | 25 | B | 26 | A | 27 | B | 28 | A |
| 29 | D | 30 | D | 31 | A | 32 | A | 33 | B | 34 | B | 35 | D |
| 36 | C | 37 | B | 38 | B | 39 | B | 40 | D | 41 | C | 42 | D |
| 43 | A | 44 | B | 45 | C | 46 | A | 47 | A | 48 | B | 49 | A |
| 50 | D | 51 | B | 52 | A | 53 | C | 54 | D | 55 | D | 56 | C |
| 57 | A | 58 | D | 59 | D | 60 | B | 61 | D | 62 | B | 63 | C |
| 64 | D | 65 | C | 66 | A | 67 | D | 68 | B | 69 | C | 70 | C |
| 71 | B | 72 | A | | | | | | | | | | |

If you have won £1,000, well done! Turn to page 121 to play for £2,000!

## £2,000

| | | | | | | | | | | | | | |
|---|---|---|---|---|---|---|---|---|---|---|---|---|---|
| 1 | B | 2 | B | 3 | C | 4 | B | 5 | B | 6 | C | 7 | D |
| 8 | A | 9 | B | 10 | B | 11 | B | 12 | D | 13 | B | 14 | C |
| 15 | D | 16 | C | 17 | B | 18 | A | 19 | A | 20 | C | 21 | C |
| 22 | C | 23 | D | 24 | D | 25 | A | 26 | C | 27 | A | 28 | A |
| 29 | C | 30 | D | 31 | C | 32 | C | 33 | C | 34 | D | 35 | D |
| 36 | A | 37 | A | 38 | B | 39 | D | 40 | B | 41 | C | 42 | D |
| 43 | B | 44 | A | 45 | B | 46 | C | 47 | B | 48 | C | 49 | D |
| 50 | D | 51 | D | 52 | D | 53 | A | 54 | D | 55 | D | 56 | B |
| 57 | D | 58 | D | 59 | D | 60 | A | 61 | C | 62 | D | 63 | D |
| 64 | B | 65 | B | 66 | D | 67 | C | 68 | B | | | | |

If you have won £2,000, well done! Turn to page 137 to play for £4,000!

# ANSWERS

## £4,000

| | | | | | | | | | | | | | |
|---|---|---|---|---|---|---|---|---|---|---|---|---|---|
| 1 | C | 2 | C | 3 | A | 4 | B | 5 | D | 6 | A | 7 | C |
| 8 | A | 9 | A | 10 | D | 11 | C | 12 | C | 13 | D | 14 | A |
| 15 | C | 16 | A | 17 | A | 18 | D | 19 | B | 20 | D | 21 | D |
| 22 | C | 23 | B | 24 | B | 25 | A | 26 | B | 27 | C | 28 | B |
| 29 | D | 30 | D | 31 | C | 32 | D | 33 | D | 34 | B | 35 | C |
| 36 | A | 37 | A | 38 | C | 39 | B | 40 | D | 41 | C | 42 | A |
| 43 | B | 44 | D | 45 | D | 46 | C | 47 | A | 48 | B | 49 | C |
| 50 | D | 51 | D | 52 | A | 53 | B | 54 | D | 55 | A | 56 | A |
| 57 | B | 58 | B | 59 | A | 60 | B | 61 | A | 62 | A | 63 | C |
| 64 | A | | | | | | | | | | | | |

If you have won £4,000, well done! Turn to page 151 to play for £8,000!

## £8,000

| | | | | | | | | | | | | | |
|---|---|---|---|---|---|---|---|---|---|---|---|---|---|
| 1 | A | 2 | B | 3 | B | 4 | D | 5 | A | 6 | C | 7 | C |
| 8 | A | 9 | C | 10 | C | 11 | A | 12 | B | 13 | B | 14 | D |
| 15 | B | 16 | B | 17 | A | 18 | D | 19 | D | 20 | B | 21 | D |
| 22 | B | 23 | C | 24 | A | 25 | D | 26 | D | 27 | B | 28 | D |
| 29 | D | 30 | D | 31 | A | 32 | D | 33 | A | 34 | C | 35 | B |
| 36 | A | 37 | D | 38 | C | 39 | B | 40 | A | 41 | D | 42 | C |
| 43 | D | 44 | B | 45 | B | 46 | A | 47 | D | 48 | B | 49 | C |
| 50 | A | 51 | D | 52 | A | 53 | C | 54 | A | 55 | A | 56 | C |
| 57 | D | 58 | C | 59 | C | 60 | A | | | | | | |

If you have won £8,000, well done! Turn to page 165 to play for £16,000!

## £16,000

| | | | | | | | | | | | | | |
|---|---|---|---|---|---|---|---|---|---|---|---|---|---|
| 1 | C | 2 | B | 3 | A | 4 | B | 5 | C | 6 | D | 7 | A |
| 8 | D | 9 | B | 10 | B | 11 | A | 12 | C | 13 | B | 14 | D |
| 15 | A | 16 | A | 17 | C | 18 | C | 19 | B | 20 | C | 21 | D |
| 22 | D | 23 | B | 24 | C | 25 | D | 26 | C | 27 | A | 28 | A |
| 29 | D | 30 | B | 31 | A | 32 | D | 33 | D | 34 | A | 35 | C |
| 36 | B | 37 | C | 38 | D | 39 | C | 40 | C | 41 | A | 42 | C |
| 43 | A | 44 | D | 45 | D | 46 | D | 47 | B | 48 | D | 49 | D |
| 50 | C | 51 | D | 52 | A | 53 | C | 54 | B | 55 | C | 56 | D |

If you have won £16,000, well done! Turn to page 179 to play for £32,000!

# ANSWERS

## £32,000

| | | | | | | | | | | | | | |
|---|---|---|---|---|---|---|---|---|---|---|---|---|---|
| 1 | B | 2 | B | 3 | D | 4 | B | 5 | C | 6 | D | 7 | D |
| 8 | A | 9 | B | 10 | D | 11 | B | 12 | D | 13 | A | 14 | B |
| 15 | C | 16 | B | 17 | D | 18 | B | 19 | D | 20 | B | 21 | A |
| 22 | D | 23 | C | 24 | D | 25 | A | 26 | D | 27 | D | 28 | D |
| 29 | A | 30 | A | 31 | B | 32 | B | 33 | A | 34 | A | 35 | C |
| 36 | D | 37 | C | 38 | B | 39 | D | 40 | B | 41 | C | 42 | B |
| 43 | D | 44 | B | 45 | C | 46 | A | 47 | B | 48 | B | 49 | D |
| 50 | B | 51 | D | 52 | B | | | | | | | | |

If you have won £32,000, well done! Turn to page 191 to play for £64,000!

## £64,000

| | | | | | | | | | | | | | |
|---|---|---|---|---|---|---|---|---|---|---|---|---|---|
| 1 | B | 2 | C | 3 | A | 4 | C | 5 | D | 6 | B | 7 | D |
| 8 | C | 9 | C | 10 | D | 11 | D | 12 | B | 13 | D | 14 | C |
| 15 | B | 16 | B | 17 | D | 18 | B | 19 | B | 20 | D | 21 | C |
| 22 | C | 23 | A | 24 | B | 25 | C | 26 | C | 27 | B | 28 | C |
| 29 | C | 30 | C | 31 | C | 32 | A | 33 | C | 34 | C | 35 | D |
| 36 | C | 37 | B | 38 | A | 39 | D | 40 | D | 41 | D | 42 | D |
| 43 | C | 44 | B | 45 | D | 46 | D | 47 | C | 48 | D | | |

If you have won £64,000, well done! Turn to page 203 to play for £125,000!

## £125,000

| | | | | | | | | | | | | | |
|---|---|---|---|---|---|---|---|---|---|---|---|---|---|
| 1 | D | 2 | B | 3 | A | 4 | B | 5 | D | 6 | C | 7 | B |
| 8 | B | 9 | B | 10 | B | 11 | C | 12 | D | 13 | D | 14 | B |
| 15 | A | 16 | D | 17 | D | 18 | D | 19 | D | 20 | A | 21 | B |
| 22 | B | 23 | A | 24 | C | 25 | D | 26 | A | 27 | D | 28 | A |
| 29 | C | 30 | D | 31 | D | 32 | A | 33 | C | 34 | B | 35 | C |
| 36 | D | 37 | B | 38 | C | 39 | B | 40 | B | 41 | D | 42 | C |
| 43 | C | 44 | C | | | | | | | | | | |

If you have won £125,000, well done! Turn to page 213 to play for £250,000!

## £250,000

| | | | | | | | | | | | | | |
|---|---|---|---|---|---|---|---|---|---|---|---|---|---|
| 1 | C | 2 | B | 3 | A | 4 | B | 5 | B | 6 | B | 7 | C |
| 8 | C | 9 | D | 10 | C | 11 | B | 12 | C | 13 | D | 14 | C |
| 15 | D | 16 | D | 17 | A | 18 | B | 19 | C | 20 | C | 21 | D |
| 22 | C | 23 | C | 24 | C | 25 | C | 26 | C | 27 | B | 28 | D |
| 29 | C | 30 | B | 31 | D | 32 | B | 33 | C | 34 | A | 35 | C |
| 36 | C | 37 | B | 38 | A | 39 | A | 40 | C | | | | |

If you have won £250,000, well done! Turn to page 223 to play for £500,000!

# ANSWERS

## £500,000

| | | | | | | | | | | | | | |
|---|---|---|---|---|---|---|---|---|---|---|---|---|---|
| 1 | D | 2 | C | 3 | D | 4 | C | 5 | D | 6 | D | 7 | B |
| 8 | B | 9 | B | 10 | D | 11 | C | 12 | C | 13 | A | 14 | B |
| 15 | D | 16 | B | 17 | A | 18 | D | 19 | A | 20 | C | 21 | B |
| 22 | A | 23 | A | 24 | A | 25 | B | 26 | A | 27 | C | 28 | D |
| 29 | C | 30 | B | 31 | A | 32 | A | 33 | A | 34 | C | 35 | A |
| 36 | A | | | | | | | | | | | | |

If you have won £500,000, well done! Turn to page 233 to play for £1,000,000!

## £1,000,000

| | | | | | | | | | | | | | |
|---|---|---|---|---|---|---|---|---|---|---|---|---|---|
| 1 | B | 2 | C | 3 | D | 4 | B | 5 | A | 6 | C | 7 | B |
| 8 | A | 9 | B | 10 | A | 11 | B | 12 | D | 13 | C | 14 | D |
| 15 | D | 16 | B | 17 | C | 18 | A | 19 | A | 20 | A | 21 | B |
| 22 | B | 23 | B | 24 | B | 25 | A | 26 | A | 27 | A | 28 | A |
| 29 | B | 30 | C | 31 | D | 32 | B | | | | | | | | |

If you have won £1,000,000, well done! You're a millionaire!

# Score sheets

Write your name and the names of any other contestants in the space provided. Shade in each of the boxes lightly with a pencil once you or one of your fellow contestants has won the amount in that box. If you or any of the other contestants answer a question incorrectly and are out of the game, use a soft eraser to rub out the relevant boxes so that the final score is showing.

# SCORE SHEET

| contestant's name | contestant's name |
|---|---|
| .................................... | .................................... |

50:50 ⚡📞 👥👥  ☐ ☐ ☐　　50:50 ⚡📞 👥👥  ☐ ☐ ☐

| 15 | £1 MILLION | 15 | £1 MILLION |
|---|---|---|---|
| 14 | £500,000 | 14 | £500,000 |
| 13 | £250,000 | 13 | £250,000 |
| 12 | £125,000 | 12 | £125,000 |
| 11 | £64,000 | 11 | £64,000 |
| **10** | £32,000 | **10** | £32,000 |
| 9 | £16,000 | 9 | £16,000 |
| 8 | £8,000 | 8 | £8,000 |
| 7 | £4,000 | 7 | £4,000 |
| 6 | £2,000 | 6 | £2,000 |
| **5** | £1,000 | **5** | £1,000 |
| 4 | £500 | 4 | £500 |
| 3 | £300 | 3 | £300 |
| 2 | £200 | 2 | £200 |
| 1 | £100 | 1 | £100 |

# SCORE SHEET

| contestant's name | contestant's name |
| --- | --- |
| ............................... | ............................... |

| 50:50 | ☎ | 👥 | | 50:50 | ☎ | 👥 |
| --- | --- | --- | --- | --- | --- | --- |
| ☐ | ☐ | ☐ | | ☐ | ☐ | ☐ |

| | | | | |
| --- | --- | --- | --- | --- |
| 15 | £1 MILLION | | 15 | £1 MILLION |
| 14 | £500,000 | | 14 | £500,000 |
| 13 | £250,000 | | 13 | £250,000 |
| 12 | £125,000 | | 12 | £125,000 |
| 11 | £64,000 | | 11 | £64,000 |
| **10** | £32,000 | | **10** | £32,000 |
| 9 | £16,000 | | 9 | £16,000 |
| 8 | £8,000 | | 8 | £8,000 |
| 7 | £4,000 | | 7 | £4,000 |
| 6 | £2,000 | | 6 | £2,000 |
| **5** | £1,000 | | **5** | £1,000 |
| 4 | £500 | | 4 | £500 |
| 3 | £300 | | 3 | £300 |
| 2 | £200 | | 2 | £200 |
| 1 | £100 | | 1 | £100 |

# SCORE SHEET

| contestant's name | contestant's name |
|---|---|
| .................................................. | .................................................. |

| 50:50 | ⚡📞 | 👥👥👥 | | 50:50 | ⚡📞 | 👥👥👥 |
|---|---|---|---|---|---|---|
| ☐ | ☐ | ☐ | | ☐ | ☐ | ☐ |

| 15 | £1 MILLION | 15 | £1 MILLION |
|---|---|---|---|
| 14 | £500,000 | 14 | £500,000 |
| 13 | £250,000 | 13 | £250,000 |
| 12 | £125,000 | 12 | £125,000 |
| 11 | £64,000 | 11 | £64,000 |
| **10** | £32,000 | **10** | £32,000 |
| 9 | £16,000 | 9 | £16,000 |
| 8 | £8,000 | 8 | £8,000 |
| 7 | £4,000 | 7 | £4,000 |
| 6 | £2,000 | 6 | £2,000 |
| **5** | £1,000 | **5** | £1,000 |
| 4 | £500 | 4 | £500 |
| 3 | £300 | 3 | £300 |
| 2 | £200 | 2 | £200 |
| 1 | £100 | 1 | £100 |

# S C O R E   S H E E T

| contestant's name | | contestant's name | |
|---|---|---|---|
| | | | |

| 50:50 | ✎⌇ | 👥 | | 50:50 | ✎⌇ | 👥 |
|---|---|---|---|---|---|---|
| ☐ | ☐ | ☐ | | ☐ | ☐ | ☐ |

| 15 | £1 MILLION | 15 | £1 MILLION |
|---|---|---|---|
| 14 | £500,000 | 14 | £500,000 |
| 13 | £250,000 | 13 | £250,000 |
| 12 | £125,000 | 12 | £125,000 |
| 11 | £64,000 | 11 | £64,000 |
| **10** | £32,000 | **10** | £32,000 |
| 9 | £16,000 | 9 | £16,000 |
| 8 | £8,000 | 8 | £8,000 |
| 7 | £4,000 | 7 | £4,000 |
| 6 | £2,000 | 6 | £2,000 |
| **5** | £1,000 | **5** | £1,000 |
| 4 | £500 | 4 | £500 |
| 3 | £300 | 3 | £300 |
| 2 | £200 | 2 | £200 |
| 1 | £100 | 1 | £100 |

# SCORE SHEET

| contestant's name | | contestant's name | |
|---|---|---|---|
| ...................... | | ...................... | |

**50:50**  📞  👥    **50:50**  📞  👥

☐  ☐  ☐    ☐  ☐  ☐

| 15 | £1 MILLION | 15 | £1 MILLION |
|---|---|---|---|
| 14 | £500,000 | 14 | £500,000 |
| 13 | £250,000 | 13 | £250,000 |
| 12 | £125,000 | 12 | £125,000 |
| 11 | £64,000 | 11 | £64,000 |
| 10 | £32,000 | 10 | £32,000 |
| 9 | £16,000 | 9 | £16,000 |
| 8 | £8,000 | 8 | £8,000 |
| 7 | £4,000 | 7 | £4,000 |
| 6 | £2,000 | 6 | £2,000 |
| 5 | £1,000 | 5 | £1,000 |
| 4 | £500 | 4 | £500 |
| 3 | £300 | 3 | £300 |
| 2 | £200 | 2 | £200 |
| 1 | £100 | 1 | £100 |

# SCORE SHEET

| contestant's name | contestant's name |
|---|---|
| ............................... | ............................... |

| 50:50 | ☎ | 👥 | | 50:50 | ☎ | 👥 |
|---|---|---|---|---|---|---|
| ☐ | ☐ | ☐ | | ☐ | ☐ | ☐ |

| 15 | £1 MILLION | | 15 | £1 MILLION |
|---|---|---|---|---|
| 14 | £500,000 | | 14 | £500,000 |
| 13 | £250,000 | | 13 | £250,000 |
| 12 | £125,000 | | 12 | £125,000 |
| 11 | £64,000 | | 11 | £64,000 |
| 10 | £32,000 | | 10 | £32,000 |
| 9 | £16,000 | | 9 | £16,000 |
| 8 | £8,000 | | 8 | £8,000 |
| 7 | £4,000 | | 7 | £4,000 |
| 6 | £2,000 | | 6 | £2,000 |
| 5 | £1,000 | | 5 | £1,000 |
| 4 | £500 | | 4 | £500 |
| 3 | £300 | | 3 | £300 |
| 2 | £200 | | 2 | £200 |
| 1 | £100 | | 1 | £100 |

# SCORE SHEET

<table>
<tr><td colspan="2">contestant's name</td><td colspan="2">contestant's name</td></tr>
<tr><td colspan="2">..............................</td><td colspan="2">..............................</td></tr>
<tr><td colspan="2">50:50   ☎   👥 <br> □   □   □</td><td colspan="2">50:50   ☎   👥 <br> □   □   □</td></tr>
<tr><td>15</td><td>£1 MILLION</td><td>15</td><td>£1 MILLION</td></tr>
<tr><td>14</td><td>£500,000</td><td>14</td><td>£500,000</td></tr>
<tr><td>13</td><td>£250,000</td><td>13</td><td>£250,000</td></tr>
<tr><td>12</td><td>£125,000</td><td>12</td><td>£125,000</td></tr>
<tr><td>11</td><td>£64,000</td><td>11</td><td>£64,000</td></tr>
<tr><td>10</td><td>£32,000</td><td>10</td><td>£32,000</td></tr>
<tr><td>9</td><td>£16,000</td><td>9</td><td>£16,000</td></tr>
<tr><td>8</td><td>£8,000</td><td>8</td><td>£8,000</td></tr>
<tr><td>7</td><td>£4,000</td><td>7</td><td>£4,000</td></tr>
<tr><td>6</td><td>£2,000</td><td>6</td><td>£2,000</td></tr>
<tr><td>5</td><td>£1,000</td><td>5</td><td>£1,000</td></tr>
<tr><td>4</td><td>£500</td><td>4</td><td>£500</td></tr>
<tr><td>3</td><td>£300</td><td>3</td><td>£300</td></tr>
<tr><td>2</td><td>£200</td><td>2</td><td>£200</td></tr>
<tr><td>1</td><td>£100</td><td>1</td><td>£100</td></tr>
</table>

# SCORE SHEET

| contestant's name | contestant's name |
|---|---|
| .......................................... | .......................................... |

50:50  ☎  👥          50:50  ☎  👥
☐     ☐   ☐          ☐     ☐   ☐

| 15 | £1 MILLION | 15 | £1 MILLION |
|---|---|---|---|
| 14 | £500,000 | 14 | £500,000 |
| 13 | £250,000 | 13 | £250,000 |
| 12 | £125,000 | 12 | £125,000 |
| 11 | £64,000 | 11 | £64,000 |
| 10 | £32,000 | 10 | £32,000 |
| 9 | £16,000 | 9 | £16,000 |
| 8 | £8,000 | 8 | £8,000 |
| 7 | £4,000 | 7 | £4,000 |
| 6 | £2,000 | 6 | £2,000 |
| 5 | £1,000 | 5 | £1,000 |
| 4 | £500 | 4 | £500 |
| 3 | £300 | 3 | £300 |
| 2 | £200 | 2 | £200 |
| 1 | £100 | 1 | £100 |

# SCORE SHEET

| | |
|---|---|
| 15 | £1 MILLION |
| 14 | £500,000 |
| 13 | £250,000 |
| 12 | £125,000 |
| 11 | £64,000 |
| **10** | £32,000 |
| 9 | £16,000 |
| 8 | £8,000 |
| 7 | £4,000 |
| 6 | £2,000 |
| **5** | £1,000 |
| 4 | £500 |
| 3 | £300 |
| 2 | £200 |
| 1 | £100 |

| | |
|---|---|
| 15 | £1 MILLION |
| 14 | £500,000 |
| 13 | £250,000 |
| 12 | £125,000 |
| 11 | £64,000 |
| **10** | £32,000 |
| 9 | £16,000 |
| 8 | £8,000 |
| 7 | £4,000 |
| 6 | £2,000 |
| **5** | £1,000 |
| 4 | £500 |
| 3 | £300 |
| 2 | £200 |
| 1 | £100 |

# SCORE SHEET

| contestant's name | contestant's name |
|---|---|
| ............................. | ............................. |

| 50:50 | ☎ | 👥 | | 50:50 | ☎ | 👥 |
|---|---|---|---|---|---|---|
| ☐ | ☐ | ☐ | | ☐ | ☐ | ☐ |

| 15 | £1 MILLION | | 15 | £1 MILLION |
|---|---|---|---|---|
| 14 | £500,000 | | 14 | £500,000 |
| 13 | £250,000 | | 13 | £250,000 |
| 12 | £125,000 | | 12 | £125,000 |
| 11 | £64,000 | | 11 | £64,000 |
| 10 | £32,000 | | 10 | £32,000 |
| 9 | £16,000 | | 9 | £16,000 |
| 8 | £8,000 | | 8 | £8,000 |
| 7 | £4,000 | | 7 | £4,000 |
| 6 | £2,000 | | 6 | £2,000 |
| 5 | £1,000 | | 5 | £1,000 |
| 4 | £500 | | 4 | £500 |
| 3 | £300 | | 3 | £300 |
| 2 | £200 | | 2 | £200 |
| 1 | £100 | | 1 | £100 |

# SCORE SHEET

| contestant's name | contestant's name |
|---|---|
| .......................... | .......................... |
| 50:50 📞 👥 | 50:50 📞 👥 |
| ☐ ☐ ☐ | ☐ ☐ ☐ |

| | | | |
|---|---|---|---|
| 15 | £1 MILLION | 15 | £1 MILLION |
| 14 | £500,000 | 14 | £500,000 |
| 13 | £250,000 | 13 | £250,000 |
| 12 | £125,000 | 12 | £125,000 |
| 11 | £64,000 | 11 | £64,000 |
| 10 | £32,000 | 10 | £32,000 |
| 9 | £16,000 | 9 | £16,000 |
| 8 | £8,000 | 8 | £8,000 |
| 7 | £4,000 | 7 | £4,000 |
| 6 | £2,000 | 6 | £2,000 |
| 5 | £1,000 | 5 | £1,000 |
| 4 | £500 | 4 | £500 |
| 3 | £300 | 3 | £300 |
| 2 | £200 | 2 | £200 |
| 1 | £100 | 1 | £100 |

# SCORE SHEET

| contestant's name | contestant's name |
|---|---|
| ......................... | ......................... |

| 50:50 | 📞 | 👥 | 50:50 | 📞 | 👥 |
|---|---|---|---|---|---|
| ☐ | ☐ | ☐ | ☐ | ☐ | ☐ |

| 15 | £1 MILLION | 15 | £1 MILLION |
|---|---|---|---|
| 14 | £500,000 | 14 | £500,000 |
| 13 | £250,000 | 13 | £250,000 |
| 12 | £125,000 | 12 | £125,000 |
| 11 | £64,000 | 11 | £64,000 |
| 10 | £32,000 | 10 | £32,000 |
| 9 | £16,000 | 9 | £16,000 |
| 8 | £8,000 | 8 | £8,000 |
| 7 | £4,000 | 7 | £4,000 |
| 6 | £2,000 | 6 | £2,000 |
| 5 | £1,000 | 5 | £1,000 |
| 4 | £500 | 4 | £500 |
| 3 | £300 | 3 | £300 |
| 2 | £200 | 2 | £200 |
| 1 | £100 | 1 | £100 |

# SCORE SHEET

| contestant's name | | contestant's name | |
|---|---|---|---|
| ...................... | | ...................... | |

| 50:50 | ☎ | 👥 | | 50:50 | ☎ | 👥 |
|---|---|---|---|---|---|---|
| ☐ | ☐ | ☐ | | ☐ | ☐ | ☐ |

| 15 | £1 MILLION | 15 | £1 MILLION |
|---|---|---|---|
| 14 | £500,000 | 14 | £500,000 |
| 13 | £250,000 | 13 | £250,000 |
| 12 | £125,000 | 12 | £125,000 |
| 11 | £64,000 | 11 | £64,000 |
| 10 | £32,000 | 10 | £32,000 |
| 9 | £16,000 | 9 | £16,000 |
| 8 | £8,000 | 8 | £8,000 |
| 7 | £4,000 | 7 | £4,000 |
| 6 | £2,000 | 6 | £2,000 |
| 5 | £1,000 | 5 | £1,000 |
| 4 | £500 | 4 | £500 |
| 3 | £300 | 3 | £300 |
| 2 | £200 | 2 | £200 |
| 1 | £100 | 1 | £100 |

# S C O R E   S H E E T

| contestant's name | contestant's name |
|---|---|
| ............................ | ............................ |

| 50:50 | ☎ | 👥 | | 50:50 | ☎ | 👥 |
|---|---|---|---|---|---|---|
| ☐ | ☐ | ☐ | | ☐ | ☐ | ☐ |

| | | | | |
|---|---|---|---|---|
| 15 | £1 MILLION | | 15 | £1 MILLION |
| 14 | £500,000 | | 14 | £500,000 |
| 13 | £250,000 | | 13 | £250,000 |
| 12 | £125,000 | | 12 | £125,000 |
| 11 | £64,000 | | 11 | £64,000 |
| **10** | £32,000 | | **10** | £32,000 |
| 9 | £16,000 | | 9 | £16,000 |
| 8 | £8,000 | | 8 | £8,000 |
| 7 | £4,000 | | 7 | £4,000 |
| 6 | £2,000 | | 6 | £2,000 |
| **5** | £1,000 | | **5** | £1,000 |
| 4 | £500 | | 4 | £500 |
| 3 | £300 | | 3 | £300 |
| 2 | £200 | | 2 | £200 |
| 1 | £100 | | 1 | £100 |

# SCORE SHEET

contestant's name

.......................................

| 50:50 | ✂📞 | 👥👥 |
|-------|------|------|
| ☐ | ☐ | ☐ |

| 15 | £1 MILLION |
|----|------------|
| 14 | £500,000 |
| 13 | £250,000 |
| 12 | £125,000 |
| 11 | £64,000 |
| 10 | £32,000 |
| 9 | £16,000 |
| 8 | £8,000 |
| 7 | £4,000 |
| 6 | £2,000 |
| 5 | £1,000 |
| 4 | £500 |
| 3 | £300 |
| 2 | £200 |
| 1 | £100 |

contestant's name

.......................................

| 50:50 | ✂📞 | 👥👥 |
|-------|------|------|
| ☐ | ☐ | ☐ |

| 15 | £1 MILLION |
|----|------------|
| 14 | £500,000 |
| 13 | £250,000 |
| 12 | £125,000 |
| 11 | £64,000 |
| 10 | £32,000 |
| 9 | £16,000 |
| 8 | £8,000 |
| 7 | £4,000 |
| 6 | £2,000 |
| 5 | £1,000 |
| 4 | £500 |
| 3 | £300 |
| 2 | £200 |
| 1 | £100 |

# SCORE SHEET

| contestant's name | contestant's name |
|---|---|
| ................................... | ................................... |

| | 50:50 | | | | 50:50 | | |
|---|---|---|---|---|---|---|---|
| | ☐ | ☐ | ☐ | | ☐ | ☐ | ☐ |

| | | | |
|---|---|---|---|
| 15 | £1 MILLION | 15 | £1 MILLION |
| 14 | £500,000 | 14 | £500,000 |
| 13 | £250,000 | 13 | £250,000 |
| 12 | £125,000 | 12 | £125,000 |
| 11 | £64,000 | 11 | £64,000 |
| 10 | £32,000 | 10 | £32,000 |
| 9 | £16,000 | 9 | £16,000 |
| 8 | £8,000 | 8 | £8,000 |
| 7 | £4,000 | 7 | £4,000 |
| 6 | £2,000 | 6 | £2,000 |
| 5 | £1,000 | 5 | £1,000 |
| 4 | £500 | 4 | £500 |
| 3 | £300 | 3 | £300 |
| 2 | £200 | 2 | £200 |
| 1 | £100 | 1 | £100 |

# SCORE SHEET

| contestant's name | contestant's name |
|---|---|
| ...................... | ...................... |

| 50:50 | ☎ | 👥 | | 50:50 | ☎ | 👥 |
|---|---|---|---|---|---|---|
| ☐ | ☐ | ☐ | | ☐ | ☐ | ☐ |

| | | | | |
|---|---|---|---|---|
| 15 | £1 MILLION | | 15 | £1 MILLION |
| 14 | £500,000 | | 14 | £500,000 |
| 13 | £250,000 | | 13 | £250,000 |
| 12 | £125,000 | | 12 | £125,000 |
| 11 | £64,000 | | 11 | £64,000 |
| 10 | £32,000 | | 10 | £32,000 |
| 9 | £16,000 | | 9 | £16,000 |
| 8 | £8,000 | | 8 | £8,000 |
| 7 | £4,000 | | 7 | £4,000 |
| 6 | £2,000 | | 6 | £2,000 |
| 5 | £1,000 | | 5 | £1,000 |
| 4 | £500 | | 4 | £500 |
| 3 | £300 | | 3 | £300 |
| 2 | £200 | | 2 | £200 |
| 1 | £100 | | 1 | £100 |

# SCORE SHEET

| 15 | £1 MILLION | 15 | £1 MILLION |
|---|---|---|---|
| 14 | £500,000 | 14 | £500,000 |
| 13 | £250,000 | 13 | £250,000 |
| 12 | £125,000 | 12 | £125,000 |
| 11 | £64,000 | 11 | £64,000 |
| **10** | £32,000 | **10** | £32,000 |
| 9 | £16,000 | 9 | £16,000 |
| 8 | £8,000 | 8 | £8,000 |
| 7 | £4,000 | 7 | £4,000 |
| 6 | £2,000 | 6 | £2,000 |
| **5** | £1,000 | **5** | £1,000 |
| 4 | £500 | 4 | £500 |
| 3 | £300 | 3 | £300 |
| 2 | £200 | 2 | £200 |
| 1 | £100 | 1 | £100 |

# S C O R E   S H E E T

| contestant's name | contestant's name |
| --- | --- |
| ........................... | ........................... |

| 50:50 | ☎ | 👥 | 50:50 | ☎ | 👥 |
| --- | --- | --- | --- | --- | --- |
| ☐ | ☐ | ☐ | ☐ | ☐ | ☐ |

| 15 | £1 MILLION | 15 | £1 MILLION |
| --- | --- | --- | --- |
| 14 | £500,000 | 14 | £500,000 |
| 13 | £250,000 | 13 | £250,000 |
| 12 | £125,000 | 12 | £125,000 |
| 11 | £64,000 | 11 | £64,000 |
| 10 | £32,000 | 10 | £32,000 |
| 9 | £16,000 | 9 | £16,000 |
| 8 | £8,000 | 8 | £8,000 |
| 7 | £4,000 | 7 | £4,000 |
| 6 | £2,000 | 6 | £2,000 |
| 5 | £1,000 | 5 | £1,000 |
| 4 | £500 | 4 | £500 |
| 3 | £300 | 3 | £300 |
| 2 | £200 | 2 | £200 |
| 1 | £100 | 1 | £100 |

# SCORE SHEET

| contestant's name | | contestant's name | |
|---|---|---|---|
| ............................ | | ............................ | |

| 50:50 | ☎ | 👥 | 50:50 | ☎ | 👥 |
|---|---|---|---|---|---|
| ☐ | ☐ | ☐ | ☐ | ☐ | ☐ |

| 15 | £1 MILLION | 15 | £1 MILLION |
|---|---|---|---|
| 14 | £500,000 | 14 | £500,000 |
| 13 | £250,000 | 13 | £250,000 |
| 12 | £125,000 | 12 | £125,000 |
| 11 | £64,000 | 11 | £64,000 |
| **10** | £32,000 | **10** | £32,000 |
| 9 | £16,000 | 9 | £16,000 |
| 8 | £8,000 | 8 | £8,000 |
| 7 | £4,000 | 7 | £4,000 |
| 6 | £2,000 | 6 | £2,000 |
| **5** | £1,000 | **5** | £1,000 |
| 4 | £500 | 4 | £500 |
| 3 | £300 | 3 | £300 |
| 2 | £200 | 2 | £200 |
| 1 | £100 | 1 | £100 |

# SCORE SHEET

| contestant's name | contestant's name |
|---|---|
| ........................... | ........................... |

| 50:50 | ☎ | 👥 | | 50:50 | ☎ | 👥 |
|---|---|---|---|---|---|---|
| ☐ | ☐ | ☐ | | ☐ | ☐ | ☐ |

| 15 | £1 MILLION | 15 | £1 MILLION |
|---|---|---|---|
| 14 | £500,000 | 14 | £500,000 |
| 13 | £250,000 | 13 | £250,000 |
| 12 | £125,000 | 12 | £125,000 |
| 11 | £64,000 | 11 | £64,000 |
| 10 | £32,000 | 10 | £32,000 |
| 9 | £16,000 | 9 | £16,000 |
| 8 | £8,000 | 8 | £8,000 |
| 7 | £4,000 | 7 | £4,000 |
| 6 | £2,000 | 6 | £2,000 |
| 5 | £1,000 | 5 | £1,000 |
| 4 | £500 | 4 | £500 |
| 3 | £300 | 3 | £300 |
| 2 | £200 | 2 | £200 |
| 1 | £100 | 1 | £100 |

# SCORE SHEET

| contestant's name | contestant's name |
|---|---|
| ........................... | ........................... |

| 50:50 | ☎ | 👥 | | 50:50 | ☎ | 👥 |
|---|---|---|---|---|---|---|
| ☐ | ☐ | ☐ | | ☐ | ☐ | ☐ |

| 15 | £1 MILLION | 15 | £1 MILLION |
|---|---|---|---|
| 14 | £500,000 | 14 | £500,000 |
| 13 | £250,000 | 13 | £250,000 |
| 12 | £125,000 | 12 | £125,000 |
| 11 | £64,000 | 11 | £64,000 |
| 10 | £32,000 | 10 | £32,000 |
| 9 | £16,000 | 9 | £16,000 |
| 8 | £8,000 | 8 | £8,000 |
| 7 | £4,000 | 7 | £4,000 |
| 6 | £2,000 | 6 | £2,000 |
| 5 | £1,000 | 5 | £1,000 |
| 4 | £500 | 4 | £500 |
| 3 | £300 | 3 | £300 |
| 2 | £200 | 2 | £200 |
| 1 | £100 | 1 | £100 |

# SCORE SHEET

| contestant's name | contestant's name |
|---|---|
| .......................... | .......................... |

| 50:50 | ☎ | 👥 | 50:50 | ☎ | 👥 |
|---|---|---|---|---|---|
| ☐ | ☐ | ☐ | ☐ | ☐ | ☐ |

| | | | | |
|---|---|---|---|---|
| 15 | £1 MILLION | | 15 | £1 MILLION |
| 14 | £500,000 | | 14 | £500,000 |
| 13 | £250,000 | | 13 | £250,000 |
| 12 | £125,000 | | 12 | £125,000 |
| 11 | £64,000 | | 11 | £64,000 |
| 10 | £32,000 | | 10 | £32,000 |
| 9 | £16,000 | | 9 | £16,000 |
| 8 | £8,000 | | 8 | £8,000 |
| 7 | £4,000 | | 7 | £4,000 |
| 6 | £2,000 | | 6 | £2,000 |
| 5 | £1,000 | | 5 | £1,000 |
| 4 | £500 | | 4 | £500 |
| 3 | £300 | | 3 | £300 |
| 2 | £200 | | 2 | £200 |
| 1 | £100 | | 1 | £100 |

# SCORE SHEET

| 15 | £1 MILLION |
| 14 | £500,000 |
| 13 | £250,000 |
| 12 | £125,000 |
| 11 | £64,000 |
| 10 | £32,000 |
| 9 | £16,000 |
| 8 | £8,000 |
| 7 | £4,000 |
| 6 | £2,000 |
| 5 | £1,000 |
| 4 | £500 |
| 3 | £300 |
| 2 | £200 |
| 1 | £100 |

contestant's name

...................................

50:50

☐  ☐  ☐

| 15 | £1 MILLION |
| 14 | £500,000 |
| 13 | £250,000 |
| 12 | £125,000 |
| 11 | £64,000 |
| 10 | £32,000 |
| 9 | £16,000 |
| 8 | £8,000 |
| 7 | £4,000 |
| 6 | £2,000 |
| 5 | £1,000 |
| 4 | £500 |
| 3 | £300 |
| 2 | £200 |
| 1 | £100 |

# SCORE SHEET

| contestant's name | contestant's name |
|---|---|
| ...................................... | ...................................... |

| 50:50 ☎ 👥 | 50:50 ☎ 👥 |
|---|---|
| ☐ ☐ ☐ | ☐ ☐ ☐ |

| | | | |
|---|---|---|---|
| 15 | £1 MILLION | 15 | £1 MILLION |
| 14 | £500,000 | 14 | £500,000 |
| 13 | £250,000 | 13 | £250,000 |
| 12 | £125,000 | 12 | £125,000 |
| 11 | £64,000 | 11 | £64,000 |
| 10 | £32,000 | 10 | £32,000 |
| 9 | £16,000 | 9 | £16,000 |
| 8 | £8,000 | 8 | £8,000 |
| 7 | £4,000 | 7 | £4,000 |
| 6 | £2,000 | 6 | £2,000 |
| 5 | £1,000 | 5 | £1,000 |
| 4 | £500 | 4 | £500 |
| 3 | £300 | 3 | £300 |
| 2 | £200 | 2 | £200 |
| 1 | £100 | 1 | £100 |

# S C O R E   S H E E T

| contestant's name | contestant's name |
|---|---|
| ........................... | ........................... |

**50:50**  ⚡📞  👥👤👥  ☐ ☐ ☐

**50:50**  ⚡📞  👥👤👥  ☐ ☐ ☐

| | | | |
|---|---|---|---|
| 15 | £1 MILLION | 15 | £1 MILLION |
| 14 | £500,000 | 14 | £500,000 |
| 13 | £250,000 | 13 | £250,000 |
| 12 | £125,000 | 12 | £125,000 |
| 11 | £64,000 | 11 | £64,000 |
| 10 | £32,000 | 10 | £32,000 |
| 9 | £16,000 | 9 | £16,000 |
| 8 | £8,000 | 8 | £8,000 |
| 7 | £4,000 | 7 | £4,000 |
| 6 | £2,000 | 6 | £2,000 |
| 5 | £1,000 | 5 | £1,000 |
| 4 | £500 | 4 | £500 |
| 3 | £300 | 3 | £300 |
| 2 | £200 | 2 | £200 |
| 1 | £100 | 1 | £100 |

# SCORE SHEET

| contestant's name | contestant's name |
|---|---|
| ........................................ | ........................................ |

| 50:50 | ☎ | 👥 | 50:50 | ☎ | 👥 |
|---|---|---|---|---|---|
| ☐ | ☐ | ☐ | ☐ | ☐ | ☐ |

| | | | | |
|---|---|---|---|---|
| 15 | £1 MILLION | | 15 | £1 MILLION |
| 14 | £500,000 | | 14 | £500,000 |
| 13 | £250,000 | | 13 | £250,000 |
| 12 | £125,000 | | 12 | £125,000 |
| 11 | £64,000 | | 11 | £64,000 |
| 10 | £32,000 | | 10 | £32,000 |
| 9 | £16,000 | | 9 | £16,000 |
| 8 | £8,000 | | 8 | £8,000 |
| 7 | £4,000 | | 7 | £4,000 |
| 6 | £2,000 | | 6 | £2,000 |
| 5 | £1,000 | | 5 | £1,000 |
| 4 | £500 | | 4 | £500 |
| 3 | £300 | | 3 | £300 |
| 2 | £200 | | 2 | £200 |
| 1 | £100 | | 1 | £100 |

# SCORE SHEET

| contestant's name | contestant's name |
|---|---|
| .............................. | .............................. |

| 50:50 | ☎ | 👥 | | 50:50 | ☎ | 👥 |
|---|---|---|---|---|---|---|
| ☐ | ☐ | ☐ | | ☐ | ☐ | ☐ |

| 15 | £1 MILLION | 15 | £1 MILLION |
|---|---|---|---|
| 14 | £500,000 | 14 | £500,000 |
| 13 | £250,000 | 13 | £250,000 |
| 12 | £125,000 | 12 | £125,000 |
| 11 | £64,000 | 11 | £64,000 |
| **10** | £32,000 | **10** | £32,000 |
| 9 | £16,000 | 9 | £16,000 |
| 8 | £8,000 | 8 | £8,000 |
| 7 | £4,000 | 7 | £4,000 |
| 6 | £2,000 | 6 | £2,000 |
| **5** | £1,000 | **5** | £1,000 |
| 4 | £500 | 4 | £500 |
| 3 | £300 | 3 | £300 |
| 2 | £200 | 2 | £200 |
| 1 | £100 | 1 | £100 |

# S C O R E   S H E E T

| contestant's name | | contestant's name | |
|---|---|---|---|
| .......................... | | .......................... | |
| 15 | £1 MILLION | 15 | £1 MILLION |
| 14 | £500,000 | 14 | £500,000 |
| 13 | £250,000 | 13 | £250,000 |
| 12 | £125,000 | 12 | £125,000 |
| 11 | £64,000 | 11 | £64,000 |
| 10 | £32,000 | 10 | £32,000 |
| 9 | £16,000 | 9 | £16,000 |
| 8 | £8,000 | 8 | £8,000 |
| 7 | £4,000 | 7 | £4,000 |
| 6 | £2,000 | 6 | £2,000 |
| 5 | £1,000 | 5 | £1,000 |
| 4 | £500 | 4 | £500 |
| 3 | £300 | 3 | £300 |
| 2 | £200 | 2 | £200 |
| 1 | £100 | 1 | £100 |

# SCORE SHEET

| contestant's name | contestant's name |
|---|---|
| .............................. | .............................. |

**50:50** ☎ 👥 ☐ ☐ ☐     **50:50** ☎ 👥 ☐ ☐ ☐

| | | | |
|---|---|---|---|
| 15 | £1 MILLION | 15 | £1 MILLION |
| 14 | £500,000 | 14 | £500,000 |
| 13 | £250,000 | 13 | £250,000 |
| 12 | £125,000 | 12 | £125,000 |
| 11 | £64,000 | 11 | £64,000 |
| **10** | £32,000 | **10** | £32,000 |
| 9 | £16,000 | 9 | £16,000 |
| 8 | £8,000 | 8 | £8,000 |
| 7 | £4,000 | 7 | £4,000 |
| 6 | £2,000 | 6 | £2,000 |
| **5** | £1,000 | **5** | £1,000 |
| 4 | £500 | 4 | £500 |
| 3 | £300 | 3 | £300 |
| 2 | £200 | 2 | £200 |
| 1 | £100 | 1 | £100 |

# SCORE SHEET

| contestant's name | contestant's name |
|---|---|
| ........................................ | ........................................ |

| 50:50 | ⚡📞 | 👥 | | 50:50 | ⚡📞 | 👥 |
|---|---|---|---|---|---|---|
| ☐ | ☐ | ☐ | | ☐ | ☐ | ☐ |

| 15 | £1 MILLION | 15 | £1 MILLION |
|---|---|---|---|
| 14 | £500,000 | 14 | £500,000 |
| 13 | £250,000 | 13 | £250,000 |
| 12 | £125,000 | 12 | £125,000 |
| 11 | £64,000 | 11 | £64,000 |
| 10 | £32,000 | 10 | £32,000 |
| 9 | £16,000 | 9 | £16,000 |
| 8 | £8,000 | 8 | £8,000 |
| 7 | £4,000 | 7 | £4,000 |
| 6 | £2,000 | 6 | £2,000 |
| 5 | £1,000 | 5 | £1,000 |
| 4 | £500 | 4 | £500 |
| 3 | £300 | 3 | £300 |
| 2 | £200 | 2 | £200 |
| 1 | £100 | 1 | £100 |

# SCORE SHEET

| contestant's name | | contestant's name | |
|---|---|---|---|
| .................... | | .................... | |

| 50:50 | 📞 | 👥 | | 50:50 | 📞 | 👥 |
|---|---|---|---|---|---|---|
| ☐ | ☐ | ☐ | | ☐ | ☐ | ☐ |

| 15 | £1 MILLION | | 15 | £1 MILLION |
|---|---|---|---|---|
| 14 | £500,000 | | 14 | £500,000 |
| 13 | £250,000 | | 13 | £250,000 |
| 12 | £125,000 | | 12 | £125,000 |
| 11 | £64,000 | | 11 | £64,000 |
| 10 | £32,000 | | 10 | £32,000 |
| 9 | £16,000 | | 9 | £16,000 |
| 8 | £8,000 | | 8 | £8,000 |
| 7 | £4,000 | | 7 | £4,000 |
| 6 | £2,000 | | 6 | £2,000 |
| 5 | £1,000 | | 5 | £1,000 |
| 4 | £500 | | 4 | £500 |
| 3 | £300 | | 3 | £300 |
| 2 | £200 | | 2 | £200 |
| 1 | £100 | | 1 | £100 |

# SCORE SHEET

| contestant's name | | contestant's name | |
|---|---|---|---|
| ............................... | | ............................... | |

| 50:50 | ☎ | 👥 | 50:50 | ☎ | 👥 |
|---|---|---|---|---|---|
| ☐ | ☐ | ☐ | ☐ | ☐ | ☐ |

| 15 | £1 MILLION | 15 | £1 MILLION |
|---|---|---|---|
| 14 | £500,000 | 14 | £500,000 |
| 13 | £250,000 | 13 | £250,000 |
| 12 | £125,000 | 12 | £125,000 |
| 11 | £64,000 | 11 | £64,000 |
| 10 | £32,000 | 10 | £32,000 |
| 9 | £16,000 | 9 | £16,000 |
| 8 | £8,000 | 8 | £8,000 |
| 7 | £4,000 | 7 | £4,000 |
| 6 | £2,000 | 6 | £2,000 |
| 5 | £1,000 | 5 | £1,000 |
| 4 | £500 | 4 | £500 |
| 3 | £300 | 3 | £300 |
| 2 | £200 | 2 | £200 |
| 1 | £100 | 1 | £100 |